T0298579

Few others alive today "do" marketing history as well as Ron Fullerton. In addition to being an intellectual *tour de force* as regards nineteenth-century German book publishing, *Foundations* is also an important scholarly contribution that all but demolishes the long prevailing ethnocentric view of marketing management as a product of mid-1950s America.

Stanley J. Shapiro, *Professor Emeritus, Simon Fraser University, Canada*

In a delightful piece of historical scholarship, Ron Fullerton has produced a splendid read about the application of the marketing mix to the German book trade. Dr. Fullerton's book is particularly fascinating because the sophisticated use of marketing tools and techniques that he so clearly describes occurred in the nineteenth century before the advent of "so-called" modern marketing of the twentieth century. A must-read for marketing historians.

Eric Shaw, *Emeritus Professor, Florida Atlantic University, USA*

# The Foundations of Marketing Practice

Between 1815 and 1890, the German book market experienced phenomenal growth, driven by German publishers' dynamic entrepreneurial attitude towards developing and distributing books. Embracing aggressive marketing on a large scale, they developed a growing sense of what their markets wanted. This study, based almost entirely upon primary sources including over 70 years of trade newspapers, is an in-depth account of how and why this market developed—decades before there was any written theory about marketing.

This book is therefore about both marketing practice and marketing theory. It provides a uniquely well-researched account of how markets were developed in very sophisticated ways long before there was a formal discipline of marketing: for example, German publishers used segmentation at least 150 years before the first US articles on the subject appeared. Much of their experience was also shared by the UK and US book markets through international interactions between booksellers and other businessmen.

All scholars of marketing will find this historical account a fascinating insight into markets and marketing, This will also be of interest to social historians, scholars of German history, the book trade and book trade historians.

**Ronald A. Fullerton** is an independent scholar living in Toronto, Canada, having held academic appointments around the globe including American University in Cairo, University of the South Pacific, Emory University, the University of Massachusetts, Visiting Professor at Quinnipiac University in the USA and most recently at California State University, Northridge, USA.

# Routledge studies in the history of marketing
Edited by Mark Tadajewski and Brian D. G. Jones

It is increasingly acknowledged that an awareness of marketing history and the history of marketing thought is relevant for all levels of marketing teaching and scholarship. Marketing history includes, but is not limited to, the histories of advertising, retailing, channels of distribution, product design and branding, pricing strategies, and consumption behaviour – all studied from the perspective of companies, industries, or even whole economies. The history of marketing thought examines marketing ideas, concepts, theories, and schools of marketing thought including the lives and times of marketing thinkers.

This series aims to be the central location for the publication of historical studies of marketing theory, thought and practice, and welcomes contributions from scholars from all disciplines that seek to explore some facet of marketing and consumer practice in a rigorous and scholarly fashion. It will also consider historical contributions that are conceptually and theoretically well-conceived, that engage with marketing theory and practice, in any time period, in any country.

# The Foundations of Marketing Practice

A history of book marketing in Germany

Ronald A. Fullerton

Routledge
Taylor & Francis Group

LONDON AND NEW YORK

First published 2016 by Routledge

2 Park Square, Milton Park, Abingdon, Oxfordshire OX14 4RN

52 Vanderbilt Avenue, New York, NY 10017

*Routledge is an imprint of the Taylor & Francis Group, an informa business*

First issued in paperback 2019

Copyright © 2016 Ronald A. Fullerton

The right of Ronald A. Fullerton to be identified as author of this work has been asserted by him in accordance with sections 77 and 78 of the Copyright, Designs and Patents Act 1988.

All rights reserved. No part of this book may be reprinted or reproduced or utilised in any form or by any electronic, mechanical, or other means, now known or hereafter invented, including photocopying and recording, or in any information storage or retrieval system, without permission in writing from the publishers.

Notice:
Product or corporate names may be trademarks or registered trademarks, and are used only for identification and explanation without intent to infringe.

*British Library Cataloguing in Publication Data*
A catalogue record for this book is available from the British Library

*Library of Congress Cataloging in Publication Data*
Names: Fullerton, Ronald A., author.
Title: The foundations of marketing practice : a history of book marketing in Germany / Ronald A. Fullerton.
Description: Abingdon, Oxon ; New York, NY : Routledge, 2016. | Includes bibliographical references and index.
Identifiers: LCCN 2015023184| ISBN 9781138848221 (hardback) | ISBN 9781315726151 (ebook)
Subjects: LCSH: Books–Germany–Marketing–History–19th century. | Book industries and trade–Germany–History–19th century.
Classification: LCC Z285.6 .F85 2016 | DDC 381/.45002094309034–dc23
LC record available at http://lccn.loc.gov/2015023184

ISBN: 978-1-138-84822-1 (hbk)
ISBN: 978-0-367-87152-9 (pbk)

Typeset in Bembo
by Wearset Ltd, Boldon, Tyne and Wear

# Contents

# Tables

# Introduction

## The role of marketing in the growth of the German book markets, 1815–1890

About a century ago the famous German political economist Karl Bucher wrote that "the book is the first modern-style product," using heavy advertising to generate sales. The book "has to be produced [and sold] in large quantities if the printing is to be financially rewarding," noted Bucher; the old method of producing books by hand was obsolete.[1] In other words, there had to be markets for books. The book trade in Germany, like that in the UK, France, and eventually the United States, pioneered the modern aggressive stance towards marketing; in the nineteenth century, for example, only the patent medicine industry rivalled the book trade's advertising expenditures.

This side of bookselling has been neglected by most writers, who are more concerned with the book as a bearer of salvation culture, especially high culture. After all, the first book to be printed was the Bible. But publishers and booksellers were businesses and had to attend to the practicalities of business if they were to survive long. And in truth, a great deal of what was published had little or no cultural or spiritual or political value. A few writers have in recent years begun to examine the business side of the German book trade, especially during the nineteenth century.[2]

This is a book about marketing practice in the German book trade starting 200 years ago and following it for seven decades. We will see that the practices were, many of them, quite sophisticated—even though all of them occurred long, long before the so-called "marketing era." Some were aggressive, others less so, but taken together they represent a considerable achievement. My topic involves Germany but similar practices were in use in Britain, France, and the United States; some references will be made to these. Because all of this took place before present-day marketing terminology was developed, I for the most part avoid using it to reduce the chance of committing the (to historians) sin of anachronism, of reading the present into the past.

I first became interested in the German book trade during a seminar conducted by Professor Fritz Ringer at Harvard University nearly half a century ago. From a seminar paper eventually came the topic for a doctoral dissertation, which in turn led to a series of journal articles and conference papers over the decades.[3]

As I penetrated the history of the trade, I found that generations of capable German scholars have studied both individual publishers and the central institutions by which the trade sought to organize and regulate itself. The markets served by the book trade, however, have been neglected. Who bought what books and why? How did such factors as social class, sex, religion, and region affect the roles played by nineteenth-century Germans as readers and purchasers of books? These questions have been seldom posed, let alone explored in a thorough scholarly manner. The day in, day out actions of bookmen have been for the most part ignored, a few of them excepted.

Moreover, although it has long been established that the market for books grew immensely during the course of the century, there has been no close analysis of how and why this happened. Scholars have contented themselves with blithe attributions of the growth to such general phenomena as the expansion of "literacy," increased urbanization, and greater prosperity. I certainly am not going to deny that such forces contributed to the growth of book consumption, for they did. But they do have to be dissected and explained much more fully than has hitherto been the case. The vaunted spread of "literacy," for example, turns out upon careful study to mean mainly that a majority of German children received a very rudimentary exposure to knowledge in crowded state schools, whose curriculum was in no way intended to make them enthusiastic readers. The work of the state elementary schools did help the book market to grow, but not in the ways in which a casual glance would lead one to believe. The growth of a middle class, and of a much better-paid working class, gave people greater incomes— yet at the same time there was an increase of objects and experiences on which that money could be spent. More money could be, and was, spent on better clothing, better housing, on jewelry, on travel, on beer, on brandy, etc., not necessarily upon books.

Again, after the traditionally advanced reasons for the growth of the book market have been studied, it becomes evident that they alone cannot explain it. Behind them, working in conjunction with them, was a factor of enormous importance—the development of an aggressive attitude towards *marketing*. Trade historians have conventionally tossed this development off by relating a few colorful anecdotes about some of the energetic booksellers of the 1830's. I am going to treat it at great length because it is the key to understanding the growth of the nineteenth-century German book market. More than a century before McCarthy spoke of the "4 Ps" of marketing, the German book trade was actively pursuing all of them. The book trade developed new products—new physical forms of reading matter, for example the inexpensive illustrated book, the magazine, the pocket book. Some products were priced aggressively. The trade excelled at segmenting and then advertising to different markets, by price, by format, by occasion of purchase, by age, by gender, and more. It developed newer methods of distributing reading matter while also keeping the traditional methods. Of course not every member of the book trade was a dynamic marketer; one of the themes of this work is the ongoing struggle between conservative, tradition-bound, bookmen and those who were aggressively entrepreneurial.

In a fascinating examination of reading habits from the seventeenth through nineteenth centuries, Engelsing (1969) found that where earlier readers read intensively, reading the same books repeatedly—people who had read the complete Bible over 50 times were common—over time the tendency became to read extensively—to read many titles once. But who was presenting readers with so many titles? Who was encouraging people to read many different books? The catalytic force was the aggressive marketing efforts of some publishers: they commissioned the writing of books that they sensed would sell well (e.g., cookbooks, how-to manuals, encyclopedias, profusely illustrated books), they introduced markedly cheaper (and usually pirated) editions of the classics, and they invented newer and cheaper ways of retailing books. Aggressive marketing utilized the advantages provided by the expansion of literacy and of printing technology; yet without these advantages publishers would not have succeeded to the extent that they did. Of course, nineteenth-century German publishers and booksellers never used the word "marketing" *(Absatzwirtschaft)*; they talked of "markets" characterized by "a disquiet, an urgency, a bustle, an aggressiveness."[4]

## A review of the German background

Germany underwent great political, economic, and social changes as the nineteenth century proceeded. Politically, Germany entered the 1800s as a collection of hundreds of basically independent states grouped together under the rubric of the centuries-old "Holy Roman Empire". The Empire was headed by the Habsburg rulers of Austria. By the eighteenth century, the Holy Roman Empire was moribund—people quipped that it was neither Holy nor Roman nor an Empire—but, inertia-bound, it kept drifting along without much opposition until the revolutionary forces were unleashed by the French Revolution, beginning in 1789, and then the conquests of the French Emperor Napoleon. Suddenly all of the existing structures became questioned. With Napoleon finally defeated in 1815, Western Europe was reorganized along conservative lines by the Congress of Vienna, yet the world of the mid-eighteenth century was irrevocably gone. There had been calls for complete German unification including Austria, but the Congress would not go that far, instead dissolving the Holy Roman Empire and creating 37 principalities and four free states, an organization which survived until the country was unified in the 1870s. Prussia and Austria were the largest and most powerful of the principalities; both were conservative, but Prussia introduced major series of reforms in political organization, education, and other areas and advanced economically faster than did Austria. When the country was unified in the early 1870s, it was under Prussian control; Austria was left out.

Regionally, Germany was quite different from today. Where today Bavaria and Baden-Wuerttemberg are now the wealthiest and best educated states,

200 years ago they were poor and comparatively backward; Saxony was the best educated and most cosmopolitan state, along with the wealthy Rhineland. Two hundred years ago, Germany had considerably sharper religious divisions than it does now, with a Lutheran North and a Catholic South, the latter poorer and more backward. Today the religions are mixed in much of the country.

Politically, Germany was ruled by conservative rulers, especially in the first half of the nineteenth century. There was censorship, but as we shall see most of what was put on the book market was apolitical and not reined in by censorship. There were major political outbreaks all over Germany in 1848, just as in much of Europe. These disrupted the economy severely but were eventually put down by conservative governments—Prussia and Austria especially.

Economically and socially Germany had (before 1815) been described as a slow-moving place where the French writer Mme de Stael (1766–1817) wrote in 1810 that, "time fell drop by drop." The country still had not fully recovered from the severe devastation of the Thirty Years War (1618–1648), in which 20–40 percent of the population had died. There were rigid rules of apprenticeship and trades stuck to existing ways. But the upsets of the French Revolution and Napoleon had shaken things up; not long after 1815 there was a tremendous birth of entrepreneurial attitudes, which conflicted with— yet was really not repressed by—the existing conservative order. And the population began to expand rapidly.

### Population growth and urbanization

Between 1820 and 1870, the population of Germany grew by more than 14,000,000 people; from 26,291,606 to 40,816,249. More significant for the book trade was the fact that an increasing proportion of the population lived in cities—urban dwellers were more likely to read than rural ones. Germany's urban population increased by 262 percent during the years from 1816 to 1871; and the rural population increased by only 43 percent. Where 90 percent of all Germans lived either on the land or in small villages at the earlier date, only 64 percent did at the later date. Moreover, the greatest increases occurred in the larger cities, which were better mass book markets than the smaller and medium-sized urban areas. Berlin gained 101,130 inhabitants between 1837 and 1844 alone, most of them from rural areas. After 1850, the trend to urban growth strengthened.

### German currencies

Up until unification, several currencies were in use across Germany, the main two being the Thaler (which had variations) and the Gulden, used largely in Southern Germany. I describe book prices in terms of the currency used by the publisher. The Thaler dated back about 400 years by the nineteenth century, and it had been used in much of the Holy Roman Empire. In 1837 the Prussian Thaler became part of a South Germany currency union, where it eventually became standard in most of Germany. A Thaler was worth 1.75 Gulden. The newly-unified Germany replaced the Thaler with the Mark but some 3 Thaler pieces remained in use until 1907, although the Mark was supposedly the only legal tender in Germany starting January 1, 1876. A Thaler was set in value at 3 Marks in 1871. A Mark had a value of 25 US cents. Of course, 25 US cents had a much greater value 140 years ago than it does today.

## Sources

As mentioned above, the main sources for this book have been primary documents—documents written at the time under discussion, above all weekly trade newspapers, which I read week-by-week, year-by-year, from 1815 until 1890. I have also used histories of the book trade, above all the classic ones by Johann Goldfriedrich (1913) and August Prinz (1855–1863) but also more modern ones. There are a few studies of reading habits that I have found particularly useful, especially those by Schenda and Engelsing. Germany's publishers have had many histories of themselves written; some are of excellent quality, for example those by Annemarie Meiner.[5]

## Notes

1 K. Bucher, "Aufsatze," p. 247, quoted in *Bilderwelt des Alltags: Werbung in der Konsumgesellschaft des 19. und 20. Jahrhunderts*, Stuttgart: Steiner 1995.
2 Examples are M. Tabaczek, *Kulturelle Kommercialisierung*, Frankfurt am Main 2003; F. Barbier, *L'empire du livre. Le livre imprime et la construction de'l'Allemagne contemporain (1815–1914)*, Paris: Norbert 1995; I. Rarisch, *Industrialisierung und Literatur* (1976), Berlin: Colloquium 1976; K.-H. Fallbacher, ed., *Taschenbuecher im 19. Jahrhundert*, Marbach (1992); and several articles by R. A. Fullerton:

  • (2012) "The Historical Development of Segmentation: The Example of the German Book Trade, 1800–1928," *Journal of Historical Research in Marketing*, 4: 56–67.
  • (2001) "Golden Images: Illustration-Driven Product Design and the Book Market in Germany." Conference on Marketing History, Duke University.
  • (1985) "Segmentation Strategies and Practices in the 19th Century German Book Trade: a Case Study in the Development of a Major Marketing Technique." in C. T. Tan and J. N. Sheth, eds., *Historical Perspective in Consumer Research: National and International Perspectives*, Singapore: National University of Singapore, 135–139.
  • (1979) "Towards a Commercial Popular Culture in Germany," *Journal of Social History* 12 (4): 489–511.
  • (1977) "Creating a Mass Book Market in Germany," *Journal of Social History* 10 (3): 265–283.

3 Older works include: G. Menz, *Der deutsche Buchhandel*, 2nd ed. rev., Gotha 1942; F. Schulze, *Der deutsche Buchhandel und die geistigen Stromungen der letzten Hundert Jahre*, Leipzig 1925; J. Goldfriedrich, *Geschichte des deutschen Buchhandels vom Beginn der Fremdherrschaft bis zur Reform des Boersenvereins im neuen deutschen Reiche,*

*1805–1889*, Leipzig 1913; H. Widmann, *Geschichte des Buchhandels vom Altertum his zur Gegenwart*, Wiesbaden 1952; and the still useful (and entertaining) work conventionally ascribed to the international erotica publisher J. A. Prinz, *Bausteine zu einer spaeteren Geschichte des Buchhandels*, 7 vols., Hamburg-Altona 1855–1863.

　　More current works include G. Jaeger, *Geschichte des deutschen Buchhandels im 19. und 20. Jahrhundert*, Frankfurt/Main 2001; R. Wittmann, *Geschichte des deutschen Buchhandels*, 3rd ed., C. H. Beck 1999.

4  F. Perthes, 1834 "Die Bedeutung des deutschen Buchhadels, besonders in der neuesten Zeit," *Börsenblatt* 1: 6.
5  R. Schendam, *Volk ohne Buch. Studien zur Sozialgechichte der popularen Lesestoffe 1770–1910*, Frankfurt/Main 1970; R. Engelsing, 1969 "Die Perioden der Lesergeschichte in der Neuzeit," *Archiv fuer Geschichte des Buchwesens* X: 946–1002; H. Kunze, *Lieblings-Buecher von Dazumal ... ein erster Versuch zu einer Geschichte des Lesergeschmacks*, Munich 1965; A. Meiner, *Cotta. Geschichte eines Verlages, 1659–1959*, Stuttgart 1959.

# 1 Separate, distinct, both sluggish

## The German book markets at the close of the Napoleonic Wars, 1815–1820

> As already, we shall have a vast chaos and confusion of books; we are oppressed with them, our eyes ache with reading, our fingers with turning.
>
> (Robert Burton, *The Anatomy of Melancholy (1621)*)

At the close of the Napoleonic Wars the German book market was small; the bulk of the German populace had little or no part in it. This was also true of every other country in the world then, but Germany considered itself the "land of poets and thinkers." Moreover, the traditionalist attitudes and business practices of the book trade and the conservatism of Germany's rulers made it seem unlikely that this situation would ever change.[1] Within a few years new attitudes and practices emerged in parts of the book trade, but immediately following the Napoleonic Wars these were scarce.

Political and religious leaders feared that reading could tempt the masses into moral depravity and political sedition. The dominant mentality in the book trade was a stately passivity, which "tended to respond to needs, but not to rush about awakening them."[2] Rarely were more than 1,000 copies of any book printed. The standard edition size was 750 to 1,000 copies, and seldom would the entire edition be sold. More titles were published annually in Germany than in any other country—over 3,000 (including reprints) in 1815, over 4,000 in 1820 (also including reprints)—but the total volume of books sold lagged far behind that of Great Britain and France. About two-thirds of the German titles were scholarly works, which usually sold 500 or fewer copies.[3]

The great number of titles published every year in Germany was due to factors other than a large book market. Contemporary bookmen often accused authors of crass profligacy; according to the Düsseldorf book dealer J. H. C. Schreiner, for example:

> The brazen industry of our writers has now burst all bounds of modesty and decency.... They debase the arts and sciences to acquire money with which to indulge themselves. To job their outrageously high royalties from publishers they concoct: new terminologies, theologies, and systems, all of which serve only to confuse and obfuscate; Romanticism

and Mysticism, which ruin good taste and seduce to silly enthusiasms; idiotic fairy tales and nonsense about magnetism, which merely revive superstition; *ad nauseam* imitations of the [Brockhaus] encyclopedia which only encourage and reward banal pedantry; and political pamphlets, which ... merely anger the censors.[4]

But Friedrich Arnold Brockhaus, the most perceptive book-man of that age, knew that there was more to it than writers' greed; he knew that publishers themselves often encouraged the flood of books; he knew too that the decentralization of the book trade, a product of the nation's political disunity, contributed to the plethora of titles:

> Germany's scribblers write too much and too much of what they write is printed. These excesses are fueled by the fact that there are so many places here which have publishers, in contrast to England and France, where they are confined to London, Edinburgh, and Paris. A result of the German situation is an atmosphere in which the personal connections of would-be authors and the over-accommodation of publishers allow the printing of stacks of manuscripts which, if judged by their scholarly or literary merits, would never find a publisher ... Perhaps half the books published in Germany have no chance in the book market; they are still-born as waste paper.[5]

Offering all of these books to the public were approximately 450 stationary book dealers, most of whom did publishing and retailing, several hundred itinerant book hawkers, or Colporteurs, and a hundred or so binders who sold books as a sideline.[6] Some binders published too. Taking Colporteurs, binders, and stationary book shops together, I estimate that, had they been equally distributed, there would have been one book retailing unit for each 25,000 to 30,000 people; in actuality, their distribution favored city dwellers. There was one school of thought in the book trade which seriously advocated shrinkage in the number of dealers.[7]

It is not surprising that "more than one book in a rural household was a peculiarity, three to five, a rarity."[8] In urban regions too, however, many people neither owned nor read books—many people had no part in the book market. Frankfurt/Main, for example, which impressed the Hamburg publisher Friedrich Perthes with its "lively ... trade, its large stocks of both old and new books, and its industrious, clever, and often well-educated bookmen,"[9] doubtless had a higher incidence of book ownership than many German cities: it was a center of the book trade of Southern and Western Germany and its population was more Protestant than Catholic. Yet in 1800 *no* books at all had been owned by:

- 73.7 percent of the journeymen artisans
- 71.7 percent of the military personnel

- 71.2 percent of the lower and middle level bureaucrats
- 68.3 percent of the workers
- 65.2 percent of the artisans
- 49.6 percent of the merchants.[10]

Members of these groups who did own books usually had only a few, i.e., one to five devotional works; in this category were:

- 15.8 percent of the journeymen artisans
- 15.2 percent of the military personnel
- 16.7 percent of the lower and middle level bureaucrats
- 23.4 percent of the workers
- 23.1 percent of the artisans
- 13.9 percent of the merchants.[11]

Thus few or no books were owned by:

- 89.5 percent of the journeymen artisans
- 86.9 percent of the military personnel
- 87.9 percent of the lower and middle level government employees
- 91.7 percent of the workers
- 88.3 percent of the artisans
- 65.3 percent of the merchants.[12]

These people composed the overwhelming majority of Frankfurt's population. Although the figures cited are from around 1800, there is no reason to assume that book ownership had increased by 1815. If anything, the economic privations and depressed condition of the book trade during the war years would indicate that it might have decreased.

There can be no doubt that at the close of the Napoleonic Wars more Germans neither owned nor bought books than those who did. Although there is too little precise statistical information available to fix exactly the size of this majority, it must have been overwhelming in the rural areas of Catholic West and South Germany and in those of the eastern reaches of Prussia and of Mecklenburg. On the land in central Prussia, Saxony, and Thuringia the majority would have been somewhat narrower. It would have been narrower yet in urban areas, especially those with cultural and educational institutions. But everywhere in Germany it would have been a majority.[13]

Of the reasons why so many people owned no books, the most important were that many people could not read and that books were expensive. Many Germans were completely illiterate. Even more were functionally illiterate, that is, able perhaps to scrawl some semblance of their names and to recognize a few written words, but not able to read sentences.

Statistics for Prussia, which had the best educational institutions in Germany, drive home the extent of the inability to read. More than 16 percent of the males, and almost 40 percent of the females, born in Prussia between 1821 and

1825 could not sign their names to their marriage contracts.[14] Among people who were adults in the period 1815–1820, and who had therefore been born during the eighteenth century, these percentages were much higher, because school attendance had been much less common during their childhoods.

In 1822, about one-quarter of the school-age children in Prussia did not go to school, the compulsory school attendance law not always being enforced. In 1815 the figure had no doubt been slightly higher. In Berlin in 1818, there were 27,000 children who were supposed to attend school. Six thousand of them did not. Rural areas had much poorer school attendance than urban ones. In both urban and rural regions, more boys than girls went to school.[15]

Some idea of the differences in educational levels between Catholics and Protestants can be gotten from 1824 statistics from the Prussian Administrative District of Aachen. There, only slightly more than half—34,140 out of 66,611—of Catholic children attended school, while almost all—1,600 out of 1,852—of Protestant children did.[16] One can imagine what the figures for Catholic Bavaria's school attendance were; unfortunately, none are available.

Most of the children who did go to school received only a very rudimentary education. That was all they were intended to get. Germany's religious, cultural, and political leaders at once feared mass education as a potential source of leveling ideas and rebelliousness and realized that it could bring economic benefits. The solution to the dilemma presented was to educate the masses—in a most limited fashion. Prussia's elementary schools, for example, aimed "not to elevate the artisan or worker above his place in society, but to give him a solid, competent school education."[17] With such an education he could best fulfill his task within the niche of society into which he had been born. If the graduate of a Prussian elementary school could struggle through a handbook or so for his trade and simple devotional literature for his soul, his schooling had fulfilled its aims. Often the schooling could not meet even these modest goals because the classes were too large, the textbooks inadequate, the teaching methods clumsy, and the teachers sorry, ill-paid wretches. In 1822, in Prussia, there was an average of nearly 70 pupils to each teacher in the elementary schools, and some schools had 200 pupils to a teacher. About two- thirds of the Prussian elementary school teachers were not really paid enough to subsist upon.[18]

Only a tiny fraction of children anywhere in Germany got more than an elementary school education, if that. The enrollment figures for the University of Berlin's winter semesters, 1815 to 1820, were:

- 1815 ... 336 students
- 1816 ... 519 students
- 1817 ... 551 students
- 1818 ... 610 students
- 1819 ... 424 students
- 1820 ... 531 students.[19]

Berlin was one of the largest German universities.

Most Germans, then, were not educated to be readers. They amused, informed, and edified themselves in other, traditional, ways. That was just as well, for if they had wanted to buy books, they would not have been able to afford them. Books were expensive; they were priced like luxury items in a country where few people had money for luxury items, and where many had difficulties in procuring necessities.[20] The two-volume edition of the poet Novalis' works cost 6 Gulden when it was published in 1802, a typical price for a work of that size. For 6 Gulden, a person in Southern Germany then could have purchased "45 kilograms of white bread, or 56 kilograms of rye bread, or 28 kilograms of beef."[21] A worker's salary at that time might have reached 100 Gulden a year, perhaps slightly more; some teachers also earned that little. People earning at that level would have been lucky to be able to buy enough rye bread, let alone white bread or beef, and they absolutely could not have afforded to have given one-tenth to one-fifteenth of their yearly income for two books.

By the 1815–1820 period, books were no cheaper. In fact, they had become slightly more expensive. The 12-volume edition of Schiller's works completed in 1815 cost 14 Reichstaler, six Groschen if printed on cheap paper, more if done on better paper—and the edition on vellum cost 34 Reichstaler, 12 Groschen. The publisher Perthes' four-volume edition of Matthias Claudius' *Werke* (1820) cost 4 Reichstaler, 12 Groschen. The fifth and sixth volumes of Karl v. Rotteck's *Universal History (Allegemaine Geschichte)*, published by Herder in Freiburg in 1818, cost two Reichstaler each; the first four (1812–1816) had cost less—one Reichstaler, 16 Groschen each. (There were 30 Groschen to a Reichstaler.) A three-volume novel by Fouqué was priced at two Reichstaler, 12 Groschen, while a three-volume effort by another popular novelist cost a full five Reichstaler.[22] These examples are of popular books, that were sure to sell.[23] Scholarly works and the works of little-known authors, which were not so sure to sell, sometimes cost a bit more.

Books were so expensive that even people who earned much more than teachers or workers complained. Authors lamented that the high prices were curtailing sales and thus their incomes. In 1819 the Diet of the Germanic Confederation, no friend of mass reading, considered imposing limits on the prices of books; this was deterred only by vigorous resistance from German publishers.[24]

## The mass book market

To the high price of books there were, however, a few exceptions:

> There were a handful of books—the Bible, parts of the Bible, catechisms (which also served as primers), songbooks, certain devotional works, calendars—which were printed in large [i.e., 2,000 to 10,000 copies] editions and sold cheaply everywhere not only by book shops but also, and especially, by binders, itinerant peddlers, and religious institutions.[25]

To this list of books should be added elementary school primers other than catechisms and simple handbooks for home, workshop, and farm.[26] Bibles could be had for 20 Groschen, very little for so large a book. Classic devotional works cost little: Johann Arndt's *The Garden of Paradise … (Paradiesgärtlein voller christlicher Tugen)* (1612) cost from two to five Groschen, depending on which of the available editions one bought. K. H. von Rogatsky's two-volume *Golden Treasure Chest of God's Children (Güldene Schatzkästlein der Kinder Gottes)* (1718, 37th printing 1819) went for four Groschen a volume. Johann Hubner's *Zweimal 52 biblische Historien* (1714, 89th printing 1825), which was used as a reader in many elementary schools in Lutheran areas, sold for eight Groschen (or six Groschen for the edition without pictures), as did Bernhard Overbeck's *Catechism of Catholic Learning for the Higher Grades (Katechismus der christkatholischen Lehre zum Gebrauch der größern Schuler* 1804, 12th printing 1819). The popular primer by Heinrich Stephani, *Learning to Read (Handfibel zum Lesenlernen* 1809, 20th printing 1820) cost two Groschen.[27]

In the period after 1815 the buyers of such books were peasants, artisans, workers, journeymen, clerks, soldiers, small merchants, and the like—ordinary Germans, in other words. Although a majority of ordinary Germans owned no books, the minority of them that did was big enough to form the numerically largest of the several German book publics. Unfortunately, study of this public has been so neglected that one could read all the standard histories of the book trade and still be scarcely aware that it existed.[28] Much of the little useful information on it lies in four studies of book ownership based upon investigation of wills and legacies.

It was a conservative public, rarely buying from beyond the narrow selection of printed matter sold by binders and Colporteurs, rarely, in fact, either able or willing to buy much at all. Although the books that ordinary Germans purchased were inexpensive compared to most books, they were not inexpensive to the people who bought them. These people did not have much disposable income. Excepting calendars, a family would seldom buy more than five to 10 printed items in as many decades; quite a few cut down even on calendar purchases by getting the 100-year calendars popular then.[29]

A study of the legacies of Tübingen's petty bourgeoisie *(Kleinbürger)* shows an average of eight books per household. The study intentionally ignored the learned elite connected with the university.[30] It is impossible to tell how many of the books listed in these legacies had been inherited rather than bought. Since some of the most popular books had been in print for decades, even centuries in a few cases, the listed copies could have been acquired generations previously. Books were treasured heirlooms, passed down from generation to generation.[31]

Books were read and re-read, usually aloud for the benefit of the illiterate members of the family, and often parts of them were memorized; the prevalent reading habit among most Germans at that time was the old one of intensive reading, the repetitive reading of a few texts.[32]

The major purpose of this intensive reading being edification, most of the books the ordinary German owned were religious. Here are some typical home libraries of citizens of Müsingen in the Swabian Alps of Württemberg:

1   Library of Matthes Mack, a cowherd and day laborer who died in 1815:
    1 Book of sermons without a title
    1 Starck's Prayer Book *(Tägliches Handbuch in guten und bösen Tagen)*
    1 Württemberg Songbook (hymnal)
2   Library of Heinrich Wagner, judge and blacksmith (d.1815):
    1 J. Arndt's Devotional Book *(Vier Bücher vom wahren Christentum)*
    1 Storr's Prayer Book
    1 Ebersdorf Songbook (probably a hymnal)
    1 Steinhofer's Sermons
    1 New Württemberg Songbook (hymnal)
    1 Wudrian's Devotional Book *(Creutz-Schule)*
    1 Bilhuber's Sermons
    1 Letter Writer's Guide
    1 Book without title
3   Library of Catharina Fink, née Gerstenmaier, widow of a tailor (d.1817):
    1 Bible, folio size
    1 Devotional book (probably Wudrian's *Creutz-Schule*)
    1 Enslen on Atonement
    2 Old Württemberg Songbooks (hymnals)
    2 Old Prayer Books
    1 Booklet of commentary (theme not listed)
    1 Mirren's Prayer Book.

A wealthy farmer of Münsingen who died in 1816 left behind 26 books, only one of which was secular—a letter writer's guide.[33]

The studies of book legacies in Tübingen and Bresigheim and in Frankfurt/Main indicate a similar predominance of religious over secular books. Of the 3,145 books listed in 408 Tübingen wills from the years 1800 to 1810, more than two-thirds (2,457) were religious. Of 299 artisan legacies in Frankfurt in 1800, 92 listed religious books, 23 also listed secular books and the rest listed no books. Analogous ratios were seen in the legacies of military people, journeymen, lower and middle-level government employees, and workers in Frankfurt. Only among merchants did the number of legacies with at least one secular work (35) approach the number of those with only ecclesiastical books (50).[34]

The religious works listed in the legacies of these ordinary Germans were seldom abstract theoretical theology or doctrinal polemics—rarely the type of works discussed in intellectual histories. Such books must have been too difficult or too uninteresting, or both, for the average reader. Although these were the testaments of Lutherans, Luther's works were seldom found and the Bible itself was not nearly as common as might be expected. Thus in Bresigheim, "quite contrary to the postulates of the Lutheran Creed, the Bible was markedly less common than prayer books, hymnals, and volumes of sermons." [35] In Tübingen, hymn books (441 copies) and prayer books (326 copies) were more numerous than Bibles (292 copies); close behind the Bible were the devotional books of Johann J. Arndt (253 copies) and of J. F. Starck (118 copies). Bibles were even less common in Münsingen, where in the wills from around the year 1810 the most common books had been: (1) J. F. Starck's *Tägliches Handbuch* (1727), a book of prayers, (2) Arndt's *Wahres Christentum* (4 vols., 1605 1610), and (3) V. Wudrian's *Die Creutz-Schule*. Arndt's *Paradiesgärtlein* was also very common.

A decade later these works were still the most common in Münsingen. The common man was not affected by fad and fashion. "The average man was conservative, preferring to read not modern books, but rather the old devotional books his forefathers had had in their book cabinets." [36]

While the examples of the three Württemberg towns and of Frankfurt/ Main could not *ex cathedra* be pronounced representative for all of such a varied country as Germany, there is other information indicating that the home libraries of that time, in so far as they existed at all, rarely contained more than a handful of books, most of which were religious in nature. [37] More people bought devotional books than any other type of book—the greatest sales successes were achieved by devotional works. [38] Although copies of the books by Arndt, Bogatsky, Starck, and others were passed down from one generation to another, they had to be reprinted regularly to meet that continual need for replacement copies as old ones wore out, and for the copies new families would need if an elder brother or sister had inherited the family copy.

The demand for Bibles was also great. The Privileged Bible Society of Württemberg, founded in 1812, printed 10,000 copies of its first edition of the Bible in 1815. It sold so well that another printing was required a year later. There were similar non-profit Bible societies in Hannover, Hamburg-Altona, Osnabrück, Berlin, and Dresden, like that in Stuttgart founded and subsidized by the British and Foreign Bible Society; but most of the Bibles sold in Germany were still published by German publishers for profit. [39] I estimate that the yearly demand for Bibles in this period exceeded 50,000 copies.

Although Catholics as a rule read less and owned fewer books than Protestants, there was a flourishing market in Catholic areas for some simple, popular religious works. The Josef Wolf publishing firm of Augsburg had to print 3,500 copies of the *The Way to Heaven for Honorable Women (Himmelswege für rechtschaffene Weibsleute)* each year to satisfy the demand. Wolf also had yearly printings of 800 to 1,000 for several other pious works. [40] Bernhard Overbeck's (1754–1826) works, including his *Biblische Geschichte des Alten und Neuen Testaments* (2 volumes 1799, 6th printing 1821) were popular with the

Catholics of Münster (Westphalia) and surrounding areas, where they were used for both school and home devotions and for religious instruction. In Bavaria, Aegydius Jais' (1750–1822) *Beautiful and Instructional Stories for Children (Schöne Geschichten und lehrreiche Erzählungen für Kinder)* (1807, 14th printing 1820) and his *Little Book of Prayer and of Learning (Lehr und Beth Büchlein)* were beloved and frequently purchased books.[41]

Among secular publications, the only ones found in the homes of ordinary Germans were: (1) crude, often brutal little stories, (2) books dispensing advice usually medical (including dreams), household, or farm matters, (3) school primers and readers, and (4) calendars.[42] Works of the first category were the least common of the three in the years 1815–1820. Not much is known about these stories, as most of them have not been preserved. Yet this type of fiction had been published all over Germany for hundreds of years. The best known example of it is the *Folk Book of Dr. Faust (Volksbüchlein von Dr. Faustus)*.[43]

Few of the advice books have been preserved either. Like the simple stories, they were scorned by the educated as drivel for the common herd. But they helped the common man deal with the intricacies of life and they often sold very well. G. E. Claudius' 1808 *General Letter Writing (Allgemeiner Briefsteller)* (also titled *Nützliche briefe auf alle fast erdenkliche Fälle*) was reprinted 12 times within the decade 1808–1818. It was but one of many letter-writer's guides on the market. Various translations and editions of the Italian Manconi's *Book of Dreams (Traumbüchlein)*, "in which one … can find out what his luck in life's lottery will be" (so ran the sub-title), did well in the German book market. The 1819 edition by the publishers Jenisch and Stage of Augsburg had 360 copperplate illustrations, yet cost only five Groschen.[44]

Sometimes the advice handbooks were intentionally fraudulent. In Bavarian Schweinfurth, for example, there were books being sold which told how to make tobacco from beet leaves, others which gave formulae for the derivation of rice, brandy, noodles, syrup, and other good things from potatoes, and still others which revealed how magic balls could be used to fatten livestock.[45] Then there were the handbooks which were cynical attempts to imitate R. Z. Becket's *Noths-und Hilfs-Büchlein*, the most beloved general handbook in rural German homes. Covering all aspects of rustic life, it was first published in 1784 and remained in print until 1837. Between these dates hundreds of thousands of copies were sold, making it the first secular book in German publishing history to sell in truly large numbers.[46]

Calendars were found in even more homes than the *Noths-und Hilfs-Büchlein* was. Most individual ones were printed in yearly editions of 10,000 copies. Some had been issued for centuries. They were the only reading matter which perforce had to be regularly purchased anew by large numbers of people. Most had a similar basic design; containing:

a chronological calendar with a list of market days and other days of local and regional significance, and a section where the reader found medical advice, helpful tips for home and farm, moral and devotional stories, anecdotes, ... poems and songs, adventure stories, horror stories, murder stories, reports of executions and misfortunes, travel descriptions, folklore, [and] bits of history.[47]

Elementary school textbooks were found in many households also. The basic schoolbooks then were primers (including catechisms), songbooks, and books of readings, which were usually religious stories. Schoolchildren were expected to buy these from teachers, binders, Colporteurs, or book shops, depending on the local rules and conditions. In Bavaria, all schoolbooks were published by the state-owned "Central Schoolbook Publishing Agency," a vestige from the eighteenth century. Elsewhere the books of private publishers were used after being approved by one or another government agency; which one, depended upon the state.[48]

In some places, schools and teachers could choose among several approved books, which motivated publishers to dangle tantalizing offers before teachers and school officials. A typical deal was that unveiled in 1816 by the well-known firm of Keyser in Erfurt, the publisher of J. G. Reinhardt's *Prayers and Songs for Town and Country Schools (Schulgebete und Schullieder ... für Stadt und Landschulen.)* Teachers or school officials could buy it in lots of 25 copies for 2.28 Groschen per copy and resell them to pupils for four Groschen a copy.[49] Considering how low teachers' salaries were, such an offer must have been tempting.

Yet there is little record of exploitation of schoolchildren with regard to schoolbooks. It was the norm then that texts remained in use so long that a single copy could be passed down from the older to the younger children in families—and often from one generation to another. Publishers and authors of textbooks had not yet begun to do frequent, usually unneeded, revisions and new editions to stimulate sales.[50] Such revisions might not have increased sales in any event, since many children could afford no books at all. The number of schoolbooks sold, however, was exceeded only by the numbers of calendars and devotional works sold. Friedrich Wilmsen's *The German Children's Friend (Der deutsche Kinderfreund)* was reprinted 42 times between 1811 and 1820. Stephani's *Handfibel* and Hübner's *Zweymal 52 biblische Historien* appear to have been equally popular.[51]

The buyers of schoolbooks, calendars, handbooks, crude fiction, and much of the popular devotional literature made up a large market. This market, and the institutions which serviced it, existed to a large degree outside of, and independent of, the "regular" book trade of publishers, book shops, and their middle to upper-class clientele.

The best-known center for the production of books for this large market was not Weimar, Leipzig, Dresden, or Berlin. It was Reutlingen in Württemberg. Some printers there had been among the first people in the German book trade to realize that the increase in literacy and semi-literacy had created a potentially large market for simple, inexpensive reading matter. Unlike most of the people in the book trade, they saw nothing wrong or degrading in attempting to cultivate this market. Not that they were fervent democrats—their principal motivation was to keep their presses running. At first the Reutlingen presses produced mainly calendars and practical handbooks, but by 1815 the Reutlingers had perceived, and were attempting to fill, a growing demand for elemental fiction.[52]

## Selling to the masses: itinerant Colporteurs

The bulk of Reutlingen's production was sold through itinerant peddlers—Colporteurs—rather than through retail book stores, which were ashamed to deal in mass-appeal books. Some production was sold through binders. Colporteurs could reach people of all classes in all regions of Germany, including the rural areas where most of the population then lived. Binders too sold to all classes but were geographically concentrated in the larger cities and towns; some binders employed Colporteurs to extend their range.[53]

The Hamburg publisher Friedrich Perthes, who journeyed through much of Germany to observe the book trade in the months July–October 1816, found that religious societies in the Rhineland and Westphalia distributed their literature "exclusively by means of their own establishments and Colporteurs."[54] The book trade of Augsburg, which astonished Perthes with its immense volume, had long been based upon sale via itinerant peddlers. Augsburg publishers found them especially effective for cultivating the "country trade."[55] In the headquarters of Matthias Rieger's Heirs, the largest firm in Augsburg, Perthes viewed "seven Augsburg natives working silently behind great iron trellises,"[56] keeping records and preparing orders for the company's Colporteurs. Rieger's Heirs sold all of its books by means of Colporteurs. Company officials told the visitor from Hamburg that:

> Two salesmen of the firm travelled winter and summer through Upper Swabia, the Rhine Basin up to Cologne, all of Bavaria, and parts of Switzerland and the Tirol. The public was so used to these salesmen that it ordered from them not only books, but also art supplies, pictures, paper, linen, jewelry-in brief, all manner of Augsburg products.[57]

Every year in September or October, Rieger's Heirs printed and distributed 3,500 copies of its book catalog, which listed both new and older books and which included some works which would appeal only to the educated. Orders were either given to the two salesmen or mailed in. There was no cost for the delivery of the books. The books were presumably delivered by freight wagons, postal services being expensive. In some ways, Rieger's Heirs' itinerant salesmen were not typical Colporteurs; they were employees of the company. In contrast, most Colporteurs were independent agents, taking books from whichever publisher they wanted. Rieger's Heirs' men sold a great variety of printed matter, where most sold only religious books, handbooks, simple fiction, and calendars. They took orders for books they did not have with them, where most sold only what they could carry on their backs.

On the usual Colporteur's back was a wooden chest with canvas shoulder straps. Filled with 40 to 50 books, dry goods, and whatever else the peddler felt that he could sell, a chest weighed about 45 lb. The more expensive ones could be quickly opened as display cases; the cheaper ones had to be laboriously unpacked at each house, tavern, or market place the Colporteur sold from. In taverns and market places, some attracted audiences by having their wives sing or by playing an instrument. That may have been necessary in cities. In little towns and villages, however, the mere presence of the Colporteur was an exciting event, sure to gather a crowd. It was a visitation from the outside world. Most towns and villages got such visitations from only one or two Colporteurs a year.[58]

After four or five weeks of tramping about, the Colporteur's chest was empty and so he went back to Augsburg, Reutlingen, or elsewhere and refilled. Some did this all year long. More common, however, was for a man to hawk books only during the fall and winter; the main selling seasons—it was then that people had time to read. The village of Eningen near Reutlingen, for example, sent out most of its adult population (including women) as Colporteurs after the harvest had been completed. All over Germany it was common for teachers to supplement their incomes with book hawking during the school vacations.[59]

Colporteurs were restless people who liked to escape the dull village life of the time by wandering about. In their ranks were people who had failed at, or had gotten tired of, being teachers, merchants, artisans, and most other occupations. That quite a few of them were illiterate was evidently no hindrance to their successfully selling books. Since no one has ever bothered to total up the number of peddler permits granted to Colporteurs in this (or any other) period, it is impossible to say exactly how many of them there were at the close of the Napoleonic Wars. I do not believe that there were more than a few hundred of them active at any season of the year.[60] Respectable Germans of the middle and upper classes, however, seeing in every vagabond a Colporteur—and grossly exaggerating the number of vagabonds—believed that there were many more.

Respectable Germans equated Colporteurs with the worst sort of degenerate tramps. Gustav Schwab's description of the Eningen Colporteurs is typical: "They sell books for the masses and for that reason as well as by reason of their physical and moral depravity should receive very careful supervision and censorship."[61]

Then there were the:

Schoolmasters, teachers, and half-educated characters who, especially during school vacations, run loose in many parts of Germany. Employing the crudest techniques of the most disgusting market hawker, they attempt to induce people to order some literary concoction or other and to pay for it in advance. In the end the customer gets either nothing at all or a wretched book.[62]

The three-hundredth anniversary of Luther's *Ninety-Five Theses* in 1817 saw a flood of mediocre religious works pour down upon Protestant Germany, peddled by "rural binders who, like huckstering Jews roamed about with sacks full of the rubbishy wares."[63]

Seeing in Colporteurs potential distributors of lascivious and of revolutionary literature, the German governments maintained over them a watch even more vigilant than that over the publishers and book shops of the regular book trade. A Colporteur had to have a peddler's permit; governments made it difficult to get one. Even with a permit, a Colporteur could be, and frequently was, arbitrarily tossed into jail as a vagrant. To keep out of trouble with the authorities, and also to avoid lugging about books the public might not buy, the itinerant book seller rarely sold anything beyond the narrow range of books Colporteurs had sold for centuries—devotional classics, handbooks, calendars, and simple fiction. Few would risk selling forbidden books. Yet the governments did have a point in keeping watch on them, for, while the normal peddler sold nothing dangerous, revolutionaries did at times distribute their books by the methods of the Colporteur.[64]

## The regular book market

A few exceptions aside, the Colporteur was the bookseller of the common people, the masses, and to leave the sphere of the Colporteur and his humble publics for those of the other publics, the other book market, within Germany is to travel worlds. It is also to travel into more familiar terrain; it is these middle- and upper-class publics which one reads about in the literary and cultural histories. There were two of these publics: one old, the other dating from the late eighteenth century, but both serviced by the regular book trade of publishers and retail book shops. Only in rural areas would such people purchase from Colporteurs.

## Upper-class customers

The older of these publics was the group of wealthy scholars—cultivated nobles and higher clergy, high government officials, and well-to-do merchants—which had been the traditional support of the regular book trade. This was an exclusive group, numbering no more than 25,000 people.[65] But it did not take many of them to keep publishers and book store owners happy, since the members of this elite spent generously to assemble large home libraries. Wittmann's study of Frankfurt legacies, for example, shows that not one high government official had fewer than 200 books; some prosperous merchants also had several hundred.[66]

Obituaries and auction notices are another source of useful information on the size which some personal libraries then attained. The writer Karl Julius Weber (1767–1832) had 11,000 volumes.[67] The learned Leipzig publisher Gottfried Heinrich Schäfer built up a collection of 6,696 volumes of rare editions of the classics.[68] Princess Christiane of Waldeck had 4,000 volumes; the Marburg professor Wilhelm Gottlieb Tennemann (1761–1819), an expert on the history of philosophy, had 4,800. There were yet larger libraries: a professor named Strickmann had a personal library of 8,361 titles, one Professor Arndt had 9,617, and in Halle in 1823 was auctioned the 50,500 book library of a Dr. Schwedler. More modest were the 1,732-title natural science library of the young professor of anatomy and physiology Samuel Christian Lucä (1787–1821), and the 854-book library of another professor which was auctioned in Cassel in 1823.[69] Other auction notices in the trade papers of the time list substantial libraries belonging to medical doctors, high government administrative and judicial officials, and gymnasium directors.[70]

While these libraries usually included the same devotional works which ordinary Germans owned, the bulk of their contents naturally varied according to the personal, scholarly, or professional interests of their owners. In Frankfurt/Main, high government officials, who were the city's intellectual elite, had many Latin works of theology and Scriptural exegesis; rich Frankfurt merchants, on the other hand, had little theology but filled their shelves with history, biography, travel descriptions, and, above all, books on contemporary events.[71]

The owners of Germany's largest personal libraries sometimes collected books from several or all branches of organized knowledge, as had been the fashion in the eighteenth century. Specialization, however, was increasingly common. Thus a historian might have hundreds of works in his area of historical interest and a surgeon might have shelves of books on surgery and anatomy.[72] Scholars liked to have personal research libraries because Germany's state, city, and university libraries existed more to hide books away than to let anyone use them.[73]

Nevertheless, there was after 1815 a growing trend among scholars to make more use of public libraries for their research. They were driven to do so by the combination of the expansion in the number of books published and of the failure of their incomes to rise fast enough to cover the costs of purchasing all the necessary works in their fields of interest.[74] Libraries were neither numerous enough nor well-financed enough to please publishers. The size of the book market presented by libraries was further reduced by the requirement, which most of the states had, that publishers give at least one free "compulsory copy" of the books they produced to one or more of the major libraries in a given state.[75]

Unpleasant too for the book trade had been the closing of "hundreds" of noble and cloister libraries as a result of the wars and upheavals preceding 1815. These libraries had been a sure market for theological books and some secular scholarly works.[76] Equally ominous was the decline in the number and size of big personal libraries. They were simply going out of fashion, especially those which aspired to universality.[77]

## The middle-class market

The traditional elite public of the regular book trade, it is evident, was a dying book market. The dynamic, expanding element in the German book market was the second of the two publics serviced by the regular book trade, the middle- to upper-middle-class reading public which had developed in the second half of the eighteenth century. It was composed of clergymen, academics, students beyond the elementary school stage, teachers, businessmen, professional people, merchants, and military officers. The wives of these people were not always literate; those who were played an ever more significant role in the book market. The exact size of this public can only be conjectured. I estimate that it was several hundred thousand members strong—a small percentage of the total German population, but the largest active public the German book trade had ever seen. Although its members hardly had the means to purchase books as freely as members of the old elite public had been able to, they had more money available for reading matter than did peasants, workers, and artisans. Moreover, reading was much more important to them than it was to most Germans. Reading conferred status. They diverted into reading the energies which could not, in the stuffy German states of the time, be channeled into political or economic endeavour.[78]

The prevalent reading habit among them was that of extensive reading, whereby many books were read once rather than a few over and over again.[79] As caustically described by August Wilhelm Schlegel, extensive reading was compounded of "an unconquerable revulsion toward a second reading of even profound works and a readiness to be satisfied by the trite, the insipid, the tasteless and the idiotic-by anything, as long as it *seems* new."[80] On the other hand, extensive reading could mean exposure to many rich intellectual experiences rather than decades of dumbly reading the same passages from *Wahres Christentum*. It all depended on who did the extensive reading: some extensive readers devoured nothing but the silliest sort of adventure and love stories, others worked their way through the great works of ancient and modern literature, philosophy, and scholarship.

Its cultural worth or lack of it aside, there is no doubt that the spread of the habit of extensive reading, which was going on unabated during the 1815 to 1820 period, encouraged the expansion of the book market. Whether the motives of the extensive reader were intellectual curiosity or a mere craving for diversion, there had to be many books available for people to read. There also had to be institutions to get these books to the middle-class public. Colporteurs and binders offered too little variety and were personally revolting to the respectable. Therefore the publishers and booksellers I have called the "regular" book trade would have to do the job.

At the close of the Napoleonic Wars, this trade was not only geograph-ically fragmented into regional and local trades, it was also moribund to non-existent in large parts of Germany. Centuries of poor transportation and particularism had fragmented the country into many markets and many book trades, each with its own institutions and often with little or no contact with the trades of other regions and with the aspiring "national" book trade cen-tered in Leipzig.[81] Perthes described the Augsburg trade, to give an example, as "a world of its own, as it has been for a long time."[82] Its unique institutions included "Latin dealers," who sold only Catholic theological works, prefera-bly those in Latin. Its dealers had no contact with either Leipzig or the Cath-olic book trade of the Rheinland and Westphalia. The religious book traders of the Rhineland and Westphalia, for their part, had "a closed religious liter-ature of which we [of the rest of the regular book trade] know nothing.... They have no contact whatsoever with the [regular] book trade".[83] West-phalia's secular scholars and book collectors, too, had little contact with their counterparts elsewhere and formed a closed book market.

Perthes noticed, however, that the isolation of places like Augsburg and Westphalia was waning. The Augsburg bookmen were anxious for trade rela-tions with Leipzig, and the new Prussian rule in the Rhineland and West-phalia was already bringing the book trades of these places into more contact with the national book trade.[84]

That in no way altered the fact that most Germans had never seen a book shop, since two-thirds of them were peasants and three-quarters of them lived on the land or in small towns and villages, while book shops were clustered in large urban areas, in residence cities, in spas, and in university towns.[85] Bonn, which in 1816 had no book dealers, had two by 1818 as a result of the founding of the university. Conversely, the closing of the university in Wit-tenberg in 1815 nearly ended the book market there. Berlin had 26 book dealers in 1816; a year later the head of the Nicolai book firm there com-plained to Jacob Grimm that "book dealers are now as numerous as the grains of sand on the ocean shore.... In Berlin ... there are at present more than thirty!"[86] These figures included second-hand book shops. In 1816 Dresden had roughly 10 book shops and Leipzig about 40. Görlitz, Bautzen, and Zittau, three cities in Lusatia with approximately 9,000 inhabitants apiece, each had one book shop. Few cities with smaller populations had book shops unless they were spa, residence, or university centers. An exception was Lübben in Lower Lusatia, which, although it fit none of these categories, had enough cultured nobles and government officials in its population of 3,000 to support a book store.[87]

In South and West Germany, even urban centers were moribund book markets. On his 1816 journey, Perthes observed that:

> In Barmen, Duisberg, Lemgo, Detmold, Paderborn, [and] Hamm book
> dealers now can survive only by the greatest effort; at that they just scrape by
> ... [In] Münster (West.) the once-notable book dealerships grew weak or

disappeared thirty years ago ... [There] a few young and capable book dealers have recently established themselves, but find it difficult to procure books from Leipzig, there being no freight service at all between the two cities and the cost of mailing through the postal services being terribly high.[88]

Further west, conditions were no better:

> Conditions in Düsseldorf are wretched: businessmen and gymnasia teachers cannot order the books they need [through a dealer]; they have, rather, to order them themselves from Frankfurt or from the firm of Bädeker in Essen.... The entire retail book trade of Coblenz is in the hands of an honest bookbinder who sells books as a sideline. In these places, as in Aachen, Trier, Wiesbaden, and others there is a great need for vigorous and competent book dealers.[89]

Perthes judged the book trade of Augsburg to be one of the liveliest in Germany. Yet the leading firms there lamented that their markets were declining.

It is unlikely, however, that these firms did anything substantial to stem the decline: the German book trade was, a handful of men excepted, anything but dynamic. As a nineteenth century historian wrote of the immediate post-Napoleonic years: "The spirit of enterprise and of speculative undertaking was still dormant; the book trade was still carried on in the traditional way."[90] The institutions of the regular book trade were simply not designed to sell as many books as possible. It was considered unworthy of the dignity of a bookseller to attempt to stir up new markets. The notion that one should strive to expand his market was sneered at by most in the trade as an expression of tawdry shopkeeper mentality.

The bookman was not a shopkeeper, not a mere merchant; he was, rather, the dispenser, sometimes even the initiator, of the higher products of the mind, which certainly could not be hawked like brooms, vegetables, or other ordinary commodities. The books he sold were genuine books, not the printed rubbish intended for the canaille:

> It has not been found possible to maintain a reputable book dealership while selling drivel for elementary schools, catechisms, primers, Bibles, and song books. The sale of such things can without envy be left in the hands of the binder [and the Colporteur].[91]

The bookman viewed himself as the trusted friend and intellectual advisor to the educated. As publisher, he made it possible for them to present their thoughts to the world; as retailer, he counseled them on what to read and purchase. The basic motive of the bookman was less the search for profit than that for status—to be looked up to as one of the intellectual elite of his community. Any attempt to blast open the book market was considered degrading to the dignity of the trade. Perthes' 1816 essay *The German Book Trade as a Precondition for a German Literature (Der deutsche Buchhandel als Bedingung des Daseyns einer deutschen Literatur)*, the most famous and influential articulation of the ideals of the regular book trade ever written, stated with pride that: "in the German book trade honesty, hard work, and good will count more than wealth, as I myself have gratefully experienced.... One can find many diligent, striving bookmen, but one never finds rich ones."[92]

These dignified figures, the bookmen of the regular trade, were content to have their books printed on slow, hand-operated presses little different from those constructed by Gutenberg in the fifteenth century. Although a German named Friedrich König had invented a revolutionary high speed press in 1808, and made it even faster four years later by coupling it to a steam engine, no German firm felt the need for one badly enough to buy it before the 1820s. Long before that, König had found customers in England. After 1817 a few German printers did import English Stanhope Presses, an improved version of the traditional book press. But as of 1820 there were still fewer than a dozen printers in all of Germany that could produce editions of more than 10,000 copies. Even these preferred to produce smaller editions, as they made more money on setting the type than on the actual printing. If perhaps there wasn't much need to do large editions, there was also no desire to do them.[93]

Still, some lucre had to adhere to the bookman's hands if he were to continue his noble operation. There was much day-to-day detail to which he had to attend. Most publishing houses were also book shops, a combination which was a product of the old Barter System still in use in some places at the end of the Napoleonic Wars. Under this system, dealers exchanged their publications with one another to get a decent selection of books to sell. This system was a hindrance to the development of the book trade, as it "made the book shops of small cities into dumping places for literature's dregs–no publisher of pretention or note would exchange his books for the less valuable ones of the small city publisher."[94] If the small city dealers wanted good books, they had to pay cash for them, since they should not return unsold copies, they would only order books sure to sell, such as famous cookbooks, the ancient classics, and a few popular reference works.

## Bulwark of the regular trade—the Sale or Return System

Fortunately, there were other ways of procuring books to retail. One could order on credit but with a firm commitment to buy. Increasingly used was the Sale or Return System, which had been developed during the last third of the eighteenth century. The Sale or Return System was based upon the use of approval. Publishers sent out books to retailers on approval. Accounts ran from January to December, but the retailer could keep books received during a given calendar year until the following year's Easter Fair of the book trade in Leipzig, at which time he either had to return the book (paying the freight himself) in good condition or, if he had either sold it or damaged it, pay for it. Often he would pay two-thirds of the cost at the Easter Fair and the remainder at the traders Michaelmas Fair in Leipzig. Most dealers did not handle their business in Leipzig personally, but rather had it done for them by agents there.[95]

Unique to Germany, the Sale or Return System was in some ways a great advance over the Barter System, and it had advantages over the purely cash transactions that were the norm in other European countries. It made it possible for the retail book seller to offer a wide range of books to his customers without risking great sums and without having to involve himself in publishing. It allowed the educated inhabitants of small cities to partake in the country's cultural life much more than their counterparts in Great Britain or France. And, by lessening the amount of capital needed to establish a book shop, it made possible a growth in the number of shops.

Under the Sale or Return System the publisher generally sent out books, on his own initiative, to any bookseller he wanted. While most retailers accepted books so sent, a growing number, feeling overwhelmed as the number of titles published grew yearly, would accept on approval only those books which they had specifically requested.[96]

The publisher still retained important initiatives. He did not have to send books on approval, and books which were steady sellers were often sold only for cash or a firm commitment to purchase. Whatever the terms he offered his book on, the publisher always set its retail selling price. The book was to be sold at this price everywhere in the country, despite differing freight costs; this was a custom found only in Germany. The retail price was conventionally 33.3 percent higher than the price the book shop paid; the 33.3 percent, in other words, was the retailer's margin. That popular books were occasionally offered at a smaller margin was considered highly improper by retailers.[97]

The chief disadvantage of the Sale or Return System was its intrinsic inefficiency, which was one reason for the high price of books. Because more books had to be printed and sent out on approval than usually could be sold, the publisher calculated the retail price so that his costs would be covered by only a part of the edition. In 1816 there was a Latin work in print whose publisher had to sell only 250 of the 600 copies he had had printed to break even. At the other extreme was the publisher of Funk's history of Frederick the Great; he gambled on selling 700 of the edition's 750 copies. The normal calculation was that two-thirds of the edition had to be sold to cover costs; thus the publisher of Niebuhr's *Roman History (Römische Geschichte)* needed to sell 600 of 1,000 copies.[98]

The greater part of the task of marketing books was assumed by the publisher, who in most cases did very little. After listing the book's author, title, publisher, and price in the Fair Catalog and perhaps one other catalog, he would passively await orders. Frequently, few came. A few publishers issued their own catalogs.[99] In a minority of cases the publisher would advertise in newspapers or journals, especially in the months before Christmas, which were the high season for book sales. Catalogs were used by book stores to inform both themselves and their customers what was available. So too was the *Allgemeiner typographische Monatsberich*, published since 1810 by Bertuch of Weimar. Each issue listed some newly published books. Eight thousand copies were printed each month and distributed gratis to book shops for further distribution to their customers. Bertuch financed this initiative by accepting advertisements from publishers.[100]

These advertisements were typical at that time. No illustrations or fancy lettering caught the eye. Ads for journals and non-fictional works were frequently composed of the table of contents and nothing more. Subtler were the laudatory "reviews," which some publishers sent in for their books; these sometimes included favorable excerpts from real reviews.

Novels and single-volumed works were seldom advertised. Large multi-volumed works, like collected works of classic authors or illustrated reference works intended for a general audience, were often elaborately advertised. Such works represented considerable effort and capital outlay by their publishers. An example was J. A. C. Löhr's *Complete Natural History for Lovers and Teachers (Gemeinnützige und vollständige Naturgeschichte für Liebhaber und Lehrer)*, a five-volume work with "more than 400 illustrations"[101] published in 1816 by Gerhard Fleischer the Younger of Leipzig. Fleischer's notice for the book exemplifies the cloying tone found in much of the advertising which was aimed at the middle-class market then:

> The author of this book, who has long been known to the public, has done his utmost to do justice to its title. It has been his intention that nothing which is significant or worth knowing and at the same time entertaining should fall prey to omission.
>
> The schoolmaster who wishes to prepare his students for their initiation into the deeper and more difficult study of natural history... yet wants to alleviate the undue rigor and sweeten the dryness of the subject, justifiably seeks and therefore will not fail to appreciate the rich measure of description, explanation, observation, and anecdote in this work; so too will the nature lover.
>
> Not only the agriculturalist, but also the artist, the horticulturist, the forester—yes! and even the apothecary and practicing doctor will find here much which they should know which will be advantageous and useful in countless ways. And of course our young, inquisitive friends and lovers of birds, animals, butterflies, insects, and plants have not been forgotten in the writing of this book...
>
> Those who understand that God and Nature are an inextricable and profound unity, and that a deeper awareness of Nature yields a closer consciousness of the wishes of the Creator, will find this book a worthwhile exercise in piety.[102]

Like most other large works then, Löhr's was offered on subscription—people would sign up for all five volumes. Sometimes the full payment had to be made in advance, as was the case with this book, whose subscription price, valid until Easter 1817, was six Reichstaler, 16 Groschen (or 12 Florins, 12 Kreuzer). After Easter the price rose. To motivate book shops to collect subscriptions, Fleischer would give them a free set for each five orders; such deals were usual.

Subscriptions with full payment in advance had been used by German publishers since the mid-eighteenth century, although they had been frequently criticized as an outrage upon the buying public, which not seldom had to wait years to receive the books it had paid so much for—publishers used the subscribers' money and not their own capital to finance these ventures. There were times when a subscriber got nothing at all.[103] In the 1815–1820 period, advance-payment subscriptions were more popular than ever with Germany's ultra-cautious publishers.

There were, to be sure, more daring publishers who required only a down-payment on subscriptions. They too enticed the customer with the promise of a lower price. An elaborate 1819 edition of *Polybius*, for example, could be had on subscription for four Reichstaler; at the end of the year no further subscriptions were taken and the price rose to six Reichstaler. The six volumes of August, Baron Steigentesch's collected writings, published by Heyer and Leske of Darmstadt in 1819, cost the subscriber one-quarter less than the non-subscriber. Those discerning enough to subscribe to the two large (quarto size), lavishly illustrated volumes of the *The Journey of His Majesty Prince Maximilian of Neuwied to Brazil in the Years 1815 to 1817 (Reise Sr. Durchlaucht des Prinzen Maximilian von Neuwied nach Brasilien in Jahren 1815 bis 1817)* got not only a favorable price, but also their names were printed in the book. Enough connoisseurs signed up to require a second printing of the first volume within a year.[104]

## Segmenting markets

Despite the general torpor of the book trade there were publishers who saw the advantage of appealing to different market segments. In January 1816, for example, the publisher Baron Cotta of Stuttgart proclaimed a new 20-volume edition of the famous writer Goethe's works, with subscription prices to be in effect until October of that year. As was then normal with ambitious works, the subscriber had a choice of paper and prices—segmenting the market according to taste and price sensitivity (see Table 1.1).

*Table 1.1* Market segmentation

| Type of paper | Price in installments | Price if paid in advance |
| --- | --- | --- |
| Ordinary | 30 Florins | 22 Florins |
| Good white | 40 Florins | 33 Florins |
| Good Swiss | 52 Florins | 44 Florins |
| Vellum | not available | 66 Florins |

Only 14 copies of the vellum edition were sold. Even the vellum (parchment) edition, however, came without binding, dust jacket, or even a paper cover—just as all other books did then.[105] The customer had to take the book to a binder, whose fees made the complete book more costly than even the high price paid to the book store.

To lessen the financial pain of purchasing a book, a few publishers began in this period to issue books in several sections, much like issues of a periodical, rather than in whole volumes. The total cost to the buyer remained the same—high—but many found it easier to get up the relatively small sum needed for each section than to get up a large sum for the entire book or volume. Karl von Rotteck's *Weltgeschichte* for example, was released by the Stuttgart publisher Hoffmann in segments costing five Groschen each. Issuing in sections was the only marketing device new to this period, and, like most of the other new ideas in marketing adopted by the German book trade during the first half of the nineteenth century, it had originated in England.[106]

## Friedrich Arnold Brockhaus

First-hand exposure to English business had helped shape the genius of Friedrich Arnold Brockhaus (1772–1823), the "intelligent speculative bookman"[107] who, more than any other German publisher of that time, knew how to lift marketing above the spheres of passivity or of mere mechanical employment of merchandising forms. A wholesale merchant in English manufactures before entering the book trade, Brockhaus always remained an aggressive businessman.

Brockhaus understood the mentality of the middle class better than any other publisher of his time, better indeed than almost any other publisher of the century. He understood its taste, and the yearnings which determined that taste; he understood as well that the traditional high prices of German books and the traditional stuffy ways in which they were marketed kept much of the middle class away from the book market. The basis of his success lay as much in the way he marketed his publications as in the books themselves. His most successful books were an edition of Luther's translation of the Bible—which had been and was being done by many other publishers—and his encyclopedia—which had been a sales disappointment to five publishers before Brockhaus bought the rights to it in 1808.[108] By setting the price for the encyclopedia about one-third lower than was conventional for a work of its size, he was able to complete the first edition by 1810, sell it by 1811, do a second edition (of 3,000 sets) in 1811–1812, and a fifth by 1818–1819. In announcing the fifth edition, Brockhaus proudly said that it "could well be called the cheapest book in the world."[109] At 12.5 Reichstaler for the 10-volume set (on ordinary paper) it was hardly that, but it was the cheapest book of its size on the German book market. Brockhaus had 12,000 sets of the fifth edition printed, some of them on costlier papers for those for whom a cheap book would never do.[110] To even his surprise, they were all sold by means of subscriptions within a year.

In March–September 1820, 10,000 more sets had to be printed. "In the entire history of the [German] book trade no work of that size had ever been so successful."[111]

Brockhaus *Conversationslexikon* (encyclopedia) created a whole new market, one which has been vital to the book trade ever since. The first great encyclopedia for the culturally ambitious middle class, it was imitated by publishers all over Europe, United States, and even England—one of the rare cases where a German achievement influenced the English book trade rather than the converse.[112]

But other German publishers were slow to follow Brockhaus' methods of marketing. A competitor encyclopedia issued by the Berlin publisher C. F. Amelang from 1809 to 1813 was only on its second edition in 1820; these editions, moreover, were markedly smaller than Brockhaus'. Although Amelang's encyclopedia had 15 volumes—one-third more than Brockhaus'—it cost over three times as much (37–40 Reichstaler, depending on paper).[113]

## Book piracy drives competition

Where Brockhaus set his prices low as a matter of policy, other publishers only lowered theirs if compelled to by lagging sales or by competition from unauthorized cheap editions of their books published by the "pirates" of the South and West German states. Baden, Bavaria, Hesse-Darmstadt, and Wuerttemberg permitted their native publishers to pirate books originally published outside the country's borders. The legal status of piracy in Prussia's Rhine Province being murky for a few years after 1815, some pirating was done there, too.[114] Cheaper than the originals and sometimes better printed as well, unauthorized editions of popular books (no other kind was pirated) dominated the book markets of Southern Germany, a situation which North German publishers, and many from the South as well, viewed as a grave threat to the existence of the German book trade. The North German trade's greatest spokesman, Friedrich Perthes, denounced piracy as a threat to the existence of German literature itself.[115]

Such assertions, countered the pirates' most candid spokesman, Johann Wilhelm Spitz of Cologne, were but the crocodile tears of gross and arrogant profiteers. Men like Baron Cotta, according to Spitz, grew rich by forcing the German public to pay through the nose for its classics (Cotta published Goethe, Schiller, and many other of the classic German writers). The Berlin publisher G. A. Reimer extorted the outrageous sum of 12 Reichstaler for his edition of Jean Paul's *Titian*, while Spitz charged no more than three Reichstaler for his pirated edition—and earned a profit of 4,000 Reichstaler on annual sales of 2,000 copies of the book. The prices of the regular trade, said Spitz, repelled customers, kept them out of the book market. He was right.[116]

Only slightly less wicked than piracy were, in the opinion of most in the book trade, the final two marketing stratagems a publisher might have used. These were: (1) selling directly either to the public or to retailers who were not part of the trade, and (2) using prizes and premiums to promote sales. The latter was rare. I have been able to unearth only one case of it, an ara- besque scheme promising 20,000 premiums, the top one of which was 800,000 Gulden plus "a beautiful plot of land."[117] To enter, one had merely to purchase four Reichstaler's worth of books "about subjects which interest everyone"[118] from the sponsors. The *Monatsbericht* denounced the offer as probably fraudulent.

Sales to non-members of the trade were considerably more common. In Bavaria, thousands of copies of a two-volume mélange of material on farming called *Der verständige Bauer Simon Struf* were sold through government offi- cials, who pushed it energetically because they could make large profits from it.[119] Book store owners all over Germany lamented that publishers sold books through the likes of postal officials, giving the stores stiff competition. Some publishers were said to be so heedless of their colleagues' welfare, so indiffer- ent to trade solidarity, that they deluged private individuals with mailed offers to buy direct. The publishers' defense to book shop complaints was that many shops were too passive, forcing the publishers to find more vigorous outlets through which to sell their books.[120]

There was a good deal of validity to that argument: book stores *were* gener- ally passive operations. They preferred to let the customers come to them unbidden, which they felt maintained their dignity. If they advertised in their local newspapers, it was almost always because a publisher had paid for the advert or because the books were their own publications.[121]

Once a potential customer entered a book shop, he or she could peruse what was in stock—generally steady-selling cookbooks, classics and reference works, as well as whatever new books publishers had been sending in on approval. He might discuss his needs with the shop owner or look at a catalog. There was no hurry, one could spend hours there. If he wanted a book that was not in stock, the book shop would order it for him; this was so even if he merely wanted to look at it. It was customary to give the customer any book he desired on approval so that he could consider at home whether or not to purchase it. The great Brockhaus judged this a ridiculous way to sell books:

> In many parts of Germany the catering to the potential customer's outra- geous whims has gone so far that he is allowed to read through prospec- tive purchases from beginning to end, cutting the pages as he goes [this was not supposed to be done] and then giving the book to his friends so that they can read them too! In the end these well-thumbed, often bat- tered books [are not purchased] ... but are sent back to the publisher.[122]

This absurd practice, Brockhaus maintained, drove operational costs up so much, that they could only be covered by setting the price of books too high for most people; the British and the French, who really knew how to sell books, would never use such methods.

There can be no doubt that the genteel ways by which most German book shops attempted to sell books were better suited to dealing with the traditional, tiny, wealthy public than with the newer middle-class public which Brockhaus understood so well. Most German booksellers, however, would have rejected any attempt to do away with giving books to customers on approval; and not only because it would have been undignified to do so, but also because they were convinced that the sight and feel of a book in the hand, in the home, generated an almost irresistible urge to purchase and possess it. And, while the price of books was high, booksellers were generous in giving credit to customers whom they knew.[123]

Some book stores did even more—they granted their customers discounts from the publishers' selling prices. These so-called "customer discounts" normally amounted to 10 percent of the publisher's selling price. In Berlin, for example, the discount was never more than 10–12.5 percent and was only given when requested. Some Leipzig firms, on the other hand, spared transportation and other costs because they operated from the most important center of the book trade, offered 25 percent discounts and sold, by mail and by messenger, so far beyond the city's limits that it was difficult for the book shops of Saxon Lusatia to compete with them. "Customer discounts" undermined the concept that the publisher should determine the retail price of a book; they were said to degrade those who granted them—and, by association, all book dealers—"to the level of the Jews, who demand such outrageous prices that one can confidently offer them half the asked-for sum."[124]

Some dealers offered these discounts unasked. Most who gave them insisted that they were compelled to do so by their adamantly niggardly customers, who would buy nothing without a sweetening discount.

For all the book stores' whining about parsimonious customers and unfair treatment by publishers, however, few of them went bankrupt in this period. Indeed, some did very well. The busier Berlin shops sold 6,000–10,000 Reichstaler's worth of books each year. More representative were the shops of Lusatia. They managed to scrape by, in no danger of going under, but hardly making big profits.[125]

### "Lending libraries" *(Leihbibliotheken)*

Yet it was true that many book stores had to do more than sell (and publish) books to keep solvent. The Aachen branch of the DuMont-Schauberg book dealership of Cologne sold toothbrushes and other items for dental hygiene in addition to books; its competitor J. A. Mayer stocked things like globes and paint boxes. These were not isolated examples.[126] The most important source of supplemental income for book shops was the lending libraries and reading circles operated by many of them. Since lending libraries could be very lucrative in themselves—people had to pay to borrow a book—and also were believed to encourage the sale of books, many were established in the years after the Napoleonic Wars. A few were independent businesses, but most were affiliates of book dealers. The famous Göttingen book firm owed by the Ruprecht family set one up in 1815. The ambitious J. S. Mayer of Aachen devoted more effort to his lending library than to the selling of books.[127]

The number of lending libraries was beginning to increase rapidly in the years after 1815, a sign of growing assertiveness in the trade. Like book shops, lending libraries were located predominantly in cities and the more cultivated towns. It was through lending libraries, and not through the sale of books, that the German book trade met the reading needs of the growing middle-class public: where the genteel, clumsy retailing institutions helped make books so expensive that middle-class readers could not afford to buy even a fraction of what they wanted to read, the circulating library provided them with all they could read at fees they could afford.[128]

The fees and terms of the Christoph Müller Lending Library in Memmingen illustrate this. The occasional user paid three Kreuzer for one to six days, six Kreuzer for seven to 12 days, and nine Kreuzer for 13 to 18 days. Mueller also offered "monthly, half-yearly, and yearly subscriptions,... to be paid in full, in advance."[129] These were, for example, six Florins for one year, with a maximum of five volumes per visit and a total of 140 volumes for the year.[130] Since novels cost nearly two Florins a volume then—for which sum one of Müller's library users could read 35 volumes—the appeal of the lending library is obvious.[131]

Interestingly, the appeal of the lending library extended even to the rich, who in many cases loaned what they could easily have bought. Of the institutions of the regular book trade, the lending library was the least affected by snobbery.[132]

The lack of snobbery, not to say squeamishness, is surprising considering the physical condition lending libraries' books often attained. Although borrowers were held responsible for maintaining the books in good condition, the management of any lending library had to contend with: (1) people who liked to tear out the pictures from illustrated volumes (which were expensive), (2) servant girls who, in picking up and returning books for their mistresses carelessly heaved them into the soft fruits and bloody meat which lay in their baskets, (3) low characters who borrowed books to sell them to used book dealers, and (4), most common, people whose unwashed and unkempt hands saturated the pages of books with grease and filthy stains. Failure to restrain such excesses caused the financial ruin of more than one lending library.[133]

The institution itself, however, remained strong. Lending libraries were the basic market for much of Germany's literary production. Fiction in particular was rarely purchased by private individuals.[134] The appetite of lending libraries for books can best be depicted by some figures on their size. Anton Sandersky's library in Landshut grew from 1,200 volumes in 1814 to 2,526 volumes in 1820. The Geigler Library in Schweinfurth had about 3,000 volumes (1813). Lindauer in Munich had almost 4,000. In large cities like Berlin, Bremen, and Munich there were a handful with more than 10,000 books; those in provincial cities, on the other hand, sometimes had fewer than 500. The tendency was for libraries to grow in size during this period. There were approximately 350–400 lending libraries in Germany. They did represent a sizeable market for books. Yet it has to be remembered that, since many people could read a single copy of a book belonging to a lending library, the most popular books frequently achieved only modest sales: they were much read, but little bought.[135]

## Understanding popular tastes in reading matter

To know what the popular taste was, therefore, it is more important to ask what the lending libraries stocked than what the sales figures were:

> Imagine that you entered a book store in Zeitz or Gera, in Bayreuth or Wiesbaden, in Flensburg or Koblenz about 1820 and inquired about the tastes of the greater part of the [reading] public. In view of the small number who actually purchase books, you would be informed, one could judge these tastes only by the records of the lending library.[136]

What were these tastes? Foreign, especially French, literature was popular in the large cities. In Frankfurt/Main, Johann Daniel Simon operated a "French and German Reading Institute." Lindauer in Munich had more foreign than German books, another Munich lending library stocked French books exclusively. In general, Munich libraries carried a wide range of books, from the lightest fiction and travel description to theology and the natural sciences. The same was doubtless true of lending libraries in other large cities, too. But most of the books in the lending libraries, in Munich as elsewhere, were light diversion literature, kept in plentiful supply because the standard patron read books to be diverted, nothing more. Many were bored women.[137]

Heinrich von Kleist's description of a Würzburg lending library is telling. He found no books by the classic German authors, but "Knight and Robber stories, on the right Knight and Robber stories with ghosts, on the left those without ghosts, and (also) true Knight and Robber stories, whichever one wanted."[138] Some of them were based (more or less) on the exploits of actual bandits like Schinderhannes, who was executed in Mainz in 1803 after orchestrating a spectacular crime spree; others were totally imaginary bandits. These stories had been a lending library staple since the eighteenth century. Some of the stories themselves were much older. Most of the authors were unknown, often anonymous hacks, but they did include such famous writers as Fouqué and Zschokke. The most popular creators of these books were Christian Heinrich Spiess (1755–1799), Carl Gottlob Cramer (1758–1817), and Christian August Vulpius (1762–1837), whose *Rinaldo Rinaldini* (3 volumes, 1798) is usually considered the definitive novel of this genre.

Characteristic titles of Knight and Robber stories were: *Aranzo the Noble Bandit Leader: Terror in Spain's Valleys and Mountains (Aranzo der edle Raüber-hauptmann: Ein Schrecken in Spaniens Thälern und Gebirge* 2 volumes, Leipzig,

1820), *The Bandits Cave of Carastro* (*Die Banditenhöle von Carastro* Quedlin-berg, 1818), and *Romando – Leader of a Band of Bandits* (*Romando, Hauptmann einer Räuberbande* 3 volumes, Leipzig 1820).[139]

Other circulating library staples included "trashy novels, horror stories... women's novels, and family pieces in the manner of Iffland and Kotzebue."[140] Horror stories chilled their readers with such titles as *The Terrible Adventure in the Dead-Filled Vaults of Bentheim* (*Das schaudervolle Abentheuer im Todtengewölbe zu Bentheim* 2 volumes, Nordhausen, 1819). The large number of works for women was composed of both syrupy romances, some of them translations from the French or English, and of novels in which love was enlivened by adventure. Examples include *Bertram and Idda, or Knighthood and Love* (*Bertram und Idda, oder Rittersinn und Liebe* Magdeburg, 1816), by an anonymous author, and *Agatha or the Vault of Graves* (*Agathe, oder das Grabengewölbe* 3 volumes, Leipzig, 1817) by August H. J. Lafontaine, which were typical love-adventure novels. The ability to enchant female readers made Lafontaine (1758–1831), as well as H. Clauren (pseudonym for Carl Heun, 1771–1854), Franz Josef Wait-zenegger (1784–1822), and August von Kotzebue writers whose productions no lending library could be without.[141] Many lending libraries also purchased works of cheerful literary fluff, like "B-r's" (1819) *The Happy Story-teller, or Character Portraits from the Folder of a Cheerful Painter* (*Der lustige Erzahler, oder Charaktergemälde und Karrikaturzeichungen aus der Mappe eines frohsinnigen Malers)*; the publisher recommended it to "lending libraries, reading circles, and everyone who wants to exterminate gloom and boredom."[142]

For other tastes, numerous libraries had "secret" shelves filled with erotic literature like *Coelestine's Stockings* (*Cölestines Strumpfbänder)* and other trans-lations of titillating French books. Illustrated works on anatomy served the same purpose. Actual pornography was seldom available for borrowing; it had to be purchased from select book shops.[143]

Some of the works in lending libraries had been popular for decades, necessitating occasional new editions as old copies wore out or as new copies were needed for new libraries. Knigge's *Dealing with People* (*Umgang mit Men-schen* 1787) was such a book, as were Joachim Heinrich Campe's children's classic *Robinson the Younger* (*Robinson der Jüngere* 1779–1780), Johann Gott-fried Schanabel's *Felsenberg Island* (*Die Insel Felsenberg* 1731–1743), like Campe's work inspired by Defoe's *Robinson Crusoe*, and Johann Martin Mill-er's *Siegwart* (1776), a Werther imitation. Some eighteenth-century poetry remained popular: L. C. H. Hölty's *Gedichte* (1783) and Moritz August v. Thümmel's *Wilhelmine, ein prosaisch komisches Gedicht* (1764). More recent poetry in steady demand then included August Tiedge's *Urania, Gedicht in sechs Gesängen*, J. P. Hebel's *Allemanische Gedichte* (1803) and his *Schatzkästlein des Rheinischen Hausfreundes* (1808–1811), and the poems of Friedrich Mat-thison (1761–1831).[144]

Poetry, erotica, adventure, horror, undying love—all of this literature was much read. The works of Goethe and the era's famous Romantics, a few of Tieck's and Chamisso's excepted, were not much read.[145]

People who had Germany's cultural welfare at heart shuddered at the thought of what people borrowed from the lending libraries. Sometimes they consoled themselves with the hypothesis that people of property and stature would never frequent these places and that "the public for this [lending library] literature was made up of petty artisans, journeymen, workers, servants, and the like."[146] Who else would read the brainless rubbish which predominated in the lending libraries?—so went the hypothesis. But the hypothesis itself was rubbish, especially at this period. It was not that journeymen and workers and the like had such good taste—they didn't—but that they were unable to afford the fees lending libraries charged. If servants read books from the libraries, these were books their masters and mistresses had withdrawn for their own reading. The users of lending libraries were solid members of the middle to noble classes.[147]

## Reading circles

Those whose reading desires were more serious, or merely more pretentious, joined "reading societies." Whether they were called "circles" or "societies," they operated upon the same principle, whereby people with similar interests pooled their resources to purchase books (and periodicals) collectively. There may have been a few hundred of these in existence in the period 1815–1820. Some were established on the initiative of book shop owners, who would advertise for members with newspaper notices and mailed prospects; they would order the required books and periodicals and would set up comfortable rooms for the members to read in. Memberships were costlier than lending library subscriptions. Groups founded by book shops generally took the fashionable literary periodicals of the day. Some even had directors to guide the reading towards maximum enrichment.[148]

Other reading societies were established independently of book shops, generally by clubs and organizations. They would have their own reading rooms. Freemasons frequently did this; their reading groups bought not only enough Masonic literature to create a steady market for it but also many classics of ancient and modern literature and other works as well.[149] In Prussia (and presumably elsewhere) people who shared similar scientific and learned interests often bought books and periodicals collectively, and so did scholars. Young academics, teachers, and clerics were forced to found reading societies because their salaries were too low to let them buy all the serious works they wanted to read. In contrast to lending libraries, reading societies could be good markets for scholarly books.[150]

The book purchases of lending libraries and reading groups made up a significant part of the regular book trade's book market. Sales to individuals made up the other major part of the market. These sales were modest. The books most frequently purchased for individual use were: the Greek and Latin classics, some German classics, devotional works, children's literature, general histories, encyclopedias, and other reference works.[151]

The ancient classics were sold to a market made up of university and gymnasia students and the very educated. Many editions vied for this market. Until 1816 those published in Halle by the Orphanage dominated the school trade, but in that year the Leipzig publisher Karl Tauchnitz (1761–1836) began to print school editions by the stereotype process, which made it possible for him to sell the books cheaply. Tauchnitz was the first Leipzig publisher to use stereotype. His editions had small print which some found difficult to read, and some scholars complained that the texts had too many errors, yet their price and quality were good enough to win them a dominance over the school market they were to hold for a quarter century.[152]

Sales of the classic German authors lagged behind those of the ancients, one reason being that the former were not part of the gymnasia or university curriculum and thus had fewer student buyers. Goethe in particular sold lethargically—"Years could pass before a provincial book shop sold one copy of Goethe." [153] Gellert, Jean Paul, and Schiller were more popular, especially in relatively inexpensive pirated editions. A Carlsruhe pirate named F. W. Müller was able to sell four editions of Schiller's works between 1814 and 1820; the authorized publishers, Christian Gottlob Körner and then Baron Cotta, sold only two within this time.[154] Spitz of Cologne, who retailed as well as published pirated books, said that he needed 400 sets of Müller 's Schiller editions to satisfy his customers alone.[155] Müller's "Bureau of German Classics" began to do the first complete edition of Germany's classics in 1815, a venture which delighted the public as it infuriated the original, authorized publishers of the classics.[156]

Another notorious pirate, Johann Jakob Mäcken of Reutlingen, helped spur the distribution of the era's most successful devotional work, Johann Heirich Daniel Zschokke's *Hours of Devotion* (*Stunden der Andacht*, 8 volumes, 1808–1816). The first complete edition (1816) was priced by its publisher H. R. Sauerländer of Aarau, Switzerland, at 16 Reichstaler or 24 Florins. Within a year Sauerländer had to halve the price to meet the competition of Mäcken's pirated version. By 1821 he had sold five complete editions, a sales success which rivalled that of Brockhaus' encyclopedia. The book was purchased by both private customers and lending libraries and became one of the great staple items of the book trade.[157]

Among the customers of the regular book trade it was important to own a few secular works of history and general information as well as devotional works like the *Stunden der Andacht*. Often-purchased works on history were: Karl Friedrich Becker's nine-volume *World History* (*Die Weltgeschichte* 1801–1805), Karl v. Rotteck's *Universal History from the Beginning of Historical Understanding to our Times* (*Allgemeine Geschichte, vom Anfang der historischen Kenntniß bis auf unsere Zeiten,* 6 volumes, 1813–1818), and Friedrich Kohlrausch's *German History for School and Home* (*Des deutsche Geschichte für Schule und Haus* 1815), a work which gave its readers stiff dosages of national self-glorifiation.[158]

These ponderous histories were not cheap—Kohlrausch's was the least expensive at one Reichstaler, 18 Groschen—to get up their purchase prices must have been difficult for many who bought them. They sold well because they met the great need for general works which would enable middle-class people to educate and enrich themselves. Typical of such people were the government officials who had been advanced because of the need for talent during the war period. Most of them had had no university education. Even more popular than the works of Becker, Rotteck, or Kohlrausch among such people was Brockhaus' encyclopedia, which was intended to be a compendium of the topics about which normal educated persons conversed (thus the German title—*Konversationslexikon*).[159]

The urge to home education motivated middle- and upper-class parents to procure suitable reading material for their children; parents transmitted to their offspring their belief in the social and intellectual importance of reading. The custom of giving children books or periodicals as gifts for Easter, birthdays, and especially Christmas, was well entrenched in the middle to upper classes by this time.[160] Aggressive book shops advertised children's literature heavily in the late autumn. There was a great body of children's material available for them to advertise—one book shop selected 200 titles to push in 1820.[161] Some of the most purchased children's books stemmed from the eighteenth century, like Campe's *Robinson* and Georg Christian Raff's *Naturgeschichte für Kinder* (in the revision of D. F. A. A. Meyers). One of the nineteenth century's most beloved Catholic children's stories first became popular in this period. It was Christoph Schmid's *The Easter Egg ... "Die Ostereier, eine Erzählung zum Ostergeschenke."* Four thousand copies of the first edition were printed in 1816; in 1818 a second printing, of more than 4,000 copies, was needed.

Books intended for women were also important to the book trade. Many cookbooks, for example, enjoyed great sales. They were considered good gifts for girls about to be married and for already married women as well. Scores were published. Publishers competed fiercely with one another to get successful ones, imitations and unauthorized editions of which were common. Sophia Juliana Weiler's venerable *Augsburger Kochbuch* (2nd edition 1788, 14th edition 1819) was one of the most popular.[162]

For those ladies whose interests transcended the domestic hearth the book shops offered more elevated reading matter such as Professor Johann Genersich's *World History for Educated Ladies with Special Attention to the Mores of Famous Ladies of All Times* (*Weltgeschichte für gebildete Frauenzimmer, mit vorzüglichen Rücksicht auf Völkersitten und auf berühmte Frauen aller Zeiten*, Leipzig 1817), a book in which "everything is presented so smoothly and easily, and the Useful so artfully blended with the Beautiful, that the fair reader, will surely prefer it to novels and romances."[163] Better-known responses to feminine reading needs then were the illustrated annual almanacs of prose, poetry, and song called "pocket books". Suitors, husbands, and lovers understood that these "always completely fulfilled their purpose, which was to be suitable gifts for educated women."[164] Many publishers had offerings in this market. Among others, Brookhaus did the *Urania*, Cotta the *Taschenbuch für Damen*,

Friedrich Fleischer the *Minerva*, Wilmans of Frankfurt/Main the *Pocket Book of Love and Friendship (Taschenbuch der Liebe und Freundschaft)*, and Leo of Leipzig both the *Rosen* and the *Forget Me Not (Vergissmeinnicht)*. Written by the popular author Clauren, the latter was "beloved by the educated and half-educated world alike."[165] Servant girls are said to have pooled their resources to get up the two Reichstaler, 20 Groschen it cost. It was sold by postal officials and fancy goods stores in addition to book shops.

It sold more than any other almanac. Yet its sales in 1819 amounted to only 4,000 copies. The book market was not very large.[166]

## Notes

1 See R. Schenda, *Volk ohne Buch. Studien zur Sozialgechichte der popularen Lesestoffe 1770–1910*, Frankfurt/Main 1970, *passim* but especially Chapter I. Schenda's is one of the best works on reading habits and attitudes towards reading in Germany that has been done in this century.

2 From an 1840 speech by the prosperous, conservative publisher F. J. Frommann. Quoted in G. Menz, *Der deutsche Buchhandel*, 2 ed. rev., Gotha 1942, pp. 128–129.

3 F. Schulze, *Der deutsche Buchhandel und die geistigen Strommungen der letzten Hundert Jahre*, Leipzig 1925, pp. 92–93; J. Goldfriedrich, *Geschichte des deutschen Buchhandels vom Beginn der Fremdherrschaft bis zur Reform des Boersenvereins im neuen deutschen Reiche, 1805–1889*, Leipzig, 1913, p. 199; W. Stieda, *Der Buechermarkt an den Hochschulen Erfurt, Wittenberg und Halle in der Vergangenheit*, Cologne 1934, p. 174.

4 *Wochenblatt für Buchhaendler, Antiquare, Musik- und Dispotenhaendler*, 1820, Nr. 34, pp. 265–266. Hereafter the *Wochenblatt* will be cited as the *Krieger'sche [after the editor] Wochenblatt*.

5 B. Friedrich Arnold, "Ueber die theuren Buecherpreise in Deutschland und die Ursachen derselben," *Literarisches Conversationsblatt*, 1821, Nrs. 169–170. Reprinted in H. E. Brockhaus, *Friedrich Arnold Brockhaus. Sein Leben und Wirken nach Briefen und andern Aufzeichnungen geschildert*, vol. III Leipzig 1881, pp. 455–459.

6 At that time unsold books were sold as waste paper, which was made into new paper. On the numbers of book shops see: "Rueckerinnerungen aus frueherer Zeit und die Miseren der Jetztzeit," *Börsenblatt fuer den deutschen Buchhandel und fuer die mit ihm verwandten Geschaeftszweige*, 1879, Nr. I, p. 3 (hereafter *Börsenblatt*); Schulze, *Der deutsche Buchhandel*, p. 11; Goldfriedrich, *Geschichte*, p. 219. The estimates on the number of Colporteurs and binders are mine.

7 Goldfriedrich, *Geschichte*, pp. 136–137.

8 R. Engelsing, "Die Perioden der Lesergeschichte in der Neuzeit," *Archiv für Geschichte des Buchwesens*, vol. X Frankfurt/Main 1969, p. 962.

9 C.T. Perthes, *Friedrich Perthes Lebennach dessen schriftlichen und muendlichen Mittheilungen*, vol. 2, 6 ed., Gotha 1872, p. 135. Hereafter cited as *Perthes Leben*.

10 W. Wittmann, *Buch und Beruf im 18. Jahrhundert. Ein Beitrag zur Erfassung und Gliederung der Leserschaft im 18. Jahrhundert*, Bochum-Langendreer, 1934, p. 134. These figures are based upon an analysis of the wills of: 299 artisans, 19 journeymen artisans, 115 merchants, 66 lower and middle-level bureaucrats, 46 soldiers, and 47 workers (See, respectively, pp. 63–64, 66, 82, 97, 127, and 130).

11 Ibid., p. 135.

12 Ibid., p. 135.

13 R. Schenda, *Volk ohne Buch*, Frankfurt/Main 1970, pp. 441–445.

14 H. Hiller, *Zur Socialgeschichte yon Buch und Buchhandel*, Bonn 1966, p. 102.

15  J. Tews, *Ein Jahrhundertpreußischer Schulgeschichte. Volksschule und Volksschullehrer-stand in PreuBen im 19. und 20 Jahrhundert*, Leipzig 1914, p. 107.

16  Ibid., p. 107.

17  *Statistik des preussischen Staats*, Berlin 1845, p. 231.

18  Figures from F. Weinstein, *Die preußische Volksschule in ihrer geschichtlichen Entwicklung*, Paderborn 1915, p. 53.

19  W. Dieterici, *Geschichtliche und statistische Nachrichten ueber die Universitaten im preußischen Staate*, Berlin 1836, p. 71

20  W. Sombart, *Die deutsche Volkswirtschaft im neunzehnten Jahrhundert*, 3 ed., rev., Berlin 1913, *passim*, but especially p. 428.

21  W. Krieg, *Materialien zu einer Entwicklungeschichte der Buecher-Preise und des Autoren-Honorars vom bis zum 20. Jahrhundert*, Vienna 1953, pp. 31–32.

22  W. Heinsius, ed. *Allgemeines Bucher-Lexicon*, vol. 6: 1816–1821, Leipzig 1822, pp. 6, 51, 145, 706, and 736–737. Hereafter cite as Heinsius.

23  H. Kunze, *Lieblings-Bucher von Dazumal*, Munich 1965, pp. 133, 167, and 367–368.

24  A. Schuermann, *Organization und Rechtsgewohnheiten des deutschen Buchhandels*, vol. I, Halle 1880, pp. 244–445.

25  R. Engelsing, *Die Perioden der Lesergeschichte*, p. 960. See also: Kunze, *Lieblings-Buecher*, p. 335.

26  "Der Buchhandel im Taschenformat," *Krieger'sche Wochenblatt*, Jg. VI (1826), Nr. 19, pp. 145–146;  G. F. Heyer, "Auch einige Woerte in und ~ueber das Wochenblatt fur Buchhandler etc.," ibid., Jg. III (1822), Nr. 1–2, p. 7.

27  *Heinsius*, vol. 3, p. 380; vol. 5, pp. 31, 64, 77, 274; vol. 6, pp. 33, 78, 93–94, 618, 814.

28  The standard histories of the book trade include those by Berger, Goldfriedrich, Schulze, and Menz, all cited above, and also those by H. Widmann, *Geschichte des Buchhandels vom Altertum his zur Gegenwart*, Wiesbaden, 1952, and the old but still useful (and entertaining) work conventionally ascribed to the international erotica publisher J. A. Prinz, *Bausteine zu einer spiteren Geschichte des Buchhandels*, 7 vols., Hamburg-Altona, 1855–1863.

29  Kunze, *Lieblings-Bucher*, p. 340. *Heinsius*, vol. 6, p. 423 lists some of these. They cost 18 to 20 Groschen.

30  Neumann, *Der Buecherbesitz der Tuebinger Buerger*, pp. 8–10.

31  Ibid., p. 82; Kunze, *Lieblings-Bucher*, p. 336.

32  This is the intelligently argued thesis of Engelsing, in "Die Perioden der Lesergeschichte," pp. 958ff.

33  Bischoff Luithlen, *Auszuege*, pp. 181–184.

34  Neumann, *Der Buecherbesitz der Tuebinger Buerger*, p. 39; Wittmann, *Buch und Beruf*, pp. 63, 66, 82, 97, 127, 131, 133.

35  Breining, "Die Hausbibliothek des gemeinen Mannes," p. 63.

36  Neumann, *Der Buecherbesitz der Tuebinger Buerger*, p. 91. See also Breining, "Die Hausbibliothek des gemeinen Mannes," p. 63.

37  Kunze, *Lieblings-Buecher*, pp. 335–336; Goldfriedrich, *Geschichte*, p. 201; Schenda, *Volk ohne Buch*, pp. 281, 315–316.

38  Kunze, *Lieblings-Buecher*, p. 335.

39  G. Frick, ed., *Der evangelische Buchhandel*, Leipzig 1921, pp. 12, 294.

40  *Perthes Leben*, pp. 138–139.

41  *Heinsius*: vol. 2, p. 480; vol. 6, p. 618; vol. 8, pp. 386–387. *Allgemeine deutsche Biographie*, vol. 13, Leipzig 1881, pp. 688–689; vol. 25, Leipzig 1887, pp. 14–17.

42  Breining, "Die Hausbibliothek des gemeinen Mannes," pp. 60–63; Neumann, *Der Buecherbesitz der Tuebinger Buerger*, p. 86; Bischoff-Luithelen, *Auszuege*, pp. 182–184.

43  Widmann, H., "Aus der Geschichte des Reutlinger Druck-und Verlagswesens," in: Hebsaker, J. U., ed., *Rueckblick fuer die Zukunft*, Reutlingen 1968, *passim*.

44 *Heinsius*, vol. I, p. 561; vol. 5, p. 110; vol. 6, p. 535.

45 M. Hahn, "Schweinfurths Drucker, Buchbinder und Buchandler," *Archiv fuer Geschichte des Buchwesens*, vol. X, 1969, p. 608. This sort of thing was common in other areas too, according to the anonymous author of "Literarischer Unfug und Buch-Hauser-Handel. Auch ein Uebel Teutschlands," *Rheinischer Merkur*, 1818, Nr. 75.

46 P. Kummer, *Sippen um Rudolf Zacharias Becker*, Goerlitz 1938, pp. 4–5.

47 Schenda, *Volk ohne Buch*, p. 285.

48 Goldfriedlich, *Geschichte*, p. 201; *Werden und Wesen des Hauses R. Oldenbourg Muenchen. Ein geschichtlicher Uberblick 1858–1958*, Munich 1958, p. 23.

49 *Monatsbericht*, 1816, Nr. X, pp. 222–223.

50 E. Berger, "Der Buchhandel in der Lausitz im 19. Jahrhundert," *Börsenblatt*, 1876, Nr. 210, p. 3219.

51 *Heinsius*, vol. 4, p. 424; vol. 6, p. 930.

52 *Rueckblick fuer die Zukunft*, essays by Widmann and Schenda.

53 On Reutlingen Colporteurs see: "w", "Etwas uber Buechernachdruck und dessen Handel," *Krieger'sche Wochenblatt*, Jg. X (1830), Nr. 11–12 (double issue), pp. 81–82. Colporteurs and binders were neglected by historians of the German book trade until very recently. The only comprehensive secondary source on Colporteurs is the work of R. Schenda in his *Volk ohne Buch*, pp. 257–269, and in his essay, "Bucher aus der Kraemerkiste" *in Rueckblick fur die Zukunft*. There is no good secondary source on binders.

54 *Perthes Leben*, p. 133.

55 Ibid., p. 138.

56 Ibid.

57 Ibid.

58 Schenda, *Volk ohne Buch*, pp. 260–261.

59 Schenda, "Buecher aus der Kraemerkiste," "Literarischer Unfug und Buch-Hauser-Handel," *Monatsbericht* 1819, Nr. I, p. 26.

60 In the 1890s it was widely believed that there were about 45,000 Colporteurs running about Germany—see W. Langenbucher, *Der aktuelle Unterhaltungsroman-Beitraege zu der Geschichte und Theorie der massenhaft verbreitetete Literatur*, Bonn 1964, p. 86. Langenbucher believes this figure himself. Yet the *Berufs und Gewerbezihlung vom 14. Juni 1895: Berufsstatistik fuer das Reich im Ganzen*, Part I, Table 4, p. 261 shows that there were only 1,714 Colporteurs in Germany. There had been an enormous growth in the number of Colporteurs between 1815–1820 and the 1890s. My conclusion is that nobody really knows how many Colporteurs there were.

61 From Widmann, H., ed., G. Schwab, *Die Neckarseite der schwaebischen Alb*, Tuebingen 1960. Original 1823, p. 87.

62 "Literarischer Unfug und Buch-Hausir-Handel," *Monatsbericht*, 1819, Nr. I, p. 26.

63 Ibid., p. 28.

64 E. Drahn, *Zur Entwicklung und Geschichte des sozialistischen Buchhandels und der Arbeiterpresse*, Gautzsch bei Leipzig 1913, pp. 9–10.

65 Engelsing, "Die Perioden der Lesergeschichte," p. 984. On this public see also G. Kohfeldt, "Zur Geschichte der Buechersamlungen und des Buecherbesitzes in Deutschland," *Zeitschrift fur Kulturgeschichte*, VII, 1900, pp. 386–387.

66 Wittmann, *Buch und Beruf*, p. 122.

67 Engelsing, "Die Perioden der Lesergeschichte," p. 1000.

68 *Bibliopolisches Jahrbuch*, 1840, Part I, pp. 59–60.

69 *Krieger'sche Wochenblatt*, 1820, Nr. 18, p. 144, Nr. 27, p. 216; 1821, Nr. 35, p. 273; 1823, Nrs. 4–5, p. 38, Nr. 27, p. 210, Nrs. 36–37, p. 292, Nrs. 45–46, p. 358.

70 *Krieger'sche Wochenblatt*, 1820, Nr. 12 (n.p.), Nr. 38, p. 300; 1821, Nrs. 51–52, p. 390; 1823, Nrs. 20–21, pp. 157–158.

71 Wittmann, *Buch und Beruf*, pp. 101–127.

72 Kohfeldt, "Zur Geschichte der Buechersammlungen," pp. 386–387; Engelsing, "Die Perioden der Lesergeschichte," p. 986.

73 The library in Hannover was typical in opening four hours a week in summer and two in winter; few libraries were open more than six hours per week until after 1850. Libraries belonging to churches and religious groups were not open at all in the cold months. See G. Leyh, "Die deutschen Bibliotheken von der Aufklaerung bis zur Gegenwort," *Handbuch der Bibliothekswissenschaft* vol. III, Part II, Wiesbaden, 1957, pp. 199–221, 248–295, 381.

74 Ibid., p. 170.

75 Leyh, "Die deutschen Bibliotheken," pp. 233, 237. "Compulsory copies" were an old institution. They were required for major libraries in Prussia until 18 October 1819 and then from 28 December 1824. See "Zur Geschichte der Pflichtsexemplare," *Börsenblatt*, 1870, Nr. 78, pp. 1188–1189.

76 *Krieger'sche Wochenblatt*, 1820, Nr. 34, p. 266.

77 Kohfeldt, "Zur Geschichte der Buechersammlungen," pp. 386–387.

78 On this public see Goldfriedrich, *Geschichte*, p. 201; Kunze, *Lieblings-Buecher*, pp. 15–17.

79 Engelsing, "Die Perioden der Lesergeschichten," pp. 968–971, 981–982.

80 Quoted ibid., p. 987.

81 Even in 1830 the fastest freight wagons hook two weeks to travel from Leipzig to Stuttgart or Cologne, nine days to reach Darmstadt, and 11 to 12 days to reach Freiburg in F. H. Breisgau–Meyer, "Mittheilungen zur innern Geschichte des deutschen Buchhandels yon 1811–1848," *Archiv fur Geschichte des deutschen Buchhandels*, vol. IX, Leipzig, 1884, p. 219.

82 *Perthes Leben*, p. 137.

83 *Perthes Leben*, p. 133.

84 Ibid., pp. 131, 133–134, 139.

85 Berger, "Der deutsche Buchhandel," p. 126; Schulze, *Der deutsche Buchhandel*, p. 11; L. Muth, *Vom Buchhaendler zum Informationshaendler*, Freiburg, Basel, Vienna 1970, p. 22.

86 Letter of 28 August 1817, reprinted in H. Widmann, ed., *Der deutsche Buchhandel in Urkunden und Quellen*, vol. I, Hamburg, 1965, p. 102.

87 On Bonn, Wittenberg, Dresden, Leipzig and the Lusatian cities see, respectively: Schulze, *Der deutsche Buchhandel*, pp. 11, 80; Stieda, *Der Buechermarkt und den Hochschulen*, pp. 175–176; "Dresdens Buchhandel sonst und jetzt, besonders seit 1863," *Börsenblatt*, 1884, Nr. 176, p. 3469; and Berger, "Der Buchhandel in der Lausitz," *Börsenblatt*, 1876 Nr. 210, p. 3219, Nr. 216, pp. 3319–3320.

88 *Perthes Leben*, p. 132.

89 Ibid., pp. 133–134.

90 E. Berger, "Der deutsche Buchhandel in seiner Entwicklung und in seiner Ein-richtungen in den Jahren 1815 his 1867," *Archiv fur Geschichte des deutschen Buch-handels*, vol. II, Leipzig, 1879, p. 125.

91 "Der Buchhandel im Taschenformat," *Krieger'sche Wochenblatt*, VI (1826), Nr. 19, pp. 145–146. The attitude had been the same before 1820.

92 F. Perthes, *Der deutsche Buchhandel als Bedingung des Daseyns einer deutschen Liter-atur*, 1816 (no place given), pp. 25–26, 28. An awareness of the lofty self-image of the bookman and his products is crucial to an understanding of the German book market. The members of the trade articulated this image when they felt threatened by innovation, as will become repeatedly manifest in the course of this book. Down to Schenda, the historians of the trade have accepted the assumption as reality. See, for example, Menz, *Der deutsche Buchhandel*, pp. 7–8.

93 The Times of London bought a Koenig Press in 1814. On press technology in Germany in this period see: Goldfriedrich, *Geschichte*, pp. 57–58; F. Schulze, *Der deutsche Buchhandel*, Leipzig, 1925, pp. 92–93.

94  Hahn, "Schweinfurths Drucker, Buchbinder und Buchhaendler," p. 608.
95  On the Sale or Return System see: C. Wolf, *Ueber den deutschen Buchhandel*, Munich 1829, pp. 3–5, 9–12, 21–25; Schurmann *Organization und Rechtsgewohnheiten des deutschen Buchandels*, vols. 1 and 2, the most detailed and legalistic account.
96  Meyer, "Mittheilungen zur innern Geschichte des deutschen Buchhandels," p. 200. Sellers who would not take all books made this known by letter and circulars; there was no national weekly trade paper until the founding of the *Krieger'sche Wochenblatt* in 1820.
97  Wolf, *Uber den deutschen Buchhandel*, p. 22.
98  Figures from Perthes, *Der deutsche Buchhandel als Bedingung des Daseigns einer deutchen Literatur*, p. 24.
99  On catalogs see: *Krieger'sche Wochenblatt*, V (1824), Nrs. 41–42, pp. 350–351, where it is maintained that other catalogs had grown up since 1800 as a reaction to the sluggishness and inaccuracy of the Fair Catalog.
100  *Monatsbericht* 1815, Nrs. I–II, p. 3; 1816, Nr. I, pp. 4–5.
101  *Monatsbericht*, 1817, Nr. II, p. 46.
102  *Monatsbericht*, 1817, Nr. II, pp. 46–48.
103  Widmann, *Der deutsche Buchhandel in Urkunden und Quellen*, II, pp. 131–138.
104  Examples from *Monatsbericht*, 1819, Nr. II, pp. 169–172; Nr. I, p. 5; Nr. VII, pp. 145–149.
105  *Monatsbericht*, (1816), Nr. I, pp. 8–11. Cotta also advertised in local newspapers all over Germany, not always successfully according to H. A. Crous, and H. Falter, *Festschrift zum Einhundertfuenfzigjahrigeh Bestehen der J. A.-Mayer'schen Buchhandlung 1817–1967*, Aachen 1967, pp. 32–33.
106  Schulze, *Der deutsche Buchhandel*, p. 101. The only exceptions were a few schoolbooks and other mass consumption items.
107  Prinz, *Bausteine zu einer spaeteren Geschichte des Buchhandels*, vol. I, pp. 25–26.
108  Ibid., p. 10.
109  On the Bible see Menz, Der deutsche Buchhandel, p. 135. On the encyclopedia see "Das Conversationslexikon und seine Gruender," *Börsenblatt*, 1873, Nr. 21, pp. 327–328, Nr. 23, pp. 357–358. The idea for the work came to a Leipzig scholar, R. G. Loebel, in the mid-1790s. Most of the original version was written by the Leipzig lawyer Christian Wilhelm Francke, who tried to publish it himself at one point.
110  *Monatsberichte*, 1818, Nr. X, pp. 211–212.
111  Ibid., p. 210. These ranged from Writing Paper at 18 Reichstaler and 18 Groschen the set to sets on English vellum at 45 Reichstaler (only 12 of these were printed); in all, there were five papers available.
112  Goldfriedrich, *Geschichte*, p. 202.
113  The *Encyclopedia Americana* began in 1821 as an unauthorized translation of the Brockhaus and remained little more than that until after 1900. See W. A. Katz, *An Introduction to Reference Work*, New York 1974, p. 123.
114  *Monatsbericht*, (1820), Nr. I, pp. 22–23.
115  Piracy had peaked in the late eighteenth century and was slowly declining by 1815–1820. Nevertheless, contemporary bookmen blamed it (not their own lack of initiative and imagination) for most of their woes, and issued a voluminous literature against it. The *Monatsbericht*, for example, had an anti-piracy essay in almost every issue until 1820. Widmann, *Der deutsche Buchhandel in Urkunden und Quellen*, vol. II, pp. 304–364, presents many documents on piracy. The fullest secondary account on it is in Goldfriedrich, *Geschichte*, Chapter 2.
116  Perthes, *Der deutsche Buchhandel als Bedingung des Daseiner deutscher Literatur*, *passim*; Perthes wrote this pamphlet to influence the Congress of' Vienna delegates to ban piracy. (They didn't.)

117 From the preface to one of Spitz' catalogs, reprinted with horror in the *Krieger'sche Wochenblatt*, Jg. I 1820, Nrs. 46–47, pp. 360–367. On Spitz see Prinz, *Bausteine zu einer spiteren Geschichte des Buchhandels*, vol. V, pp. 53–64.
118 *Monatsbericht*, 1818, Nr. X, pp. 227–228.
119 Ibid., 1819, Nr. I, p. 27.
120 *Krieger'sche Wochenblatt*, 1820, Nr. 37, pp. 288–290.
121 There were exceptions: see Crous and Falter, *Festschrift der J. A. Mayer'schen Buchhandlung*, pp. 36–43.
122 Quoted in H. E. Brockhaus, *Friedrich Arnold Brockhaus*, vol. III, p. 457.
123 Prinz, *Bausteine*, vol. I, pp. 10–11.
124 *Krieger'sche Wochenblatt*, (1820), Nr. 7.
125 Berger, "Der Buchhandel in der Lausitz," p. 3218; Vollert, *Die Korporation der Berliner Buchhaendler*, p. 44.
126 Crous and Falter, *Festschrift der J. A. Mayer'schen Buchhandlung*, p. 47; Hahn, "Schweinfurths Drucker, Buch-binder und Buchhaendler," p. 610; *Perthes Leben*, p. 132.
127 Crous and Falter, p. 41; W. Ruprecht, *Vaeter und Soehne. Zwei Jahrhundert Buchhaendler in einer deutschem Universitätsstadt*, Goettingen 1935, p. 152. On lending libraries in general see: H. W. Eybel, "Aus der Arbeit des Leihbuchhandels. Kurzer Streifzug durch die Geschichte des Leihbuchhandels," *Börsenblatt* (Leipzig edition), 123 Jg., Nr. 49, 8 Dec. 1956, pp. 778–779; "Fuer und wider die die Leihbibliotheken in frueheren Tagen," *Börsenblatt* (Frankfurt edition) 1957, Nr. 38, pp. 581–583; "Miszellen zur Geschichte der Leihbibliotheken," *Börsenblatt* (Frankfurt edition), 1957, Nr. 5, pp. 60–63; S. Wangert, "Das Entstehen des Leihbuchereiwesens in Deutschland. Ein Beitrag zu seiner Geschichte," *Reichsnachrichtenblatt der Buchverleihe*, Nr. 7 Sept. 1932 (no pagination). W. Nutz, *Der Trivialroman*, Cologne and Opladen 1962, pp. 99–101.
128 A. Martino, *Die deutsche Leihbibliothek*, Harassowitz, Wiesbaden, 1990, especially pp. 174ff.
129 Widmann, *Der deutsche Buchhandel in Urkunden und Quellen*, vol. II.
130 Ibid., p. 269. 129.
131 See *Heinsius*, vol. 6, section entitled *"Romane"*–novels cost about one Reichsthaler a volume; a Reichsthaler then was equal to 1.8 Gulden/Florin.
132 Schenda, *Volk ohne Buch*, p. 205.
133 Wangart, "Das Entstehen des Leihbuchereiwesens," *passim*.
134 Langenbucher, *Der aktuelle Unterhaltungsroman*, cited above, pp. 46–47.
135 Hahn, "Schweinfurths Drucker, Buchbinder und Buchhaendler," p. 609.
136 Schulze, *Der deutsche Buchhandel*, p. 3.
137 J. W. Appell, *Die Ritter-, Raeuber- und Schaueromantik*, Leipzig, 1859, pp. 5–6; Wangart, "Das Entstehen des Leihbuchereiwesens," *passim*; "Miszellen zur Geschichte der Leihbibliotheken," *Börsenblatt* (Frankfurt edition) 1957, pp. 60–61.
138 Quoted in Schenda, *Volk ohne Buch*, p. 204. The description dates from 1800 but is equally valid for the period 1815–1820 (and on up until about 1830).
139 *Heinsius*, vol. 6, section "Romane," pp. 8, 9, 5, 40. The prices of these novels were, repectively, three Reichsthaler, one Reichsthaler, 18 Groschen, one Reichsthaler, and three Reichsthaler, 12 Groschen.
140 Hahn, "Schweinfurths Drucker, Buchbinder und Buchhaendler," p. 610.
141 Book titles from *Heinsius*, vol. 6, Section "Romane," pp. 5, 6, 10. On the authors' popularity see Kunze, *Lieblings-Buecher*, pp. 133, 171, 175–176, 308; Perthes, *Der deutsche Buchhandel als Bedingung des Daseyns einer deutschen Literatur*, p. 28.
142 *Monatsbericht*, 1819, Nr. IX, pp. 218–219.
143 Kunze, *Lieblings-Bucher*, pp. 15, 38–39.
144 Kunze, *Lieblings-Buecher*, pp. 43, 60, 87, 256, 264–265, 274–275, 277–279, 357, 415–416.

145 Ibid., p. 7.
146 Berger, "Der deutsche Buchhandel," p. 129.
147 Schenda, *Volk ohne Buch*, pp. 205–206.
148 Over 600 groups were founded between 1760 and 1820. See Muth, *Vom Buch-haendler zum Informationshandler*, p. 22; *Börsenblatt*, 1876, Nr. 216, p. 3320.
149 *Bibliopolisches Jahrbuch fuer 1836*, Leipzig 1836, p. vii.
150 *Statistik des preussischen Staats*, 1845, p. 256.
151 Berger, "Der deutsche Buchhandel," pp. 126–127; A. Meiner, *G. J. Manz, Person und Werk 1830–1855*, Munich 1957, pp. 22, 24.
152 Berger, "Der deutsche Buchhandel," p. 133. On Tauchnitz see C. B. Yorck, *Die Druckkunst und der Buchhandel in Leipzig durch vier Jahrhunderte*, Leipzig 1879, p. 30.
153 Berger, "Der deutsche Buchhandel," p. 126.
154 Cotta bought the rights to Koerner's edition. About 1816; he issued an edition of his own. See: L. Lohrer, *Cotta. Geschichte eines Verlages*, 1659–1959, Stuttgart, 1959, p. 60; and C. G. Kayser, *Vollstaendiges Buecher-Lexikon, (vols. I-6) alle vom 1750 bis zu Ende des Jahres 1832 in Deutschland und in den angrenzenden Laendern gedruckten Buecher* (printed as a single volume, Leipzig 1834), part V, p. 81. Here-after this work, which was continued up until 1910, will be referred to as *"Kayser."*
155 Prinz, *Bausteine*, vol. V, p. 56.
156 Mueller had obtained the permission of the Wurrttemberg government to pirate the works of all the classic German authors who were dead. See: *Monatsbericht*, 1816, Nr. II, pp. 45–48, (1817), Nr. XII, pp. 252–254.
157 The book had been issued as a periodical from 1808 to 1816.
158 Dr. Adalbert Brauer gave me helpful information on these histories. See Schulze, *Der deutsche Buchhandel*, pp. 131–132.
159 Prinz, *Bausteine*, vol. I, p. 7.
160 Schenda, *Volk ohne Buch*, pp. 74–76; there was a periodical called *Der neue deutsche Kinderfreund*, which, according to Schenda (p. 76), sold 100,000 copies an issue about 1815.
161 Crous and Falter, *Festschrift. der J. A. Meyer' schen Buchhandlung*, p. 47.
162 Meiner, *G. J. Manz*, p. 24.
163 *Krieger'sche Wochenblatt*, 1821, Nr. 12, p. 91, Nr. 17, p. 126; *Monatsbericht* 1818, Nr. VI, pp. 114–115, 1820, Nrs. VI–VII.
164 From the publisher's advertisement, *Monatsbericht* 1820, Nr. VIII, p. 144.
165 *Börsenblatt*, 1850, Nr. 94, pp. 1311–1312. On the pocket books see also the charming illustrated history by M. Lanckoronsk and A. Ruemann, *Geschichte der deutschen Taschenbuecher und Almanache aus der klassisch-romantischen Zeit*, Munich, 1954. Pocket books had been popular since the later 18th century.
166 Berger, "Der deutsche Buchhandel," p. 128.

# 2 The regular book market explodes, 1820–1843

Proud and secure in its dignity, content with the limited income derived from a small market, the regular book trade glided into the 1820's on a gentle tide of indolence and complacency. There was nothing to indicate that the rate of growth in the number of dealers and titles from 1820 to 1843 would be the fastest of the entire nineteenth century. In 1820, 4,375 titles were published. By 1826 the number had risen to over 5,000; by 1830 to over 7,000; by 1834 to over 9,000; and by 1838 to over 10,000 titles published annually. 1840 saw 10,808 titles published, a number not exceeded for 30 years thereafter. Within two decades the number of titles issued had increased by 147 percent.[1]

Even more striking was the rise in the number of dealers. "Where once there were no book dealers there are now two or three,"[2] exulted an article in the *Börsenblatt* in 1834; a phenomenon Perthes observed simultaneously, but in more dour terms—"now practically every half-important provincial burg has a book dealer."[3] Between 1822 and 1842 the number of dealers increased by 183 percent, the number of cities with book dealers by 127 percent.[4]

Of the 1,274 dealers in 1842, about one-quarter did only publishing. Some of the remaining three-quarters were retailers exclusively but most still practiced both publishing and selling. In all of Germany there were only four cities in which the number of book dealers decreased between 1822 and 1842—Augustenberg, Göttingen, Hadamar, and Halberstadt. Two-hundred-and-ninety-four cities gained dealers. Table 2.1 shows some examples.

Nearly 200 cities and towns got their first book dealerships during this period. Prussia's rule being favorable to the trade, more than half (102) of these were founded in her domains.[5] In the Rhineland and Westphalia, where Perthes had found the book trade so moribund, book shops were established for the first time in 27 cities; by contrast, this happened to only 12 cities in Saxony and 15 in Bavaria. The vast, largely rustic area in the East of Germany was brought into closer contact with literary culture by the founding of book shops in eight cities in the province of Posen, nine cities each in the provinces of Prussia and Pomerania, and 18 in Silesia. The expansionist spirit spilled from Prussia over into Mecklenburg-Schwerin, where eight cities got book dealerships for the first time

*Table 2.1* Book dealers in 1822, 1832, 1842[1]

| City | Dealers in 1822 | Dealers in 1832 | Dealers in 1842 | Number of people to one dealer in 1842 |
|---|---|---|---|---|
| Augsburg | 5 | 20 | 16 | 2,500 |
| Berlin | 51 | 81 | 106 (16)* | 2,690 |
| Bremen | 3 | 5 | 5 (1) | 10,000 |
| Cassel | 4 | 4 | 7 | 4,286 |
| Cologne | 5 | 9 | 21 (1) | 3,381 |
| Dresden | 4 | 15 | 28 (14) | 2,857 |
| Erfurt | 4 | 8 | 13 | 2,154 |
| Frankfurt/Main | 18 | 38 | 33 | 1,818 |
| Halle | 12 | 14 | 15 (1) | 1,893 |
| Hamburg | 7 | 17 | 24 (3) | 5,000 |
| Hannover | 2 | 6 | 9 (2) | 2,778 |
| Konigsberg | 3 | 5 | 7 (1) | 10,000 |
| Leipzig | 59 | 79 | 130 (10) | 400 |
| Mainz | 2 | 5 | 10 (3) | 3,500 |
| Munich | 8 | 15 | 20 (10) | 4,750 |
| Nurnberg | 19 | 26 | 26 (4) | 1,711 |
| Posen | 1 | 3 | 7 | 5,571 |
| Stettin | 0 | 3 | 8 | 3,750 |
| Stuttgart | 5 | 14 | 37 (4) | 1,083 |
| Trier | 3 | 4 | 6 (2) | 2,500 |
| Weimer | 3 | 5 | 7 (1) | 1,571 |

Notes
* Numbers in parentheses are the numbers of art and music dealers, who did sometimes sell books. Figures for 1822 and 1832 also include art and music dealers, but no exact breakdown is possible.
1 Figures for the municipal states given above, *Börsenblatt* 1843, Nr. 8, p. 211.

during these two decades. Württemberg attracted new dealerships to 13 cities with its liberal policies, the king there actively encouraging publishers and booksellers to set up shop in his kingdom.[6]

The slowest growth occurred in West Central to North Central Germany—in Nassau (four cities), Hessen-Darmstadt (two cities), Hessen-Cassel (five cities), Oldenburg (two cities), and in Hannover (five cities). The relative economic sluggishness of these regions was one reason for this, the absence of government encouragement another. Hannover's government had a deliberate policy of keeping the number of book dealerships small.[7]

All the growth of the regular book trade took place in urban areas. As before, there were no book shops or publishing operations on the land. But the growth of the trade was hardly confined to the larger cities, in fact, about one-third—411 out of 1,274—of all the firms in the trade in 1842 were located in cities with 5,000 to 15,000 inhabitants. Sixty-nine towns with under 4,000 people had book dealers. There was even a tiny (population 600) Rhenish village named Gummerbach that boasted its own book dealer.[8]

And yet there were no book dealers in numerous larger cities which certainly could have provided better markets than such small towns, and there were still regions which could have supported many more dealers than they had, both of which factors point up the sometimes erratic quality that characterized the distribution of book dealerships in these decades. The book trade of much of East Prussia and Lithuania was in the hands of two Konigsberg firms until the 1830s, and three until the late 1840s. There was business for more than that. In 1826, the publisher Bernhard Friedrich Voight published in a trade paper a list of 111 cities which in his judgment were capable of supporting book shops, none of them had fewer than 4,000 inhabitants, many had between 5,000 and 7,000. Few bookmen had a better understanding of the book market than Voigt. Nevertheless, 16 years later more than one-third (43) of these places were still without book dealers.[9]

At the other extreme were those places into which new book operations clustered to the point of suffocating both themselves and already established firms. Typically these were towns that could scarcely support one book dealer. The city of Plauen in Saxony had three dealers in 1832, too many for a city of 9,500 without a large cultivated middle class. By 1843 only one of them was left. The Pomeranian city of Stolp, whose 6,000 inhabitants lived by trade and factories, had no book dealers until the mid-1830s, when, absurdly, three were suddenly founded. Two of them just as suddenly expired. Adorf an der Elster in Saxony—a town which was neither a resort nor a government center, whose population of 2,500 was composed largely of weavers and paper mill laborers, and which had neither a gymnasium (academic high school) nor any other type of higher school—had two book dealers in the late 1830s and early 1840s.[10]

These extreme situations are only understandable in light of the fact that the great expansion of the book trade in this period was an expression, not of a sober, systematic plan, but rather of the chaotic exuberance of the early Industrial Age in Germany. People founded book shops wherever they wanted, recklessly, over-optimistically, and often without adequate financing.

Still, in most places an invisible hand seemed to see to it that the number of book operations formed a sensible counterpart to the number of potential customers. For the 13,000-inhabitant city of Burg in Prussia's province of Saxony, one book shop was adequate, most of the populace being employed in weaving and in the tobacco trade. Bad Ems had less than one-sixth the population (2,000) of Burg but also one book shop; the difference was that this shop got many customers from the well-heeled visitors to the mineral springs there. With far more book buyers per capita than most cities, university towns also had far more book dealers per capita than most cities. GieBen had one to every 2,000 inhabitants, Heidelberg one to every 1,350, Göttingen one to every 1,100, and Jena one to every 750, to cite a few examples from 1843. Gotha (one dealer to every 1,100 persons) had no university but an unusually large number of cultured people.[11]

The densities of book dealerships in the German states varied as follows in 1843; I exclude the municipal states:

Central Germany thus had the densest concentration of book dealers, far North and far Eastern Germany the least dense. West Central and Southern Germany stood between these poles of density. Much of the far west of Germany was barren of book establishments. Within the Rhineland, however, in an area inscribed by a triangle whose points were Cleve, Bonn, and Dortmund, the density of book shops and publishers rivalled that of Central Germany itself.[12]

Taking the country as a whole, there was approximately one regular book dealer to every 25,900 people in 1843; a considerable increase from the one to every 55,000 people I estimated for 1820. The regular book trade was growing much faster than the population, which rose by 30 percent between 1820 and 1845, from 26,291,606 to 34,396,055 souls.[13]

*Table 2.2* Concentrations of book dealers by state

|  | Number of dealers | Number of cities with dealers | Inhabitants per dealer |
| --- | --- | --- | --- |
| Saxony | 194 | 23 | 8,763 |
| Hohenzollern-Hechingen | 2 | 1 | 9,700 |
| Saxony-Coburg-Gotha | 14 | 3 | 10,071 |
| Anhalt-Dessau | 6 | 2 | 10,433 |
| Saxony-Weimer | 19 | 5 | 13,160 |
| Saxony-Altenburg | 9 | 4 | 13,666 |
| Schwarzburg Rudolstadt | 5 | 2 | 13,772 |
| Brunswick | 18 | 4 | 13,944 |
| Schwarzburg Sondershausen | 4 | 2 | 14,310 |
| Reuß (both lines) | 7 | 3 | 15,286 |
| Saxony-Meiningen | 9 | 6 | 16,888 |
| Wuerttemburg | 85 | 21 | 19,764 |
| Mecklenburg-Strelitz | 4 | 3 | 22,375 |
| Hessen-Homburg | 1 | 1 | 23,700 |
| Prussia | 473 | 133 | 24,023 |
| Baden | 46 | 12 | 28,261 |
| Waldeck | 2 | 2 | 28,600 |
| Hessen-Darmstadt | 27 |  | 30,037 |
| Nassau | 12 | 3 | 33,083 |
| Bavaria | 124 | 35 | 35,224 |
| Hessen-Cassel | 20 | 9 | 35,400 |
| Mecklinburg-Schwerin | 13 | 8 | 38,461 |
| Oldenburg | 7 | 3 | 38,571 |
| Anhalt-Cothen | 1 | 1 | 41,000 |
| Hohenzollern-Siegmaringen | 1 | 1 | 44,000 |
| Anhalt-Bernburg | 1 | 1 | 46,000 |
| Holstein | 10 | 4 | 50,000 |
| Hannover | 33 | 15 | 52,182 |
| Lippe-Detmold | 1 | 1 | 102,000 |

Note
Figures for the municipal states given above, *Börsenblatt* 1843, Nr. 8, p. 211.

It is certain, too, that the regular book trade was growing faster than the number of educated people, that is, people educated beyond elementary school level. The social and economic barriers which kept those with elementary school and less education—the masses—out of the regular book market remained erect and impenetrable during this period. The market for the products of the regular book trade was found among Germans who attended such schools as middle schools, *Realschulen*, normal schools, gymnasia, and universities. Students at these schools not only used more textbooks than elementary school pupils, they also grew up to be the people who placed greater emphasis on reading.[14] Statistics on the number of such students are unfortunately not as complete as those on the elementary schools, but contemporaries agreed that their number was increasing at a good clip, except at the universities, where attendance leveled off after the early 1830s.[15] In the early 1840s there were over 100,000 academic pupils and students in Prussia.[16] Nonetheless, they represented only one pupil to every 20 in the Kingdom's elementary schools. In the mid-1830s it was calculated that every six or seven Prussians attended an elementary school, while every 603 pupils attended a gymnasium.[17]

The growth of the academic schools produced increases in the sizes of groups whose members were customers, actual or potential, for the regular book trade. Some examples: Prussia had 2,260 full-fledged medical doctors in 1834 but 2,735 six years later; it had 337 professors in 1834 but 500 a decade later. With salaries averaging 973 Reichsthaler per year, the professors were certainly earning enough to buy books regularly. In no case, however, was the growth of such groups as rapid as that of the book trade.[18]

The book trade had grown faster than population, education, or income levels. Believing that these three factors completely determined the size of the book market, many people both within and outside of the book trade insisted that its growth had outstripped that of the book market. They saw in rapid growth a dangerous self-destructive process. As early as 1823, a Darmstadt bookseller lamented: "The number of book dealers has increased far beyond the natural and desirable limit ... five-sixths of all books printed remain unsold."[19] That same year another bookseller fervently hoped "that the number of titles would cease this year-in, year-out increasing, (as) many readers are already satiated and can read no more."[20] An analysis of the book trade by a newspaper correspondent in 1828 stated:

> Production is out of proportion to needs; much more is printed than can be consumed, enjoyed, and digested. The more dealers there are, the more pressing the problem. Every dealer trains apprentices. These apprentices then grub up or marry a few thousand Thaler and crash onto the scene as book dealers in their own right. Such parasites sap the strength of the old, established dealers, who lose both the will and the means to undertake anything of significance.[21]

The belief that the trade was over-expanding was strengthened by the sky-rocketing number of bankruptcies. In the early 1820s it was said that "a bankrupt bookman is as rare as a white raven;"[22] a decade later the sad truth was that "many fall into debt or into bankruptcy every year."[23] Stories about young dealers whose lack of capital and experience (purists found less than 20 years inadequate) had doomed them to rapid financial ruin were played up on older bookmen to dissuade new people from setting up book shops. Powerfully told, these stories seem nevertheless not to have deterred anybody.[24]

The established bookmen could do more than recite scare stories: in barrages of petitions to government licensing authorities, as in countless trade circulars and articles in trade papers, they asserted that their cities and regions had absolutely no need for more book dealers and, furthermore, that candidates for new licenses were invariably ignorant of, and unfit for, the book trade. They raged at publishers who dared to undermine the trade's solidarity by extending credit to new dealers, especially to the hordes of new men who had entered from other, less august, trades and occupations. A characteristic reaction to a new dealer was that of two Giessen book shop owners in 1832—tendered to the trade—in the following circular:

> It used to be said that there was "nothing new under the sun." In point of fact, however, this venerable truth has now been unhappily refuted by a case so dreadfully unique, so unprecedented, so unheard-of, that it behooves us to make our colleagues fully aware of its true particulars. For a widow to inherit a book shop and to operate it in the interests of her children is a not unheard-of event. But in *this* case a young woman, to wit Miss Johannette Christine Eckstein, the daughter of a University actuary here,—a young woman who can present evidence neither as to where she has learned our honorable trade, nor that she has been initiated into it with the proper and time-honored formalities and assurances—in this case such a young woman has become *our* colleague.[25]

And so on. It seemed that she had been able to charm a license out of the same board which had turned down her fiancé; actually, the fiancé was a trained bookman.

Attempts by Heyer and Ferber, the two dealers, to have the license of Miss Eckstein revoked were futile, however. Most efforts to have the governments limit the number of newcomers were. Most of the German states set fewer restrictions for entry into the book trade than for into many other trades and did not always enforce even these regulations, a paradox in view of their stiff censorship and lukewarm attitude towards mass readings.[26] The explanation for this paradox is that most states looked favorably upon economic growth and also that they associated the growth of their book trades with the advance of culture within their borders.

Thus the trade went on growing. To the older and the more traditionalist dealers, growth brought only rampaging instability, loss of dignity, and progressive economic deterioration. Among such men it was axiomatic that the trade was swirling down into ruin: "cries about the fall of the book trade are being raised from all sides," wrote one in 1834; "the ruin of the book trade is generally acknowledged," asserted another four years later.[27] So harsh were conditions, some could find solace only in impressionistic evocations of a past Golden Age of the book trade. This happy time had ended sometime between 1780 and 1822, depending mainly on the writer's age.[28]

From an economic standpoint, such views were over-gloomy; from a social and psychological standpoint, entirely justified. The very growth of the trade proved that many more firms survived than went bankrupt. Most financial failures were due to overcrowding in some cities and to poor business practices, not to a general over-expansion of the trade. And, although it seemed impossible to many then, the book market of the regular book trade had expanded faster than population and schooling—its expansion had kept pace with the growth in the number of book titles and dealers. But its expansion had been brought about by methods of producing and marketing books which traditionalists could not but find anathema. These methods and their results are the topic of the next chapter.

## Notes

1 Goldfriedrich, *Geschichte*, p. 199. These figures include reprints and also the production of Austria and Switzerland. The year 1838 saw 5,678 titles issued in France and 3,376 in England (both figures including reprints)—see *Bibliopolisches Jahrbuch fuer 1840*, Jg. IV (Leipzig, 1840), p. 40.

2 "Ueber die große Vermehrung der Buchhaendler," *Börsenblatt* 1834, Nr. 39, p. 741.

3 F. Perthes, "Die Bedeutung des deutschen Buchhandels, besonders in der neuesten Zeit," *Börsenblatt* 1834, Nr. I, p. 6.

4 These figures include Holstein, but omit Austria and Switzerland. Those for 1822 derived from Wolf, "Ueber den deutschen Buchhandel," pp. 79–86; for 1832 from J. C. Gaedicke, *Zur Statistik der deutschen Literatur und des deutschen Buchhandels*, Berlin, 1834 pp. 16–19; and for 1842 from the *Börsenblatt* 1843, Nr. 8, pp. 211–212.

5 B. F. Voigt, "Ueber Vermehrung der Buchhaendler-Etablissements," *Krieqer'sche Wochenblatt*, V, Nr. 50–51, p. 417.

6 Derived from Table 2.1.

7 Goldfriedrich, *Geschichte*, p. 389.

8 *Börsenblatt* 1843, Nr. 8, pp. 212–213; *Bibliopolisches Jahrbuch fuer 1842/43*, Jg. VI, Part II, p. 16.

9 B. F. Voight, "Ueber Vermehrung der Buchhaendler-Etablissements," *Krieger'sche Wochenblatt* V, cited above, pp. 419–422.

10 *Bibliopolisches Jahrbuch fuer 1837*, Part II, pp. 4, 154; *Bibliopolisches Jahrbuch fuer 1842*, Part II, pp. 12, 34.

11 Schulze, *Der deutsche Buchandel*, p. 80; *Bibliopolisches Jahrbuch fuer 1837*, Part II, pp. 54–55, 64–65, 74–75, 79–80.

12 See the map on the inside rear cover of the *Bibliopolisches Jahrbuch fuer 1836*.

13 *Statistisches Jahrbuch fuer das deutsche Reich*, Jg. I, (1880), p. 5.

14 The importance of such schools to the regular trade is indicated by the detailed lists of them in a trade periodical which aimed to give bookmen important information, the *Bibliopolisches Jahrbuch*. See, for examples, 1837, Part III, pp. 55–63; 1838, pp. 33–38.

15 This was true at any rate of the Prussian universities, where during the Winter Semester of 1833–1834, 5,362 students attended. See: *Statistik des preussischen Staats* (1845), p. 253.

16 Ibid., pp. 231–233, 242–248, 253.

17 Ibid., pp. 247–248.

18 Ibid., pp. 253–254; Dieterici, *Geschichtliche*, pp. 106, 128. Dieterici, p. 113, and the 1845 *Statistik*, pp. 192–193, 544, give good descriptive statistics on the sizes of other groups which patronized Prussia's regular book trade: in 1834 there were 5,740 Protestant ministers in the Kingdom; in the mid-1840s there were approximately 9,500 officers in the army and 150,000 bureaucrats of all levels; the number of legal and judicial officials in 1844 was 15,903.

19 Letter of G. F. Heyer to Johann Krieger, October 13, 1823, *Krieger'sche Wochenblatt*, IV, Nr. 3–4, p. 21.

20 S-gg, "Sendschreiben an Herrn Joh. Chr. Krieger in Marburg," *Krieger'sche Wochenblatt*, III, Nrs. 47–48, p. 378. (Numbers of the paper did not go precisely by calendar years.)

21 *Allgemeine Zeitung*, 1828, no page or number given; quoted in Wolf, *Ueber den deutschen Buchhandel*, p. 35.

22 Prinz, *Bausteine*, vol. IV, p. 40.

23 Gaedicke, *Zur Statistik der deutschen Literatur*, cited above, p. 20.

24 For examples of bankruptcy scare stories see "Ein Practicus, 'Ueber einige Odiosa im Buchandel,'" *Krieger'sche Wochenblatt*, X, Nrs. 14 and 15, p. 113.

25 "Vor fuenfzig Jahren. Blaetter aus der Geschichte des deutschen Buchhandels, aus Anlaß des fuenfzigjahrigen Jubilaeums der Firma J. Ricker in Gießen," *Börsenblatt* 1882, Nr. 216.

26 Schulze, *Der deutsche Buchandel*, pp. 32–33; Wolf, *Ueber den deutschen Buchandel*, p. 32.

27 er, "Einige Bemerkungen ueber des stets mehr und mehr einreissende Schleudern beim Buchverkaufe," *Krieger'sche Wochenblatt* XV, Nrs. 13–14, p. 142.

28 On the Golden Age see: S-gg in L., "Ueber das Rabattgeben der Buchhaendler," *Krieger'sche Wochenblatt*, Nrs. 9–10, p. 66.

# 3 Engines of growth

## Dynamic and entrepreneurial marketing, 1820–1843

"The sphere of the German book trade has been expanded significantly (in recent decades)," the readers of Germany's leading book trade paper were told in 1841; "where once it embraced only a small circle, it now embraces an entire nation of readers."[1] This "nation" was a middle- and upper-class one, to be sure, but far larger than that which had composed the market for the regular trade in 1820. Sales of books had risen; more copies of the average title were sold than had been the case in the years immediately following Napoleon's fall.[2]

The growth of the book market is demonstrated by the increase of the lending libraries—still the basic market for fiction—in both number and size. From 350–400 of them in 1820, there were approximately 600 in 1842. Before 1820, a large library had been one with 4,000 volumes, but by the late 1820s, libraries of 4,000 to 6,000 volumes were commonplace. Before 1820, only a handful of lending libraries had had more than 10,000 volumes; by 1836 there was one of that size in the small city of Bautzen. In the early 1840s Aachen, a medium-sized city, boasted one lending library with about 15,000 volumes and another with over 30,000. The measure of a big city lending library at that time was set by the establishment of Gustav Adolf Oehler in Frankfurt/Main, whose patrons could choose from over 100,000 volumes in 1842. All of these books had been purchased since 1828, when Oehler had founded the library.[3]

Moreover, the lending libraries absorbed even more books than these figures suggest, since literary fads and styles now came and went more rapidly than they had previously, and libraries had to discard unfashionable works to make room for the currently desirable ones.[4] During the years around 1830 for example, both almanacs and Knight/Bandit stories went out of fashion in the larger and medium-sized cities.[5]

The sales achieved by some of the books which replaced these old favorites further indicate how the book market had grown. Between 1826 and 1850 the Frankfurt/Main publisher J. D. Sauerländer sold 258,000 copies of novels by James Fennimore Cooper, and he was only one of many who published this author.[6]

Even more popular was Sir Walter Scott—"the works of this Briton are almost as popular as the Bible," wrote Wilhelm Hauff in 1828.[7] Hauff estimated that a minimum of 60,000 copies of Scott had been sold by 1828. A legion of publishers offered Scott's works, of which countless thousands of copies were sold after 1828 as well. Figures are available for the poet and playwright Schiller (1759–1805), who grew increasingly popular in this period. In 1837–1838 his publisher, Cotta, sold 100,000 copies of a cheap edition of the great author's works.[8]

## Aggressive marketing

Behind the success of these editions of Schiller, Scott, Cooper and others lay a new attitude towards bookselling, an attitude which dispelled the complacency and tranquility of the book trade with a "disquiet, an urgency, a bustle, an aggressiveness,"[9] an attitude which brought the penetration of the regular book shop trade deep into the middle class. "Mass production of literature had made its appearance, accompanied by the exploitation of a newly discovered market by speculative booksellers concerned to stimulate demand artificially, without regard to the method used."[10] The new attitude represented an influx into the book trade of the dynamic capitalistic ideas beginning to sweep Germany at that time: "Critics, publishers, and booksellers alike attributed the extension of the book market chiefly to the intrusion into the literary field of the economic factor characteristic of the time."[11]

Publishers infected by this attitude sloughed off the traditional passivity of the book trade. Considering themselves businessmen first and cultural emissaries second—if at all—they proclaimed and practiced their credo of Grow and Profit. An anonymous essayist captured the essence of their attitude in 1841: "We are businessmen. We publish in order to sell, and the more we sell, the better. How, through whom, and at what price sell-to these considerations we are indifferent, because anything goes as long as it brings a profit."[12]

This aggressive attitude towards producing and selling books fired the growth of the German book market. Population increase, more education, higher incomes, the spread of the habit of extensive reading—all of these factors heightened the potential of the market, but without aggressive bookselling that potential would have been realized only weakly.

The first significant move towards the New Way of merchandising books was made by the publisher August Schumann, father of the composer Robert Schumann. In 1815 Schumann began his '*Pocket Library of the German Classics*' (*Etui-Bibliothek der deutschen Classiker*), which by its end in 1827 had 100 volumes, most 160 pages long with a frontispiece of the author or main character and a brief biographical note. The books cost eight Groschen unbound, nine Groschen in brochure form, and 12 Groschen if bound; the final price inbook stores was 50 percent over these figures.

Germany's most arrogant, aristocratic publisher, Baron Cotta was a surprising second to enter the "pocket book" market. In 1822, alarmed at the inroads that pirated editions of Schiller were making into his sales, Cotta issued a cheap edition of Schiller. Both its size and its price were unusually small. Each of the edition's eighteen volumes measured only 3⅞ inches by 5⅜ inches when bound, had from 200–300 pages, was made of decent gray-white paper, and was printed with small but clear type. A set sold by subscription for only 4⅔ Reichsthaler (in advance); the full-sized 1818 edition of Schiller had sold for nearly 14 Reichsthaler. Cotta called these little books a "pocket edition." Part of the inspiration for this format came from England, but more was Cotta's own idea. Between 1822 and 1824, 50,000 sets were sold.[13] Predictably, "pocket editions" aroused the consternation of the book trade's many traditionalists. An 1827 report of the Exchange Union of German Booksellers spoke of "the universal revulsion towards these editions … (which) bring the greatest disadvantages to both good literature and to all branches of the book trade."[14] An article in the *Krieger'sche Wochenblatt* gratuitously allowed:

> This format is all right for children and for those of slender means but exceptional eyesight. Apparently these editions increase the desire to read and bring good authors more into everyday life than previously.... [They are, however,] disrespectful at once to authors and to the book trade.[15]

Traditional bookmen believed that cheap books cheapened the dignity of books and of the trade. They also feared that there was too little profit on each copy sold. In doing so, they ignored the concept that lower prices could increase the volume of sales so much that the total profit would be greater. It does have to be kept in mind, though, that this concept, a tedious commonplace of supermarket advertising today, was not widely known then; even if it had been, most bookmen would have disdained it. Many booksellers also worried that the public would become spoiled by cheap editions and refuse to buy more expensive books.[16]

## Speculative publishing explodes

But all of this worrying and all of this resistance was to no avail. Half unwittingly, more than half unwillingly, Cotta had tapped the potentially vast market of middle-class people who wanted to own good books but who were unable to afford them at the usual high prices. This was the market which Friedrich Arnold Brockhaus had revealed a decade earlier. But where few bookmen had sought to capitalize on the market then, now the climate had changed, and into the breach which Cotta had made in traditional marketing soon charged a horde of other publishers, most of them more energetic and less inhibited by past marketing forms than Cotta. Some of them were literary pirates and plagiarizers who evaded the spreading ban on piracy by going legitimate in the new, dynamic way.[17] The most important of the speculative publishers were: Ernst Friedrich Fuerst in Nordhausen, Joseph Meyer in Hildburghausen, and several men who made Stuttgart their headquarters—

Friedrich and Johann Franckh, Johann Scheible, and Carl Hoffmann. These men speculated especially in foreign novels, handbooks and other practical works, and classics.

There being no international copyright then, foreign authors received no royalties, which made their books inexpensive items to speculate with. That such authors as Sir Walter Scott and James Fennimore Cooper, and later Edward Bulwer-Lytton, Charles Dickens, and the Frenchman Eugene Sue, wrote more entertaining novels than most German writers of that era made these foreign books even more enticing.

Scott, whose novels had been published in German translation at a conventional price even before 1820, was a lending library staple by the mid-1820s, when publishers vied with one another to see who could bring out his new works most quickly. The first edition to appear would command the market, even if terribly done.[18] In 1825 the Schumann brothers of Zwickau, former pirates, brought out a new treat for the Scott fans—a complete works in 19 volumes at only eight Groschen per volume (nine Groschen if bound). The year 1826 saw the Scott war warm up, as F. S. Gerhard of Danzig countered with a rival edition selling for 6 Groschen per volume. The following year Stuttgart's Franckh brothers, hitherto known only as cut-rate booksellers and sometime pirates, trumped all the competition with small volumes at two Groschen each. Despite its "wretched paper, awful print, and pitiful covers,"[19] 30,000 sets of the Franckh's edition were sold within a short period, and the brothers are said to have made a profit of 100,000 Gulden in 1828. The low price of their Scott edition enabled small provincial lending libraries to purchase multiple copies; the edition was even purchased by some private individuals—very unusual for novels then.[20]

The Franckhs were soon considered by their peers to be the masters of speculative publishing. Not all of their gambles were successful, however. Of the five firms they founded in Stuttgart between 1822 and 1842, four went under. They constantly risked printing large (i.e., 3,000–5,000 copies on the first editions) editions of the books they did, and thus were often heavily in debt to printers and paper suppliers. In the mid-1830s Friedrich Franckh hit upon the idea of having outside investors put up the capital for a publishing venture he called the "House of Classics." The plan was to do fancy editions of translations of French books, but poor public response ended the venture.[21]

By that time other publishers, inspired by the Franckhs' early successes, had long since been issuing cheap translations. The most notable of these imitators were Säuerlander of Frankfurt/Main, who did editions of the Americans Washington Irving and James Fennimore Cooper, and Metzler of Stuttgart, who began with cheap translations of the Greek and Latin classics and later did such books as a complete edition of Bulwer-Lytton's works (1840–1853).[22]

Another speculator, Carl Hoffmann of Stuttgart, had tried in the late 1820s to cut in on the Scott mania, but soon perceived that there was no more room. An inveterate gambler, unstable as a businessman (he founded a total

of eight firms), but rich in ideas, Hoffmann then decided to attempt marketing broad-appeal history books on the scale which the Franckhs had used for
cheap novel translations. He chose his books well: the first edition of
Rotteck's 1831 *Allgemeine Weltgeschichte*, a briefer version of the *Allgemeine
Geschichte*, sold 20,000 copies; translations of Segur's *History of the 1812 Campaign* and Mignet's *History of the French Revolution* sold a total of 40,000 copies
in one year. Hoffmann issued all of these books in small inexpensive
installments rather than large and costly volumes.[23]

Continued good sales of Rotteck's book and also of Oken's *Naturgesghichte*
spared Hoffmann the fate of Johann Scheible, who had a run of luck in the
late 1820s and early 1830s with books on popular medicine, child-rearing,
and the like. Scheible's fortune peaked with a translation of the Pole, Soltyk's
*Poland*, an impassioned novel about the course and repression of the Polish
Revolution of 1830–1831. Scheible brought it onto the market just when
German interest in, and sympathy with, the Polish rebels were at their strongest. Because he had enormous numbers of the book printed, he was able to
sell it for a low price, which further drove sales upward. But success warped
his judgment, and Scheible began issuing all his publications in huge editions
that could not be sold. To meet his expenses he had to sell stacks of these
books to a notorious Cologne used-book dealer named Heinrich Tonger.
Tonger took the books, but went bankrupt before he could pay for them.
That finished Scheible.[24]

Ernst Friedrich Fürst, and Gottfried Basse, the former disdained by
respectable bookmen as a disgusting and ignorant man, the latter in the
opinion of most a gross literary pirate, both began their careers with the
publication of numerous low-grade Knight and Robber stories. Among
Fürst's stable of hacks was one with the absurd name (or pseudonym)
Eduardo Antonio Bartels. Furst himself was disrespectfully known as "the
Prince of Nordhausen."[25]

Both of these publishers had diversified into the lucrative fields of books
on popular medicine and practical handbooks by the time Knight and Robber
novels ebbed in popularity. Fürst's 1832 list included: J. C. Marcker's *Advice
and Help for those who Suffer from Bad Indigestion and Lower Body Difficulties
(Rath und Hülfe für diejenigen Personen, welche an schlechten Verdauung und Unter-
leibsbeschwerden leiden)* and Dr. Abicht's *The Doctor for those Suffering Diseases of
the Breast, or the Helper for Diseases of the Breast (Der Artz fur diejenigen, welche an
brustkrankheiten leiden, oder der Helfer bei den Krankheiten der Brust)*. These sold
for eight Groschen. A principal source of such books was one Dr. Schöpffer,
who wrote under 33 different pseudonyms, and his wife, who wrote under
five; productions from the Schöpffer household covered hemorrhoids, insom-
nia, venereal disease, and other common ailments. One of Germany's most
prolific publishers, Basse also got several of his books from plagiarists, and he
himself stole titles from successful works to make those that he published
more attractive. The health books done by Basse and Fürst were not especially inexpensive; their success was due to the natural appeal such books

always have to the sick and worried, and to heavy advertising. Basse and Fürst pleased retailers by their generosity in placing frequent advertisements in local newspapers.[26]

## The master of aggressive marketing: Carl Josef Mayer

The greatest of the speculative publishers of the 1820s, 1830s, and 1840s was Carl Joseph Meyer (1796–1856), the founder of the famous Bibliographisches Institut. Meyer was one of the most creative, and most energetic, German publishers of the nineteenth century. As a child he had given an early demonstration of his vigor by breaking the arm of a fellow student in a Gotha gymnasium. (He was expelled.) As an adult, he broke all the rules and traditions of the German book trade.

Like Brockhaus, he knew England first hand and had begun his career as a merchant. He then turned to stock speculation. He lost his fortune of 100,000 *Reichstahler* in a daring attempt to corner the German coffee supply in 1820. He entered the book trade in Gotha in 1824 as an editor (of business books and periodicals) and translator (of Scott and Shakespeare). Each of his first four Scott translations received a printing of 21,000 copies. His translation of Shakespeare was thoroughly mediocre, particularly in contrast to the Tieck-Schlegel version, but since it hit the market earlier, and at a lower price, it outsold the classic translation at first. Eleven thousand volumes of Meyer's Shakespeare were in print in 1825. By the following year he had earned enough to establish his own firm in Coburg-Gotha. He called it the Bibligraphisches Institut.[27]

Most new book dealers began their careers slowly and cautiously, producing only retail sales until they were well established enough to begin publishing; Meyer began with an immense publishing venture, his "Library of the German Classics." This was projected as a 150-volume collection of Germany's classics. Its format (3 by 5½ inches) was inspired by the "pocket editions" of Cotta and others.[28] He was deterred neither by the failure of two analogous ventures after 1815 nor by the fact that he would have to pirate many of the works of recent classic authors.[29]

Meyer, who united broad vision with a marvelous capacity to expedite details, plotted the marketing of the "Library" like Hannibal or Napoleon plotted their military campaigns. The series was unveiled with salvos of advertising whose volume far surpassed anything the German book trade had yet seen: Meyer placed advertisements "in almost all of the German newspapers"[30] and had them plastered on walls and windows all over the country.[31] To ensure that all who heard about the series could place their orders, the publisher sold it not only through retail book stores but also through many types of merchants and Colporteurs. He had selected and trained the Colporteurs himself so that he could be certain of their respectability. The books were issued from July 1827 until early 1834, usually at the rate of one per week; in all, 184 volumes appeared. They were sold by subscription, customers having to pay in advance only for the following volume, not for the entire series.

By September 1827, 337 book stores had either placed orders or indicated that they soon would. Several had ordered more than a thousand sets. The Hahn Book Store in Hannover, for example, ordered 1,600 sets. The Library was most enthusiastically accepted by younger retailers and by book stores in general in the West, South, and Center of Germany, where pirated editions had long been sold.[32]

Dealers in the great book market centers like Berlin, Leipzig, and Magdeburg, however, considered it a sleazy example of literary piracy and of pandering to a market which the trade could do well enough without. This opposition spread, especially among traditionally-minded dealers, and by 1828 there was a tremendous uproar against Meyer. Baron Cotta himself led the attack, which caused the government of Coburg-Gotha to close down Meyer's offices and the Leipzig book forwarders to refuse to handle his business. Meyer, unfazed, deflected the attacks by moving his operation to Hildburghausen, by sending shipments to Leipzig without listing his name, and by going into the printing business on a large scale. In 1830 Meyer had the fourth largest printing operation in Germany and was turning out cheap classics by the hundreds of thousands. From June 1, 1829 to June 1, 1830 his sales in Germany and Austria brought in 58,000 Gulden. The attacks on him had failed utterly.[33]

By 1830 the shape of his operations had gelled. He always initiated his own publications, commissioning writers and editors to do them rather than passively waiting for suitable manuscripts to come to him. He always did his own printing, made lavish use of advertising, and placed increasing reliance on his own Colporteurs and on direct letters to potential customers; his reliance on books shops, on the other hand, decreased. Meyer's ventures in the 1830s and early 1840s included: a cheap library of the ancient classics (9,000 copies of volume 1 were sold in its first four weeks of publication), an inexpensive atlas (30,000 copies were sold between 1832 and 1834), a Protestant Bible (Meyer sold 180,000 of these in the decade 1834–1844), an encyclopedia inaugurated in 1839, and the *Universum*, a unique illustrated book which appeared periodically As against these commercial successes, there were a few failures, like an English-language collection of British classics which never got past the first volume.[34]

Meyer did more than any other publisher of the first half of the nineteenth century to make the classics of German literature and other good books available to the majority of the German middle class. Underlying his success was his realization of the great hunger among many middle-class Germans to own such books. This was a public which old-line bookmen disdained as fit only to read to greasy lending library copies of Knight and Robber stories. Brockhaus had understood this public: Meyer's understanding of its anxieties and aspirations rivaled that of Brockhaus. Meyer sensed the insecurity of those who made up his market, people who wanted desperately to better themselves yet needed to be told how to do it, people who needed both their national and their personal pride flattered.

His advertising for the *Bibliothek der deutschen Classiker (Library of German Classics)* stressed that it was an enduring investment in both national glory and in personal, moral, and cultural elevation. A prospectus of May 1827 intoned:

> Time cannot render the content of this Library obsolete; age cannot lessen its worth. It is eternal, for the works which it contains will never die—Germany's great classics will live forever, like Greece's Homer. As it pleases us, so too will it please our posterity centuries hence...
>
> The father who purchases it as a worthwhile gift for his children, the friend who buys it for a close friend, and the swain who buys it for his beloved fiancé ... all are conscious that the reading which it contains will germinate the seeds of Greatness, Goodness, and Beauty in the soul of youth, and ill ennoble the spirits of grown men and of matrons ... He who sees on his bookshelf the means to elevate himself from the spiritual oppression of work and worry—who sees in books the staff upon which his soul will lean as it climbs out of the mire of everyday life ...—to him above all is our Library dedicated.[35]

## Others follow the aggressive paths of Meyer, Basse, *et al.*

The process inaugurated by Meyer, Fürst, Basse, Scheible, and the other pioneers of speculative publishing inspired—or infected, as some contemporaries had it—other publishers to emulation. There was a greater awareness and appreciation of the technological advances which had made large editions more economical. The main technological advances of the period were the invention of steel engraving in 1820 and the discovery of a way to lithograph in several colors by Alois Senefelder in 1826. Koenig's high-speed press found much more acceptance than previously; by 1840 there were more than 1,100 steam-driven presses in the Prussian territories. At times, indeed, the mere possibility of creating huge mounds of books must have acted like a narcotic stimulus on some publishers; for there were cases of absurd over-production. Production simply did not create its own demand.[36]

To make certain that they had sufficient and inexpensive material to feed the presses, publishers employed many hack writers and hack translators. An example was the Berlin writer Barda, who would write a Knight and Robber novel for a mere six *Reichsthaler*; a publisher had only to give him a title, he did the rest—usually by plagiarizing large segments from other novels. Numerous low-level bureaucrats supplemented their incomes at the rate of 25 Reichsthaler per month by doing anonymous hackwork.[37]

In a charming satire written for Cotta's *Morgenblatt für gebildete Stände* in 1827, Wilhelm Hauff described an imaginary translation factory in an imaginary place he called Scheerau. It employed, said Hauff, 30 translators and 15 presses and could turn out 120 octavo pages of Scott per day.[38] At the very time he wrote, Scott translations were being produced at a heady clip by G. v. Alvensleben, who wrote under the pen name "Gustav Sellen." Alvensleben did not bother to ponder over and write out his translations; rather, he dictated them, chattering away so rapidly that he required a crew of four high-speed scribes.[39]

The counterpart to the increased production of books was a more aggressive attitude towards selling them. An 1837 article in the *Börsenblatt* is subtly indicative of the change away from passivity. It analyzed the effect of weather upon retail sales, concluding that inclement weather aided sales because it caused people read more.[40] Nothing very profound in that—but it was a sign that bookmen were pondering the reasons for sales more than they had earlier.

Most of the new aggressiveness was on the part of publishers, not retailers, though many publishers also refused to allow the new ways to affect them. Among those who were affected, some began to realize that the physical form of a book could influence sales. Since the seventeenth century, German books had been fat, heavy, dowdy things. And until the late nineteenth century, they were sold unbound and without enticing wrappers. But in the 1820s it was clear to the more perceptive that the popularity of the "pocket editions," while mainly due to their low price, owed something to their physical form—there was something very attractive about the little books.

When the novelty of the "pocket editions" faded in the early 1830s publishers came up with a new delight for the public: the single volume collected writings of a major author. Throughout this period illustrations were found to help sales, especially of encyclopedias, handbooks, histories, and natural histories. Meyer had all of his books illustrated. New technology made lithographed and steel-engraved illustrations inexpensive to reproduce.[41] In the 1830s, some publishers realized that cheap gray paper hindered sales by making books look cheap and impermanent. The public wanted inexpensive books, but it expected them to last.[42]

Advertising became much more common. As early as the mid-1820s, some form of advertising or other announcement beyond a listing in the Fair Catalog was considered a necessity for any book. Unless retail bookmen and the public were made aware of a book's existence and virtues by such announcements, wrote the author of a trade handbook in 1825, even a good book had little chance of succeeding in the marketplace.[43]

## Advertising becomes more common

Publishers could choose from a broad spectrum of ways in which to publicize their books. They would place adverts in the several trade papers and catalogs, or in newspapers and journals; they could print up their own catalogs or have their offerings listed on the inside wrappers of books;[44] they could send retail shops "order blanks, posters, subscription forms, sample copies of books, (and) printed advertisements";[45] and they could mail letters and prospects directly to the public, this last a technique used with great success by Joseph Meyer.[46]

The ever-growing numbers of newspapers made comprehensive advertising campaigns increasingly expensive. It was difficult for publishers to select which newspapers and periodicals to use, especially as these, greedy for revenue, made hyperbolic claims. There were other problems with advertising. A large Berlin dealer complained that book advertising was placed in degrading proximity to adverts for butter, meat, and domestics.[47] There were retailers who, refusing to accept a publisher's books unless he paid for the advertising, either kept part of the money for themselves or got it in the form of kickbacks from the local newspaper.[48]

But no one in the trade would consider giving up newspaper advertising. It was a rule of thumb then that one notice in a local newspaper would sell 20 to 30 copies of a general book.[49]

The art of book advertising was still in an embryonic stage. Few advertisements were illustrated. The *Börsenblatt* and trade manuals had to remind publishers that long, bare author–title–price listings were not as effective as advertisements in which books were enumerated singly, or those in which the book was described.[50]

The extravagant claims and outright lies made by some publishers in their advertising were frequently denounced and ridiculed in both the trade and the general press, as for example by Ludwig Bauer in an 1830 number of the *Morgenblatt für gebildete Staende*:

> Bright tears well up in my eyes as I read in every newspaper the announcements of new books. And what announcements! Not a single book is issued which does not fill an important gap in the literature; not a single pamphlet which does not meet some long-felt need; not a single historical work which does not throw an entirely new light on this or that epoch.... Most compelling of all are the advertisements for new poems and romances for the sweet sex.... Here it sparkles of dewdrops, there swarm forget-me-nots and periwinkles, and here the brightest blooms of love and longing are entwined in fragrant wreaths.[51]

From within the trade came complaints that hyperbole in advertising would soon be self-defeating because the public was coming to associate it with books which no one would want to buy.[52]

## Publishers introduce other marketing techniques as well

But there was no going back to the Golden Age when advertising had not been necessary. And not only advertising, but also other marketing techniques were used by publishers more frequently and more energetically than previously; these devices were: (1) issuing books in sections, (2) cutting prices to spur sales, (3) altering titles, (4) subscriptions, and (5) promises of premiums.

Both Meyer and Scheible used premiums, the latter in ways which misled people. Subscribers to Meyer's encyclopedia received the first eight (of a planned 252) sections gratis as a premium. Fortunately for the old-fashioned in the trade, lotteries to promote book sales remained rarities.[53]

The custom of issuing books in inexpensive sections grew gradually during the 1820s, when many novels and encyclopedias were released in this manner. From the late 1820s, the speculative publishers began doing yet more with them. All of Joseph Meyer's publications were issued in installments. Scheible and Hoffmann used them. The use of these sections enabled the book trade to penetrate into the broad strata of the middle class.[54]

Subscriptions, especially those involving payment in advance, were the marketing rage of the late 1820s. In the middle years of the decade they were used even for books costing less than one Reichsthaler. In the heat of the subscription mania, some publishers abused their prerogatives; trumpeting their subscription prices as unbelievably low, then later raising them; or manipulating customers to buy in a rush by offering subscription prices for brief periods of time, then later extending these deadlines. These abuses angered those who had bought at the original subscription prices before the first deadline. Worse were the frauds when publishers failed to deliver books for which advance payment had been made. The excesses eventually generated such resistance from both retailers and the public that by the middle of the 1830s, the use of subscriptions with payment in advance was in sharp decline. The other forms of subscription remained fairly common, however.[55]

The next rage in marketing was price cutting by publishers. It was done at times to meet the competition of similar (or pirated) books and at other times to spur sales. A publisher could reduce the price of a book permanently; more often he reduced it only for a period of time, hoping thereby to induce the public to buy quickly.[56]

There was a widespread view among the public and retailers that books were only reduced in price if they were so wretched that no one would buy them at the original price.[57] Publishers therefore took pains to give high-sounding reasons for cutting prices, and who is to say that these reasons were not sometimes true? In 1825 the publisher Starck of Chemnitz offered L. Lang's *Treasure Chest for Good Boys and Girls (Raritätenbureau für gute Knaben und Mädchen)* (16 small volumes, bound) at two *Reichsthaler* eight *Groschen* instead of three *Reichsthaler*; this offer, which was in effect only until the end of December, 1825, aimed "to make it easier for parents without great means to purchase ... (this) welcome Christmas gift for children."[58] The Brockhaus Company asserted in 1830 that it lowered the price of Dr. Vollmer's *The Nature and Customs of the Tropics (Natur und Sittengemälde der Troepländer)* from three *Reichsthaler* to one *Reichsthaler* twelve *Groschen* only to lighten the financial burden its purchase entailed. In 1833 the Guttenberg Book Company of Tubingen claimed that steadily rising demand had enabled it to reduce the price of its seven-volume translation of Swedenborg by 25%.[59]

Some publishers were reproached by other bookmen for lowering prices when sales of a book were still good, an action which would, it was believed, make the public tend to withhold all book purchases unless prices were cut.[60] There was something to these reproaches. As one regular book buyer wrote, it made little sense to purchase books when they first appeared, since it was inevitable that after a year and a half to two years their prices would be dropped.[61] Analogous to this were the remarks of a scholar who wrote the *Börsenblatt* in 1839 to complain that when the price of a book was cut within a few years of its publication, those who had invested in it at first were made to feel gulled, the owners of products which too-rapidly depreciated.[62]

Despite such attitudes, however, both publishers and retailers were, on the whole, satisfied with the practice of reducing prices. Book shop owners were content as long as they were reimbursed for the difference between the original and the lower price in cases where they had bought the book, or as long as the margin remained at 33.3 percent in cases where they had gotten the book on approval.[63]

In the early 1830s a few enterprising used-book dealers bought up stocks of reduced-price books and issued catalogs on these. A. Weinbrack of Leipzig published a list of reduced-price novels and sent it to lending libraries. The firm of J. D. Classische in Hellbronn did a series of *Listings of Good Reduced Price Books (Verzeichniß gutter Bücher ... welche zum herabgesetzte Preise zu haben sind)*. Number 11 in this series, for example, covered books on history, geography, biography, statistics, travel-description, mythology, genealogy, and other topics. In 1839 the Jena publisher Friedrich Frommann invited other publishers to list their reduced-price books in a new catalog he had created rather than sell them to second-hand dealers. It would cost little to put a listing in this catalog, which would be sold so cheaply to retailers that they could buy many copies for themselves and for distribution to their customers. Books on which the margin was less than 25 percent would not be listed—Frommann knew that retailers would not touch them. The catalog quickly achieved considerable success, selling 20,000 copies by January of 1841.[64]

Reducing the price of a book to spur its sales was considered more honest than changing its title. The conventional wisdom then was that price and content were more potent attractions than the title. Yet title changes were fairly common, usually as last desperate efforts to rescue unsold books from being rendered into waste paper. A title change is said to have been partially responsible for one of the era's greatest sales successes: the guide to letter writing and related matters by an elementary school teacher named C. W. Schmalz. Schmalz published the book himself but had no luck selling it. He sold all rights to the book to the Glogau publisher Heymann, who dropped the original, now-unknown title, renamed it the *Home Secretary (Haussecretär)*, and sold 50,000 copies. Contemporaries ascribed much of this success to the book's new title.[65]

It is clear by this point that the major initiatives and innovations towards more aggressive bookselling were made by publishers, not by retail book shop operators, who as a group were the most conservative element within the trade. It was the retailers who spearheaded the resistance to trade expansion, to cheap editions, to issuing books in sections, to stirring up new strata of book buyers from the less affluent mass of the middle class; as well as to any-thing which could be construed to increase the work that they would have to do, to lower their 33.3 percent margin, or to corrode the august stature of the trade.

## Tendency towards specialization of function

In this period there was more and more separation between publishers and stationary retailers, as many publishers gave up their retail operations and many retailers abandoned publishing. The trend was towards specialization and concentration of function, although most dealers continued to have the traditional multiple functions. The Barter System, which had once made it necessary for bookmen to both publish and retail, was dying even by 1820; during the course of the 1820s it evolved into a sporadically used exchange system by which booksellers would swap unsold books or odd numbers of large works like encyclopedias.[66]

## The Sale or Return System

As the Barter System faded, retailers made greater use of the Sale or Return System, which placed most of the risk onto the shoulders of publishers. Retailers were very timid in risking their own capital, from customers and trade figures alike came complaints that few book shops would purchase a stock of books to keep on hand. They would not even purchase such sure-to-sell items as classics, despite the general awareness that a good stock encouraged people to visit the shop. The veteran Berlin bookseller Johann Christian Gädicke (1763–1837), no friend of the new trends, said that stock was second only to location in determining how well a book shop would do.[67]

The typical book shop of the 1820s and 1830s received books on approval from publishers and in turn distributed these among its customers for approval. A growing minority, reacting against the over-exuberant use of approval by some publishers, would take on approval only those books which they had specifically requested. In a notice in the *Krieger'sche Wochen-blatt* in 1828 a Paderborn book shop owner announced that he would no longer accept unrequested "novels, plays, poems, works of local interest, old works with new titles,... and very small works." [68] J. N. Fischer of Reutlingen gave notice in 1829 that the only unrequested books he would take on approval were: almanacs, devotional works, histories, geographies, works on natural science, children's books, theologies, and writings intended for the broad masses. These categories of book were generally considered less risky than fiction.[69]

Motivating the retailers' seeming largesse in permitting their customers to examine books on approval for indefinite periods was the hallowed rationale that this practice enabled the "contents of a book to drive themselves into (the customer's) ... consciousness with the force of lightning bolts," which of course meant that the customer "will sacrifice much, very much to possess" the book—so enthused a writer in the *Börsenblatt* in 1834.[70] With cunning timidity, many retailers allowed their customers to read on approval book after book, without ever having to buy. However, the customer did have to pay a fee, just as in a lending library; the only difference was that the books were cleaner. When his customers had tired of such books, the retailer would send them back to the publisher. Numerous readers, however, read approval books without paying fees, then gave them back in battered condition.[71]

Understandably, there was criticism of the retailers' use of approval. The writer Gutzkow accused them of being "naive to the point of absurdity (*Abgeschnacktheit*)."[72] In the absence of restraints upon customers, of course they would read without paying—"Who will blame me for wanting to save a few Thaler?"[73] More seriously, he argued, this ridiculous system discouraged the actual sale of books, and hence reduced the income of authors. Several bookmen replied to Gutzkow that the German book trade was too refined and decent to begrudge its customers a bit of cheating; furthermore, efficient business methods were better left to the British and French, who lived only for superficialities and appearances anyway.[74]

## Price cutting—underselling and discounts

Yet much as they longed to isolate themselves from the crasser aspects of the age, increasing numbers of book shops found it necessary to edge into the hubbub of the marketplace, there entering into vigorous, often anarchistic, combat with other book shops for what was incorrectly perceived as a small and inelastic body of custom. Customer discounts and underselling were the weapons of the struggle; the wounded could assuage themselves by counter-attacking their adversaries in the trade papers: the backbiting and bitter accusations reached a crescendo in the last years of the *Krieger'sche Wochenblatt* (1829–1834).[75]

> Underselling, whereby a retailer on his own initiative sold books for less than the publisher-established prices, had spread from Leipzig to most large and many medium-sized cities by the late 1830's. Since those who undersold normally took mail orders, they siphoned off business from small cities as well as from book shops in larger ones.[76]

Discounts to customers came to reach 20, 25, and even 33 percent of the selling price—and were frequently given. Once one bookseller in a city began to increase his discounts, the others felt compelled to follow suit. An old Paderborn bookseller named Wesener complained in 1830 that he had been in business for 20 years before having to give his first customer discount (of 10 percent) in the mid-1820s to match a competitor's deals. But as soon as he granted 10 percent discounts, the competitor gave 15 percent *and* free delivery, at which point a third retailer charged into the fray with 20–25 percent discounts. These discounts to customers were a terrible blow to the cherished institutions of the trade, said Wesener, but he had no choice but to use them too—"Shall I and my large family starve?"[77]

Despite the use of customer discounts and underselling, however, retail book shops were unable to sell enough books to satisfy the more aggressive publishers. Such publishers were convinced that the stationary retail shops were too passive and too mired in the past. Bernhard Friedrich Voight spoke for many publishers when he spoke of "the boundless inactivity of too many retail booksellers, (who) ... by doing business with neither joy nor ambition undermine even their own interests."[78] Another publisher asserted in 1842 that since stationary retailers did not understand their trade, were disorderly in business matters, and treated their customers with excessive arrogance, they had only themselves to blame for their small profits.[79] Still another publisher characterized them as blind, arrogant, rigid, and greedy boors unable to comprehend the modern business maxim that if they took a smaller margin, the resulting lower prices would enable them to sell so many more books that their profits would increase:

> Viewing books as mere material commodities, they are as a rule indifferent to their content and push mainly those on which the publisher has given the largest margin. They go so far as to tell publishers that they will not order books from them unless a suitably inflated margin is given.[80]

## New places to sell books

Considering the inadequacies which they ascribed to the book shops, it is understandable that ambitious publishers would seek supplementary retail outlets. As shown above, some had done this even before 1820. After 1820, many more did so, and much more extensively. In one of the most important developments of the period, publishers sold books on a vast scale through direct correspondence with the public, through government officials, through merchants and innkeepers, through used-book dealers, and through a new type of Colporteur. Book shop owners and traditionally-minded publishers viewed this process with glum anger as an attack upon both the cherished institutions of the trade and their own solvency. But the swelling volume of denunciatory letters they sent to the trade papers could not stop the process—they could only document it for the historian.

In the *Krieger'sche Wochenblatt* for 1820, there are furious letters revealing that the well-known publishers Palm of Erlangen and Frommann of Jena were selling directly to private persons, who got books at the same price book stores did.[81] Another typical letter of a decade later revealed that a Württemberg publisher had contacted scholars in Baden, Bavaria, and Württemberg to offer them his books at half the normal retail price.[82] It was later demonstrated in the *Börsenblatt* that many publishers, among them the large Hannover firm of Hahn, did similar things.[83]

More numerous than the complaints of direct sale to the public were accusations that publishers were supplying government officials with stocks of popular books and allowing them to sell these under the established retail prices. Most of these accusations were true—most publishers scorned to deny them. Postal officials and teachers were the usual government outlets for books, although other bureaucrats were not slighted.

Schmalz' *Haussecretär* was sold largely through government officials. In 1820, postal officials in Ehrenbreitstein and Coblenz sold the popular "almanacs" for slightly less than the set price. By 1842 the postal services of both Saxony and Prussia sold a full range of periodicals and popular books. Saxony's, for example, offered illustrated Bibles, several encyclopedias, a law lexicon, a fancy edition of Cicero's works, popular biographies of Luther, Napoleon, and Gustavus Adolphus, and other books.[84]

Merchants and publicans also offered a variety of books in some places. Joseph Meyer sold through merchants in regions where book shops would not stock in his books. Voight used them in regions where there were few book shops. He also dealt with innkeepers, as for example in the early 1840s, when he sent a lithographed prospectus offering to let them sell Biedenfelds *Compendiöses Conversations-Lexikon*, an inexpensive encyclopedia which he published. This work would practically sell itself, according to Voigt's prospectus:

> You'll be able to sell this book in a big way by merely mentioning it to friends and acquaintances at the right moment, or by letting some talkative, clever fellow show the subscription list about among the educated and prosperous. It will sell especially well among those who don't yet have an encyclopedia and among those who find the other encyclopedias on the market too expensive.[85]

When criticized for permitting the likes of publicans to sell his books, Voigt replied that such methods people whom the book stores didn't; furthermore, he continued, once these people were exposed to books, they might well become customers of the retail book stores.[86] His argument mollified no one, however.

In addition to innkeepers, binders and itinerant salesmen, earlier disdained by the proud stationary retailers as the book venders to the *hoi poloi*, became feared competitors. Long having sold elementary schoolbooks and such, binders were now given "real" books by publishers who appreciated their sprightly use of discounts and door-to-door selling.[87]

It was an even greater blow to the pride of the stationary book shops when publishers devised ways to adapt itinerant salesmen to the needs of the regular book trade. The pioneer here was Benjamin Herder of Freiburg, the founder of the great Herder publishing house. In the early 1820s he sent out salesmen to collect subscriptions for some of his publications, especially Rotteck's *Allgemeine Geschichte*. Unlike traditional Colporteurs, Herder's salesmen did not carry all their wares about with them; rather, they had demonstration copies and subscription forms. Again unlike traditional Colporteurs, Herder's were carefully selected so that they appeared to be educated people who were at home with fine books. Soon a few other publishers found that they too could sell serious works by means of travelling salesmen.[88]

But it was the increase in the number of books issued in inexpensive sections in the 1830s that really got this trend going. The installments were so light that a salesman could easily carry many samples with him. He could also deliver them easily once orders had been placed. Hoffman, Scheible, and Meyer appear to have realized these things simultaneously. Their success with travelling salesmen was much imitated, to the point where such salesmen became a pestilence in some regions—one man complained in 1837 that he had been visited by five different salesmen before noon on a single day.[89]

Publishers who retained tight control over their salesmen were able to preclude frauds and dishonest selling. On the other hand, free agents hired carelessly—they might use "street urchins, and even streetwalkers"[90]—and employed without much supervision, thus creating problems by making extravagant promises to customers which they could not fulfill, or by pestering people for so long that they either signed up or "threw the salesman out the door,"[91] or by absconding with the payments that customers had entrusted to them.

It was no wonder that the old aristocratic publishers of North Germany, who like the retail shop owners were upholders of the traders stately traditions, were reported in 1842 to:

> believe that a publisher who employs Colporteurs damns himself irrevocably as one of the pernicious outsiders who have pushed their way into the old and honorable fraternity of bookmen.... These artificial marketing techniques [i.e., Colporteurs] stupefy the public, engender revulsion towards booksellers, and degrade all of us.[92]

## A new way of retailing—Modern Second-Hand bookshops

Equally disturbing to such traditionalists was the development of the so-called "Modern Second-Hand" or "Modern Antiquarian" bookshops, which in addition to selling used books also sold new ones at low prices. Such shops were unknown before the 1820s. They were "entirely a product of the new era [and] could first appear only when publishers printed editions much larger than could be sold," wrote a trade historian who had watched them develop.[93]

The earliest attempts by used-book dealers to sell new books had been fueled more by dishonesty than over-production, however. They occurred in the early 1820s, when some second-hand dealers began to sell new books which had been stolen by printers' apprentices and warehouse employees in centers like Leipzig and Frankfurt.[94] When this source of supply was largely cut off by the police and the criminal courts, a number of second-hand dealers found another source of supply in pirated editions. The problem with pirated editions, however, was that they were illegal in more and more of Germany and were dwindling in supply.

The rise of speculative publishing and the growth of the trade ended all supply problems. The penchant of the speculative publishers and their imitators for big editions saw the volume of remaindered books mushroom. A Crefeld publisher named Cramer, for example, would do only editions of 20,000 copies—most of which remained unsold.[95] But because of the demands of the Sale or Return System, even cautious publishers found themselves with an increasing number of remainders: they had to print ever-larger editions so that they could send books on approval to the ever-increasing number of book shops, and the book shops returned the many books they were unable to sell.[96] Some publishers originally sold their piles of remainders to auctioneers, others to waste-paper concerns. The first to sell his to a used-book dealer was the ingenious Scheible, soon followed by Hoffmann and others.

Because remainders did not have the obvious sales attraction of pirated and stolen books, most used-book dealers were initially unwilling to take them. The flamboyant Cologne bookseller Heinrich Tonger was the first to buy remainders. He was soon surpassed by Joseph Baer and Michael St. Goar, two Frankfurt Jews who had good connections with the speculative publishers of Stuttgart. Then the other large cities developed Modern Antiquarian booksellers too. Berlin had 10 to 12 of them in the 1840s. Almost all of these dealers were Jews, but in the face of the deals they offered, whatever prejudice publishers had was forgotten.[97] They always paid cash. They never asked publishers to take back the books they had been unable to sell. Aside from Tonger, most of them were extremely reliable businessmen. They took enormous numbers of books. For these reasons publishers not only gave them favorable deals on remainders, they also permitted them to sell some still-successful books as well. Some of the proudest and most prestigious publishing houses in Germany, including those of Cotta, Brockhaus, and Carl Tauchnitz, dealt with Modern Second-Hand booksellers.

As retailers, these booksellers were extremely effective. Unlike most new book retailers, they were not inhibited by the old conventions, which assumed a tiny, elegant, and rich public. Their customers had to pay cash and were not permitted to examine books on approval. In return, the customers got bargains—Modern Second-Hand dealers sold books for far less than the publishers' retail prices, even very popular books like those of Schiller and Rotteck. Thus in Dresden during the latter part of the decade of the 1830s, one Modern Second-Hand dealer sold more copies of Schiller than the city's five new book shops combined.[98]

It seemed to some that the Modern Second-Hand dealers would attract all the customers away from regular book shops. Georg Reimer, a respected Berlin publisher, wrote in 1835:

> Once they are spoiled by such gross and undignified deals [as the Modern Second-hand shops offered], book buyers will no longer want to buy their new books [in retail shops]: instead, they will prefer to wait until they can pick them up at the terms offered by these so-called Modern Antiquarian booksellers.[99]

Such fears were exaggerated. Even in the large cities, where most of the Modern Second-Hand operations were located, the number of traditional book shops grew throughout this period. This growth could only have been sustained by a growing volume of patronage. Other retail institutions might be able to sell a limited number of books more cheaply, but they could offer neither the variety of books nor the personal service and exclusive atmosphere of the traditional book shops, where the customer was treated "as a close acquaintance [and] as a full member of the prestigious Society of Those Who Read."[100] An old Munich bookseller who looked back upon conditions in the 1820s decades later remembered:

> Relations with the public were personal and *gemütlich*. We still recall with pleasure, nay with enthusiasm, the almost daily personal contact with the cultivated ... government officials, scholars, and artists who came in person to the shop every week to make their selection of the new books.[101]

Some retail book shops were more like literary salons or literary coffee houses than mercantile establishments. In the Berlin shop of Cosmar and Krause "associated all the literary greats, the literary insignificants, and all types of people who were obsessed with keeping up with the latest in literature; midday was the time when these assemblies took place."[102] Neither the anguished rhetoric in the trade periodicals of the time, nor the truly impressive development of other retail outlets for books, should be allowed to obscure the vitality of the traditional bookshops.

Similarly, the spectacular market successes of the speculative publishers, particularly with novels, should not be allowed to give a misleading impression of the regular trade's book market during this period. Although the book market did grow enormously in sales and in volume from 1820 to 1843, its basic structure did not change very much. Its customers were still entirely from the upper and middle classes. As in the past, a very large number of books were not purchased by individuals for their personal libraries, but rather by lending libraries, reading groups, scientific societies, and the like.[103]

The relative importance of the various subjects of the books on the market remained much what it had been in the years 1815–1820.

The decline in the number of titles on history was only temporary and did not reflect any great decline in sales; the drop in the number of titles on poetry, in contrast, can be ascribed to lower sales. The most significant increases were in the last three categories and reflect the growing importance of the natural sciences and commerce as well as the growing complexity of government. Yet even during the 1836–1840 period, the largest single category of titles was religion, just as it had been since the fourth and fifth centuries AD.[104]

## "Which books are most often bought?"

The number of titles was not an infallible guide to actual sales, of course. In the years 1838–1840, an average of 725 titles on philology were issued each year, but it is unlikely that many of them sold more than 1,000 copies. "Which books are most often bought?" asked the bookman Johann Bergk rhetorically in 1825. His answer was a brilliant analysis:

> Books which correspond to the interests, and fulfill the needs, of the greater part of the public. Those which aid physical, cultural, and spiritual wellbeing will find the most applause. Books, therefore... which contain basic information; which instruct in the various branches of knowledge; which are indispensable for advancement in the world;

*Table 3.1* Titles published by subject, 1816–1840

| Subjects | Percentage of titles | | |
|---|---|---|---|
| | *1816/1820* | *1826/1830* | *1836/1840* |
| 1 Theology | 10.1 | 12.2 | 10.8 |
| 2 History, Politics, Biography | 12.2 | 11.4 | 9.7 |
| 3 Medicine | 7.4 | 6.5 | 9.7 |
| 4 Mathematics | 2.4 | 2.2 | 2.4 |
| 5 Children's Books | 7.2 | 5.7 | 5.7 |
| 6 Philology, Mythology, Freemasonry | 7.3 | 8.2 | 8.5 |
| 7 War, Cavalry | 1.4 | 1.6 | 1.4 |
| 8 Poetry, Fine Arts | 8.1 | 7.5 | 5.8 |
| 9 Novels | 5.9 | 5.9 | 6.8 |
| 10 Plays | 2.8 | 2.4 | 2.6 |
| 11 Natural Sciences | 4.3 | 5.3 | 6.2 |
| 12 Trade, Mining | 0.8 | 1.7 | 2.2 |
| 13 Public Administration, Agriculture, Veterinary Science, Hunting | 5.8 | 10.4 | 14.1 |

Note
Figures from 1838 and 1839 from "Einige allgemeine und besondere Betrachtungen ueber den Buchhandel," *Börsenblatt* 1840, Nr. 30, pp. 773–776.

which teach us about peoples, mankind, the earth, and religion; which tell how to keep body and soul well or how to restore their wellbeing: which teach us how to count and calculate, and so forth—these find the most buyers.[105]

The mass of the book-buying public of the regular book trade, then, was practical. It bought religious books for its spiritual wellbeing; encyclopedias, histories and classics for its cultural wellbeing; and handbooks for its physical and material wellbeing—just as it had during the years immediately after Napoleon's fall.[106] The contemporaries who feared that German culture, taste, and morality were drowning in a flood of cheap foreign novels did not realize that most of these novels sold well under 1,000 copies.[107] A careful investigation by the Berlin bookseller Gädicke in the mid-1830s showed that fictional works were seldom reprinted: of 30 books which had been reprinted for the tenth or greater time in 1833, only two were works of fiction. These were Matthison's long-popular *Gedichte* (12th reprinting) and Ernst Beckmann's *Eckensteher Nante* (1833) 15th reprinting 1833), the purported observations of a Berlin street-corner loafer and the most fashionable book of that year.[108] The rest were either mass-market items like primers and simple devotional books, or such serious works as Buttmann's *Greek Grammar (Griechische Grammatik)* (14th reprinting, price one Thaler), Stein's *New Atlas of the Whole World (Neuer Atlas der ganzen Erde)* (12th reprinting, price four Thaler, eight Groschen) and Kohlrausch's *German History (Deutsche Geschichte)* (10th reprinting, price one Thaler, 12 Groschen) and Zschokke's *Hours of Devotion (Stunden der Andacht)* (17th reprinting).[109] The *Stunden der Andacht* far overshadowed all the others in the marketplace—it was the most successful full-sized book of the entire era. Were the precise statistics on its sales known, they would probably make the triumphs of the speculative publishers look insignificant.[110]

Sales of the ancient classics grew throughout the 1820s, then leveled off.[111] Some of the great German classics, on the other hand, became increasingly popular—to the advantage of the Cotta publishing house, which enjoyed an almost total monopoly in this field.[112] Schiller (1788–1805) was easily the most-purchased of the German classical authors; a conservative estimate would be that 250,000 copies of his works were sold between 1820 and 1843, most of them in inexpensive editions. Twenty-thousand sets of the famous *Ausgabe letzer Hand* of Goethe's (1749–1832) collected writings (1827–1830) were sold, the high sales due largely to the fact that the edition was available in the inexpensive "pocket" format as well as in an elegant octavo version. Cotta also issued two other editions of Goethe between 1836 and 1840.[113] Eckermann's *Conversations With Goethe*, however, appealed to the public as little as did the productions of the Romantic School.[114] The most popular younger German author then was Wilhelm Hauff. So strong and consistent was the demand for his works, that they were considered an essential part of the stock of any book shop.[115]

The encyclopedia market discovered by Brockhaus continued to grow rapidly in this period, despite outcries that "encyclopedias intend only to convey superficialities, not to probe deeply," and were causing "true scholarship and serious learning to collapse in ruin."[116] Twenty thousand sets of the fifth edition of Brockhaus' *Conversations-Lexikon* were sold between 1820 and the great publisher's death three years later; 12,000 had been sold between 1818 and 1820. Brockhaus' son continued the firm ably along the lines which his father had laid down. The seventh edition of the *Conversations-Lexikon* (1827–1830) sold 26,000 sets, and the eighth edition sold (from 1837–1842) 32,000. Two smaller versions, the *Conversations-Lexikon der neuesten Zeit und Literatur* (4 volumes, 1832–1843) and the *Conversationslexikon der Gegenwart* (4 volumes, 1838–1841), sold 27,000 and 18,000 sets, respectively.[117]

These brief versions were issued to counter some of the many competitor encyclopedias that were swarming into the market—six of them in 1834 alone.[118] The best of the competitor works was Pierer's *Encyklopädisches Wörterbuch* (26 volumes, 1822; 2nd edition 36 volumes, 1840). Some said it was better than the Brockhaus.[119] But since it, like encyclopedias today, was intended as a straight forward reference work, while Brockhaus' encyclopedia aimed to entertain as well as instruct, it did not sell as well. Most of the other general encyclopedias were brazen imitations of either Brockhaus or Pierer. The most serious threat to Brockhaus' hegemony in this market was posed by the encyclopedia Joseph Meyer began issuing in 1839. Designed to appeal to people who would find both Brockhaus and Pierer too difficult, it sold very well.[120]

## Notes

1 "Ueber den Einfluss des deutschen Buchhandels," *Börsenblatt* 1841, Nr. 2, pp. 28–29.
2 *Börsenblatt* 1836, Nr. 51, p. 1660.
3 *Börsenblatt* 1957 (Frankfurt edition), Nr. 5, pp. 582–583; W. Hauff, "Die Buecher und die Lesewelt," *Morgenblatt fuer gebildete Staende* 1827, Nrs. 85–90.
4 Hauff, "Die Buecher und die Lesewelt," cited above, *passim* but especially pp. 21, 55–60; "Ueber Fabrication und Absatz von Romanen," *Börsenblatt* 1840, Nr. 104, pp. 2758–2760.
5 *Börsenblatt* 1842, Nr. 36, p. 955.
6 Nutz, *Der Trivialroman*, p. 54.
7 Hauff, "Die Buecher und die Lesewelt," p. 32.
8 Lohrer, *Cotta*, p. 109.
9 F. Perthes, "Die Bedeutung des deutschen Buchhadels, besonders in der neuesten Zeit," *Börsenblatt* 1834, Nr. 1, p. 6. This famous and often-reprinted essay opened the first issue of the *Börsenblatt*.
10 Magill, "The German Author and his Public in the Mid-Nineteenth Century," p. 494.
11 Ibid., p. 494.
12 "Ist das Colportieren erlaubt oder nicht?," *Börsenblatt* 1841, Nr. 95, p. 2369.
13 I saw a copy of this "Pocket edition" in the Deutsches Buch und Schrift Museum in the Deutsche Buecherei, Leipzig in 1972. On the pocket books see *Krieger'sche Wochenblatt* III, Nrs. 47–48, p. 378.

14  H. Widmann, *Der deutsche Buchhandel in Urkunden und Quellen*, vol. II, p. 147.

15  *Krieger'sche Wochenblatt* VI, Nrs. 50–51, p. 416.

16  "Worte eines alten Sortimentshaendlers," *Krieger'sche Wochenblatt* VII, Nrs. 15–16, pp. 113–114.

17  The regular book trade generated intense pressure against piracy. By the late 1820s few book retailers would sell pirated editions openly. In 1837 the Bundestag of the German confederation essentially made piracy illegal everywhere in the Confederation—which included most of Germany.

18  Prinz, *Bausteine*, vol. I, pp. 11–12.

19  Berger, "Der deutsche Buchandel," p. 131.

20  On the cheap Scott and other editions see Prinz, *Bausteine*, vol. I, pp. 13–14.

21  Ibid., vol. III, p. 36.

22  Ibid., vol. I, pp. 14–15; "Johann David Sauerlaender," *Börsenblatt* 1869, Nr. 291, pp. 4169–4170.

23  Ibid., vol. I, pp. 25–27; Menz, *Der deutsche Buchandel*, p. 141.

24  On Scheible and Tonger see Prinz, *Bausteine*, vol. III, pp. 35–39.

25  See ibid., vol. I, p. 18.

26  *Krieger'sche Wochenblatt* VII, Nrs. 5–6, pp. 33–34; X, Nrs. 9–10, pp. 65–66; XII, Nrs. 45–46, p. 359. Also "Ueber Fabrication und Absatz von Romanen," *Börsenblatt* 1840, Nr. 104, pp. 2758–2760.

27  He founded it in his wife's name so that he would not be able to gamble away earnings on wild speculations that he had trouble resisting. See J. Hohlfeld, *Das Bibliographische Institut*, Leipzig 1926, p. 32. See also Prinz, *Bausteine*, vol. I, p. 15.

28  There are copies in the Deutsches Buch und Schrift Museum in Leipzig. The paper is still soft, the small Gothic type is easy to read.

29  Hohlfeld, *Das Bibliographische Institut* Leipzig 1926, pp. 45–46.

30  *Krieger'sche Wochenblatt* VII, pp. 387–390.

31  Goldfriedrich, *Geschichte*, p. 384.

32  *Krieger'sche Wochenblatt* VII, Nrs. 43–44, pp. 343–344; Nrs. 49–50, pp. 387–389.

33  Menz, *Der deutsche Buchhandel*, p. 137.

34  Hohlfeld, *Das Bibliographische Institut* Leipzig 1926, pp. 71–106.

35  Ibid., pp. 47–48.

36  G. Jaeger and D. Langwiesche, eds., *Geschichte des deutschen Buchhandel im 19. Und 20. Jahrhundert*, Frankfurt/Main, 2001, p. 19; Menz, *Der deutsche Buchhandel*, p. 138; Prinz, *Bausteine*, vol. I, pp. 66–71; Uhlig, *Geschichte des Buches und des Buchhandels*, pp. 64–65.

37  "Ueber Fabrication und Absatz von Romanen," *Börsenblatt* 1840, Nr. 104, pp. 2758–2760.

38  Hauff, "Die Buecher und der Lesewelt," pp. 32–36.

39  Prinz, *Bausteine*, vol. I, pp. 12–13.

40  *Börsenblatt* 1837, Nr. 21, pp. 417–419.

41  Uhlig, *Geschichte des Buches und des Buchhandels*, p. 65.

42  "Chronik des deutschen Buchhandels—Jahr 1833," *Börsenblatt* 1834, Nr. 8, p. 125; J. C. Gaedige, *Der Buchhandel von mehreren Seiten betrachtet*, 2nd ed., Grelz 1834, p. 63. Hereafter cited as Gaedicke, *Der Buchhandel*.

43  J. A. Bergk, *Der Buchhaendler, oder Anweisung wie man durch den Buchhadel zu Ansehen und Vermoegen kommen kann* Leipzig 1825, pp. 38–39.

44  *Krieger'sche Wochenblatt* V, Nr. 46, p. 392.

45  Quoted in *Kleine Geschichte der Buchhandlung Friedrich Schaumburg in Stade* Stade 1965, p. 13.

46  Hohlfeld, *Das Bibliographische Institut* Leipzig 1926, p. 90.

47  *Börsenblatt* 1839, Nr. 95, pp. 2345–2346.

48  "Einige Mittheilungen ueber den jetzigen deutschen Buchhandel," *Krieger'sche Wochenblatt* VI, Nrs. 48–49, p. 389.

49  Prinz, *Bausteine* vol. II, pp. 58–59.
50  Gaedicke, *Der Buchhandel*, pp. 80–82.
51  "Genialitaet und Buchhandel," *Morgenblatt fuer Gebildete Staende* 1830, Nrs. 95–96.
52  C., "Ueber Anzeigen," *Krieger'sche Wochenblatt* XIII, Nrs. 9–10, pp. 66–67.
53  On the use of premiums see: Meyer, "Mittheilungen zur inneren Geschichte des deutschen Buchhandels," p. 234; *Börsenblatt* 1845, Nr. 26, p. 315.
54  E. Drahn, *Geschichte des deutschen Buch-und Zeitschriften-Handels* Berlin 1914, pp. 29–30.
55  M. F. in H., "Stimme eines Zuschauers," *Krieger'sche Wochenblatt* III, Nrs. 8–9, pp. 62–63; *"Ansicht ueber Subscription und Praenumeration,"* *Krieger'sche Wochenblatt* VI, Nrs. 20–21, pp. 153–155; Gaedicke, *Der Buchhandel*, p. 71.
56  Gaedicke, *Der Buchhandel*, pp. 74–75, Wolf, *Ueber den deutschen Buchhandel*, pp. 18–19.
57  Gaedicke, *Der Buchhandel*, pp. 74–75.
58  *Monatsbericht* 1825, Nr. 11, pp. 186–187.
59  *Kreiger'sche Wochenblatt* IX, Nrs. 49–50, p. 396.
60  *Börsenblatt* 1835, Nr. 36, pp. 983–984; 1842, Nr. 12, p. 301.
61  Cited in Meyer, "Mittheilungen zu inneren Geschichte des Buchhandels," p. 198.
62  Dr. Schellwitz, "Ueber die Grunduebel des deutschen Buchandels," *Börsenblatt* 1939, Nr. 12, pp. 259–260.
63  *Börsenblatt* 1835, Nr. 50, p. 1413; Nr. 52, pp. 1474–1476.
64  *Krieger'sche Wochenblatt* XIII, Nrs. 21–22, pp. 173–174; Nrs. 29–30, p. 236.
65  Prinz, *Bausteine*, vol. I, p. 17; Krieg, *Matelialien zu einer Entwicklungsgeschichte der Buecher-Preise*, p. 132.
66  Schulze, *Der deutsche Buchhandel*, p. 79. On the Barter System, see *Krieger'sche Wochenblatt* I, Nr. 26, pp. 283–285; IV, Nr. 44, pp. 345–346.
67  Gadicke, *Der Buchhandel*, p. 20.
68  J. Wesener, "Bitte an die loeblichen Buchandlungen Deutschlands," *Krieger'sche Wochenblatt* VIII, Nrs. 17–18, pp. 131–132.
69  *Krieger'sche Wochenblatt* IX, Nrs. 5–6, p. 46.
70  "Ueber die grosse Vermehrung der Buchhaendler," *Börsenblatt* 1834, Nr. 39, pp. 743–744.
71  Bergk, *Der Buchhaendler*, p. 40; O. Wigand, "Der deutsche Buchhandel," *Börsenblatt* 1842, Nr. 96, pp. 2657–2658.
72  *Börsenblatt* 1837, Nr. 56, pp. 1241–1242.
73  Ibid.
74  *Börsenblatt* 1837, Nr. 71, pp. 1649–1654; Nr. 74, pp. 1729–1734.
75  For examples see *Krieger'sche Wochenblatt* X, Nrs. 1–2, pp. 2–5; Nrs. 11–12, pp. 85–86.
76  R. M. "Ueber das Rabatgeben," *Börsenblatt* 1839, Nr. 94, pp. 2313–2315.
77  *Krieger'sche Wochenblatt* X, Nrs. 7–8.
78  *Suddeutsche Buchhaendler-Zeitung*, 1838, Nr. 6—quoted in Goldfriedrich, *Geschichte*, p. 385.
79  *Börsenblatt* 1842, Nr. 82, pp. 2194–2195.
80  Quoted in Goldfriedrich, *Geschichte*, p. 385. On the retailers' obsession with the 33.3 percent margin see "Ueber die Frankh'sche Zwei Groschenausgabe des Walther Scott," *Krieger'sche Wochenblatt* VIII, Nrs. 35–36, pp. 310–311.
81  *Krieger'sche Wochenblatt* I, Nr. 19, pp. 149–150.
82  *Krieger'sche Wochenblatt* X, Nrs. 19–20, pp. 145–147.
83  *Börsenblatt* 1846, Nr. 97, p. 1289.
84  *Börsenblatt* 1842, Nr. 19, pp. 241–242.
85  *Börsenblatt* 1844, Nr. 59, p. 1467.

86  *Börsenblatt* 1842, Nr. 1, pp. 1–7.

87  On retail sale by binders see: G. F. Heyer, "Auch einige Worte in und ueber das Wochenblatt fuer Buchhaendler, etc.," *Krieger'sche Wochenblatt* III, Nrs. 1–2, pp. 5–7; B., "Stimme eines reisenden Buchhandlers," *Krieger'sche Wochenblatt* III, Nrs. 45–46, pp. 355–356.

88  "Auszug eines Schreibens," *Krieger'sche Wochenblatt* III, pp. 73–75.

89  *Börsenblatt* 1837, Nr. 98, pp. 1156–1157.

90  *Börsenblatt* 1836, pp. 1156–1157.

91  Ibid.

92  "Ist das Colportiren erlaubt oder nicht?," *Börsenblatt* 1841, Nr. 95, p. 2369.

93  Prinz, *Bausteine*, vol. V, p. 13. See pp. 13–21 of this for the best account of the second-hand trade.

94  Prinz, *Bausteine*, vol. I, pp. 68–69.

95  Ibid., vol. V, p. 15.

96  "An Verleger zur Berathung von dem geheimen Maculatur-Rath von H," *Krieger'sche Wochenblatt* IX, pp. 257–258.

97  There was a plea to the trade to accept the Jews as equals—Anton, Eduard, "Vorschlag," *Krieger'sche Wochenblatt* VII, Nrs. 11–12, pp. 81–83.

98  Richter, "Zur Vorgeschichte und Geschichte der vormals Walther'schen jetzt Burdach'schen Hofbuchhandlung," p. 156.

99  *Organ des deutschen Buchandels* 1835, Nr. 34, quoted in Vollert, *Die Korporation der Berliner Buchhaendler*, pp. 14–15.

100  *Der deutsche Buchhandel im Spiegel der Vossischen Zeitung*, Berlin 1925, p. 14.

101  F. Senior, "Streiflichter zu dem Aufsatze 'Der Muenchener Sortimentshandel von heute'," *Börsenblatt* 1868, Nr, 39, p. 439.

102  Prinz, *Bausteine*, VII, p. 18.

103  Gaedicke, *Der Buchhandel*, p. 19; *Statistik des preussischen Staats* 1845, pp. 256–261.

104  Goldfriedrich, *Geschichte*, pp. 220–221.

105  Bergk, *Der Buchhandler*, p. 14.

106  Ibid., pp. 17–20.

107  For an example of a fearful contemporary reaction see Appell, *Die Ritter-, Raeuber, und Schauerromantik*, cited above, entire. On the small sales of novels see Bergk, *Der Buchhandler*, p. 22.

108  See Berger, *Der deutsche Buchhandel*, pp. 137–138.

109  Gaedicke, *Zur Statistik der deutschen Literatur*, pp. 26–44.

110  "Ueber den Einfluss des deutschen Buchandels," *Börsenblatt* 1841, Nr. 4, pp. 65–66.

111  Schulze, *Der deutsche Buchhandel*, p. 138.

112  Lohrer, *Cotta*, p. 100.

113  Ibid., pp. 59–60, 109–111.

114  Widmann, *Der deutsche Buchhandel in Urkunden und Quellen*, vol. II, p. 65.

115  *Börsenblatt* 1843, Nr. 64, p. 2086.

116  Prinz, *Bausteine*, vol. VI, p. 32.

117  Goldfriedrich, *Geschichte*, pp. 202–203.

118  Vinzer, "Chronik des Jahres 1834," *Börsenblatt* 1835, Nr. 16, pp. 402–404.

119  Ibid., pp. 402–404.

120  Menz, *Hundert Jahre Meyers Kexikon*, pp. 26–33.

# 4   The mass book market, 1820–1870

For all its growth, the regular book trade never dealt with more than 5 to 10 percent of Germany's population. Its clientele was the middle and upper classes; everyone else was disdained. As noted in Chapter 1, however, the German masses—the peasants, domestics, artisans, industrial workers and their families—did not have to go without reading matter. Their needs were serviced by a separate, distinct book trade, which I shall call the "mass book trade."

During the half-century after 1820, the mass book market grew considerably. Increased urbanization, the spread of literacy, technological advances in bookmaking, and slightly higher incomes in some segments of the masses created conditions in which publishers could bring a growing proportion of Germany's mushrooming population into contact with books. "It is now not uncommon to see lady fruit vendors; peasants, and artisans buried enthusiastically in books and newspapers," wrote a contributor to the *Börsenblatt* in 1861 with only moderate exaggeration.[1]

## Literacy and semi-literacy

Literacy among the masses grew faster than their numbers. In 1820, approximately 50 percent of all Germany's males and 70 percent of its females were illiterate or semi-literate. By 1870 not only had the gap between males and females been drastically narrowed, but also a large majority of each group had become literate.[2] The decline of male illiteracy is clearly shown by statistics on Prussian army recruits.[3]

The Prussian census of 1871 revealed that roughly 10 percent of males over nine years of age in the Kingdom were illiterate; among Catholic males, the rate was 18 percent. Elsewhere in Germany at this time the rates would have been lower because of the absence of the large, poorly educated Polish minority found in Prussia's eastern reaches.[4] Semi-illiteracy was more common than illiteracy. It has been estimated that about one-fifth of the adult males in Germany were semi-literate during the period of national unification.[5] One-quarter of the females were semi-literate, too. The higher figure for females was caused mainly by the presence of older women who had received little education—Prussian school statistics show that after 1830, almost as many girls as boys attended elementary schools.[6] For the book market, the decrease in female illiteracy and semi-literacy was especially important, because women tended to read more than men did.

There were, however, two factors that severely limited *how much* the masses read: (1) most books remained far beyond the limited incomes of many lower-class Germans, and, more important, (2) reading did not become the important, prestige-conferring activity among the masses which it had long been for the upper and middle classes.

"High prices prevent most people from buying books," wrote the social reformer Karl Preusker in 1835; "they are not used to spending much for books—and are often unable to do so even when they earnestly want to buy them."[7] The same was true in 1870. Even the industrial workers, the most prosperous group in the masses, did not have much disposable income for books, and during periods of economic crisis they had none. Most German books remained as expensive as they had been before 1820. The books produced by the regular trade's speculative publishers were relatively less expensive, but still beyond the reach of the many Germans who lived at the level of bare subsistence. Furthermore, many of these books were not the kind of thing the masses had either the training or the inclination to read. This was particularly true of the classics, which had been written by elites for elites. For Germany's masses, literate but barely so, even encyclopedias and translations of popular foreign novels were abstruse and difficult fare.[8]

The most diligent and capable elementary school graduate was ignorant and unlettered. His education had not been designed to make reading an important part of his life; rather, it had been designed by people who feared that reading should become important to him. Throughout the nineteenth century the philosophy underlying the elementary schools remained unchanged—to instill the barest rudiments of learning and nothing more. A Prussian Edict of June 14, 1844 declared that:

> The only books which elementary school children need use are: a primer, a catechism, a collection of stories from the Bible (the Lutheran children get Bible stories and a songbook), a collection of exercises in calculation, and, for those children who have learned to read, a reader containing the essentials of natural science, geography, and history.[9]

In the 1850s and 1860s, the curriculum was broadened to include drafting and (in rural schools) gymnastics. An elementary school education was all the masses got. Perhaps it was all they wanted: there was no German counterpart to the movement for self-education that developed among some British working men and artisans.[10]

The trend towards mass reading engendered by a growing population, increased urbanization, and greater literacy among the masses, was, then, tempered by the factors of limited education, limited income, and a limited inclination to read. The result was that individual book consumption by literate members of the lower classes did not increase very much—but also that there was an ever-growing number of literate people among these classes. Each of these people only required a few books. But there were millions of them.

The types of books which they required were the same ones that had long been on the mass market: the staples of the mass book trade after 1820 were the same types of books which had been the staples before 1820. These were: schoolbooks, devotional works (including songbooks), calendars, pictures, pamphlets describing spectacular current events, advice and handbooks, and simple stories. The lower-class German decorated his walls with pictures and kept himself informed of the world's condition with pamphlets and calendars. A variety of handbooks and advice manuals provided him with information on his livelihood, his personal interests, and his problems. He sometimes edified himself and his family with readings from the Bible and devotional works, or entertained them with the simple stories contained in the so-called "folk literature" (*Volksbücher*). Many of the individual books which had been popular before 1820 remained so.[11]

## Primacy of religious literature

An examination of the books most frequently bequeathed in the village of Feldstetten in 1840 showed them to be the same ones which had been most frequently bequeathed in 1810 and 1820—Starck's *Prayerbook (Gebetbuch)* and Arnd's *True Christianity (Wahres Christentum)*, followed by the devotional works of Brastberger, Wudrian, and Schmolck. Of secular works, only letter writer's-guides and schoolbooks were common. Much the same result emerges from an examination of the wills of 1,169 average Tübingen citizens who died between 1840 and 1850. Religious works were almost six times as common as secular books. Most often mentioned were, respectively, song-books, Bibles, miscellaneous devotional works, Starck's works, and Arnd's works. Zschokke's *Hours of Devotion (Stunden der Andacht)* was mentioned in 20 wills, good evidence of its vast popularity.[12]

Although some of the long-popular devotional works mentioned in these legacies could have been very old copies, it is likely that many had been printed and purchased more recently. These books were the basic stock of many Colporteurs well into the nineteenth century and were continually reprinted.[13] Between 1835 and 1841 there were six editions of Arnd's *Wahres Christentum* (1605–1610) published by five different publishers; four of these editions also included his *Paradiesgärtlein*. Seven editions of *Wahres Christentum* were issued between 1847 and 1851. Other books by Arnd were occasionally reprinted too.[14]

Arnd's works declined somewhat in popularity in the 1860s, while books written by Johann Friedrich Starck in the first half of the eighteenth century grew more popular than ever. Starck's most beloved book, the *Daily Hand-book for Good and Bad Days (Tägliches Handbuch in guten und bösen Tagen,* 1727) was published in no less than eight editions by various publishers between 1862 and 1867. Twenty years before, only three had been in print. Judging from the frequency of editions, Starck's *Morning and Evening Devotions (Morgen und Abendandachten)*, his *Das Communion Buch*, and his *Prayers (Predigten)* also enjoyed a steady market, though not so large a one as that for the *Tägliches Handbuch*.[15]

There were other Protestant devotional classics which were reprinted again and again deep into the nineteenth century. One of the most popular of these was Carl Heinrich v. Bogatsky's *Golden Treasure Chest of God's Children (Güldenes Schatzkästlein der Kinder Gottes* 1718). Contemporary works of great popularity were Johann Wilhelm Löhe's (1808–1872) *Seeds of Prayer (Samenkörner des Gebetes,* 1840) and Johann Christian Lavater's *Words from the Heart (Wort des Herzens),* edited by Hufeland in 1825.[16]

There was a large market for Catholic devotional books among the masses, too, although per capita ownership of these (and other) books was lower among Catholics than among Lutherans and Calvinists because of the higher incidence of illiteracy, the greater poverty, and the still substantial vestiges of the traditional antipathy towards reading among Catholics.[17] And there were fewer Catholics than Protestants. Like the Protestant market, the Catholic one continued to absorb some venerable books: translations of the Frenchman, St. Francis of Sales' (1567–1622) *Philothea* and some of his other writings; Kaspar Neumann's (1648–1715) *The Seeds of All Prayer (Kern aller Gebete,* 1680), a book of ascetic prayers; and Leonhard Goffine's *Christian Education for all Sundays and Devotional Days for the Whole Year (Hand-Postill, oder christkatholische Unterrichtungen auf alle Sonn-und Feiertage des ganzen Jahres,* 1690). These books were never out of print. Five editions of the *Philothea* were on the market between 1835 and 1841, eight between 1847 and 1851, and six between 1857 and 1861. In the period from 1828 until 1867 the publishing firm of Coppenrath in Munster (Westphalia) reprinted the *Kern aller Gebete* 15 times—and it was only one of several firms which were publishing the book.[18]

There were some nineteenth-century devotional works whose popularity rivaled that of the older books, among them Aegydius Jais' *Lehr Und Beth Büchlein* (1807, 27th edition 1834) and Michael Sintzel's beloved *Gertrudenbuch*, which was reprinted 22 times between 1842 and 1886.[19]

The most frequently reprinted of all religious works outside of the Bible was a medieval classic read by both Catholics and Protestants—Thomas a Kempis' (1380–1471) *Imitation of Christ*. Those who purchased this book could choose among a great variety of editions; there were: cheap stereotype editions for as little as five Groschen, elaborate luxury editions for more than three Reichsthaler, editions for Protestants, editions for Catholics, editions with steel-engraved illustrations, editions with woodcut illustrations, editions with devotional exercises, and editions with all manner of commentary, exegesis, prayers, and other filler. As was true of all the other devotional books I have mentioned here, the *Imitation of Christ* was published mainly by commercial publishers anxious to make a profit, not by subsidized religious institutions which would give the book away. Again like the other books, it was purchased willingly by the masses. Among the publishing houses doing the *Imitation* were such masters of the mass trade as Bönner in Frankfurt/ Main, Wolff in Augsburg, B. G. Teubner in Leipzig, and Fleischhauer and Spohn in Reutlingen. At times, Teubner had several editions of the book on the market simultaneously, each appealing to a different taste and purse.[20]

Devotional books were the most often-purchased items on the mass book market, just as they always had been. Not until after 1870 was their hegemony threatened.[21]

## Elementary schoolbooks

Second in popularity were schoolbooks used in the elementary schools. The sales achieved by a few of these surpassed those of all books except the Bible. Of course, it would be misleading to make too sharp a distinction between schoolbooks and religious books, since religion was a major part of the elementary school curriculum. The children read Biblical stories to exercise their reading skills, and sang hymns to polish their singing abilities. Thus, many of the most widely circulated schoolbooks were religious in nature. One million copies of Christian Gottlob Barth's *Two Times Fifty Two Biblical Stories for Schools and Families (Zweimal zwei und fünfzig biblische Geschichten für Schulen und Familien)* were sold between 1832 and 1869. It was used in the Protestant elementary schools in Bavaria as well as in many other places. In Hannover, many elementary schools used Friedrich Wilhelm Bodemann's reader, *Biblical Stories Told in the Bible's Words (Biblische Geschichte, mit den Worten der Bibel erzählt* 1844, 15th printing 1870). Approximately 100,000 copies were sold between 1844 and 1870. The publisher Carl Bertelsmann sold 200,000 copies of Friedrich Eickhoff's *80 Lieder nach dem Urtext und mit Berücksichtigung der preßischen Schul-Reputation* in the 1830s, 1840s, and 1850s. Another songbook published by Bertelsmann and used in schools as well as in homes became one of the largest selling books of the nineteenth century. It was Johann Hinrich Volkening's *The Little Mission Harp (Die kleine Missionsharfe)*, of which two million copies were sold in the several decades after it first appeared in the 1830s.[22]

Numerous elementary schools in Catholic areas used Bernhard Overberg's *Biblische Geschichte des Alten und Neuen Testaments* (1799, 33rd edition 1888) and his *Katechismus der christkatholisches Lehre*, Aegydius Jais' *Beautiful Stories and Valuable Lessons for Children (Schöne Geschichte und lehrreiche Erzählungen für Kinder* 1807, 26th edition 1846), and Christoph v. Schmid's *Biblische Geschichte für Kinder*. Eventually all of these books were surpassed in the marketplace by the schoolbooks of Ignaz Schuster—*Katechismus der katholischen Religion* (1848), *Kleiner Katechismus der katholischen Religion* (1846), and the *Biblische Geschichte des Alten und Neuen Testaments* (1848).[23]

Many elementary school textbooks were in print for decades. *The Child's Friend, a Reader for Urban and Country Schools (Der Kinderfreund, ein Lesebuch für Bürger und Landschulen)*, written in the early 1770s by the Prussian school reformer Friedrich Eberhard v. Rochow (1734–1805), was in print until the early 1850s; often there were several editions offered simultaneously by different publishers. Wesener of Paderborn did 16 printings between 1808 and 1851, and Hahn of Hannover produced 10 between 1819 and 1851.[24]

In addition to a songbook and perhaps a reader, every elementary school pupil also had a primer *(Fibel)* to teach him how to read. Because so many primers were needed, scores of publishers strove energetically to publish ones which would sell well. The most successful primers in this period were Heinrich Stephani's *Handfibel zum Lesenlernen nach der Lautirmethode* (1809, 52nd printing 1835, 102nd printing 1868) and Albert Haester's 1850 *Fibel*, of which three million copies were published by 1883—the highest figure achieved by any secular work during the entire nineteenth century. Some other types of schoolbooks were also widely circulated, for example little geography texts. H. A. Daniel's *Leitfaden für den Unterricht in der Geographie* (Halle 1850, 270th printing 1913) sold 1,400,000 copies by 1898.[25]

The market for calendars was as impressive as the market for schoolbooks. A total of 1,075,535, copies were published in Prussia alone in 1855—one to every 15 Prussians.[26] These calendars were issued by 103 different publishers. The largest calendar publishing firm, Trowitzsch and Son of Berlin, had about 15 percent of the market that year, with 157,479 copies of its several calendars. The Nursing Institute of Kaiserswerth issued nearly 50,000 copies of its popular *Christliche Volkskalender*.

Of course sales had not been that high in the 1820s and 1830s, but even then the yearly calendar production of Reutlingen had averaged about 200,000 copies.[27]

The traditional formats of Germany's calendars did not change during this period. Each offered a blend of information, entertainment, and, sometimes, edification in addition to a chronological scheme of the days and months. Most were 50 to 100 pages long, and a few were as long as 150 pages. They usually cost eight to 10 Groschen.

Despite the similarity of general structure, however, the contents varied according to the audience for which the calendar was intended. The *Christliche Volkskalender* omitted the fiction found in many calendars in favor of brief inspiring biographies of great Protestants, a daily plan of Bible readings, and condemnations of such evils as alcohol, card-playing, and anti-monarchical sentiments. The *Neuer bayerischer Volkskalender* offered "many practical and expedient essays for the welfare of both urban and rural people."[28] Quite a number of others promised the same things. Then there were the humorous calendars, like the *Humoristischer berliner Volkskalender für das Jahr* 1856, which was compiled "by leading humorists under the editorship of Jokosus the Younger" and which had "numerous illustrations."[29] Humorous calendars did especially well in the Berlin market. There were also calendars devoted to most of the larger cities, as well as many regions.[30]

Calendars were a major source of information on contemporary events for the masses of Germany. The events described were more often market days and weather patterns than political occurrences. The masses' other chief source of current information was the printed flier. These seldom dealt with politics either; instead, they thrilled the reader with news about murders, executions, child-beating and other brutal perversions as well as major natural and accidental disasters at home and abroad. Such fliers had been common across much of Europe for centuries. The true forerunners of the sensationalistic mass circulation newspaper which developed in the last quarter of the nineteenth century, they offer insights into a mentality which never thought of news in abstract terms, in terms of trends and developments; for the common man, news was sensational, isolated, individual events.[31]

News fliers were five to 10 pages long. As improvements in printing technology made illustrations very inexpensive to reproduce, the fliers were more and more often illustrated. Reutlingen was a major center for their production. Here are some characteristic—and descriptive—titles:

1   *A Brief Life of M. Joseph Brehm of Reutlingen ... Including a Detailed Description of his Execution on July 18 1829. Also Included is a Brief Description of his Reaction to his Death Sentence and his Behavior on the way towards his Execution on July 18 1829* (*Kurzer Lebens-Abriß des M. Joseph Brehm, gewesenen Helfers zu Reutlingen nebst ausführlicher Darstellung seines im Monat August 1828 verbüten Verbrechens und der hierauf erfolgten Hinrichtung am 18, Juli 1829. Nebst einer kurzen Schilderung seines Verhaltens bei der Verkündigung seines Todesurtheils sowohl, als auch auf dem Wege zum Blutgerichte* (Reutlingen 1829)).

2   *The True and Shocking Misfortune which befell the big American Steamship Amazon, which on the 5th of May 1852 burned at sea, ending the lives of over 400 German Emigrants in a Fearful Way* (*Wahrhaftes und schreckliches Unglück von dem grossen amerikanischen Dampfschiffe Amazone, welches am 5. Mai 1852 auf der See in Brand gerieth, und uber 400 deutsche Auswanderer auf furchtbare Weise ihr Leben verloren haben* (1852, place of publication not known)).

3   *Horrible Murder of five innocent Schoolchildren of Bolkenhain by a 12 year old Boy* (*Schreckliche Mordthat, verübt von einem nur 12 Jahre alten Knaben an fünf unschuldige* (sic) *Kinder zu Bolkenhain* Hamburg 1857. Also published by different publishers in Bremen and Oldenberg).[32]

For the historically-minded, there were fliers describing past atrocities, perversions, and disasters, for example:

4   *A look back at the great fire in September of 1726 which left the city of Reutlingen in ashes. Towards a hundred year memorial.* (*Zurückblick auf das große brand-Unglück durch welches die Stadt Reutlingen im September des jahres 1726 in Schutt und Asche gelegt worden ist. Zur hundertjährigen Gedächtnißfeyer desselben* (Reutlingen 1826)).[33]

The gruesome monotony of the news fliers is in sharp contrast to the great variety of advice books and handbooks available on the mass book market. There were: letter-writer's guides, collections of phrases with which to wish people well, books on how to play games, books on all facets of human health, manuals on the health of livestock, trade manuals, cookbooks, works on farming and gardening, and many others.[34]

Social and technological developments were constantly creating a new need for manuals. The growth of large-scale emigration to the United States and elsewhere, for example, made a sizeable market for books advising people how and where to go. August Rauschenbusch's *Some Advice for Emigrants to the Western States of North America. With Illustrations* (*Einige Anweisungen für Auswanderer nach den westlichen Staaten von Nordamerika und Reisebilder* 3rd edition, Elberfeld 1848) cautioned prospective emigrants to avoid the Southern US and Texas, South America, and Australia and go instead to Illinois, Wisconsin, Indiana, Missouri, or Iowa.[35] The temperance movement and its opponents made "medical" books for and against brandy hot sellers. Technological changes produced new occupations, which required manuals.[36]

The total market for advice and handbooks was very large. One reason for this was that they were frequently purchased by middle- and upper-class Germans as well as by the masses. In this realm the lines between the mass and regular book markets were not always distinct. By 1870, the Brockhaus *Encyclopedia*, once the very symbol of the striving middle class, was also found "in the possession of our less-cultured and less-fortunate fellow citizens,"[37] as the *Gartenlaube* magazine put it. The popular health and medicine books of publishers like Basse and Fürst were sold to Germans of all social levels. So were cookbooks. Agricultural works could have been bought by both farming nobles (*Junkers*) and by reasonably prosperous peasants.[38]

## Voight's handbooks

People from peasants, artisans, and workers to engineers and industrialists bought books belonging to the greatest series of handbooks done in Germany in the nineteenth century, Bernhard Friedrich Voigt's *Neuer Schauplatz der Künste und Handwerke*. Begun in 1817, it was expanded throughout the entire century, until almost 300 volumes were published. Voigt (1790–1859) got the idea for the venture from a series of books which had been published in France from 1761 to 1789 and translated into German as the *Schauplatz der Künste und Handwerke* from 1762 to 1805.[39]

## Voight as a marketer

The *Neuer Schauplatz*, however, was far from a mere imitation. It was much more ambitious than the earlier French work. Voigt involved himself actively in the project, both in the creation and in the marketing of the books. Many of the series' volumes were written by experts at Voigt's initiative. The first volume, *The Complete Pastry Baker* (*Der vollkommene Conditor*, 1817, 10th edition revised 1873) was done at Voigt's request by the well-known Gotha pastry cook Johann Christian Eupel. Even before Joseph Mayer, Voigt advertised heavily and attempted to reach all possible customers by means of a sophisticated multi-faceted approach to retailing. While the books were available in book stores, he knew very well that buyers from the lower classes would not enter a book store. Thus he also sold them through innkeepers and by means of a skilled staff of itinerant salesmen, which he himself had recruited and trained. Such a staff was more reliable than the usual sleazy book peddlers of the time.[40]

By the end of its first decade, the *Neuer Schauplatz* included 30 titles; it grew more rapidly thereafter—to 79 titles by 1835, 130 by 1844, 200 by 1851, and 278 by 1879. In the 1840s the series covered, among other subjects; gold- and silversmithing, masonry, chocolate making, milling, sugar making, metallurgy, piano repairing, silk making, machinery, fireworks, and railroading.[41]

Voigt successfully kept up with the rapid development of nineteenth-century technology: a glance at the titles of the *Neuer Schauplatz* over the decades is like a summary of the progress of the Industrial and Agricultural Revolutions. By the 1850s it included handbooks on: photography, gas lighting, telegraphy, the manufacture of rubber, the use of chemicals in manufacturing, heating systems, and new ways of making brandy and sugar.[42]

## Traditional tastes in the mass book market

Handbooks like those in the *Neuer Schauplatz* were actually something of an anomaly on the mass book market, which was based so largely on books that had either been done in the sixteenth or seventeenth centuries, or were reminiscent of books done then. Much more characteristic than handbooks on railroading and chemicals were the dream books and "folk literature," which were found in the tiny home libraries of many German common people. Dream books were often based upon such venerable founts of wisdom as: Tycho Brache's divinations, "the time-proven writings of the Greeks and Romans," and "ancient Egyptian ... and Arab manuscripts."[43] A typical title was, *The Genuine Egyptian Guide to Dreams, or Truthful Depiction of all Dreams which Befall One in Llife. Following the Egyptian Fortune Tellers* (*Der ächte ägyptische Traumdeuter, oder wahrhafte Auslegun aller Träume, welche im menschlichen Leben vorkommen. Nach den ägyptische Wahrsagern*, 5th edition 1866).[44] This book was used to explain what dreams signified.

There were also two other types of dream books. One was used to analyze dreams to obtain winning lottery numbers. Examples are *Nanconi's Traumbüchlein* and the *Vollständiges Traumbüchlein*, published by the house of Jacquet in Augsburg, both of which were in print for decades. The second type of dream book presented dream analysis as a form of amusement and presumably appealed to a more sophisticated audience than most dream books.[45]

## "Folk literature"

"Folk literature" is a large, little-studied category of literature. It included both fiction and non-fiction, the latter usually history. In essence, "folk literature" was made up of stories whose simplicity and vigor made them understandable and entertaining to the masses. Most of this literature was based upon themes, motives, and stereotypes which dated to the sixteenth century and earlier—even when its topic was something as recent as Napoleon.[46] Some folk literature was nothing more than a clever, simple retelling of stories which had first appealed to middle- and upper-class readers; for example an 1853 book entitled *Parzival, Gedicht von Wolfram v. Eschenbach, als Erzählung für das deutsche Volk bearbeitet von E. Wild* (Dresden). The great folk literature publishing house of Ensslin and Laiblin in Reutlingen had *Uncle Tom's Cabin* (1852) retold for the masses in 1869.[47]

The core of German folk literature was made up of stories which had been read and told for centuries: the ancient tales about Apollonius, St. Helena, and St. Christopher; Carolingian sagas about Roland, Siegfried, the saintly Countess Genovesa of the Palatinate, Melusine and Magelone, and the four *Haimonskinder*; the medieval stories of Tristan and Isolde, Friedrich Barbarossa, and Doctor Faustus; the legendary narratives of the Wandering Jew, the Seven Swabians, the Swan Knight, Til Eulenspiegel, Reinecke the Fox, and Count Münchhausen. These beloved stories were reprinted again and again during the decades after 1820. Issued in inexpensive editions by such publishing houses as Jacquet in Augsburg, Brönner in Frankfurt/Main, Ensslin and Laiblin in Reutlingen, and Fleischhauer and Spohn in Reutlingen, they played an ever-larger role in the mass book market.[48]

## Knight and Bandit stories

Until mid-century, an equally large role was played by Knight and Bandit stories, whose "sweet delights were happily devoured in the servants' chambers and the guard rooms."[49] Some say that they were more popular than folk literature itself among the masses.[50] To meet the demand, Fürst and Basse re-issued some of their old stocks of these stories in the 1840s. Fürst produced the complete works of Spiess in 1840–1841, for example. Three different publishers produced editions of Vulpius' *Rinaldo Rinaldini* during the decade of the 1840s.

Some publishers risked more ambitious ventures, like the 20-volume *Bibliothek von Ritter, Räuber-und Criminal Geschichten* published by the Schreck Publishing Company of Leipzig from 1839 to 1841. Supposedly "edited by several scholars,"[51] it included: a revised version of *Rinaldo Rinaldini*, a story based upon the wicked life of Marie Lafarge *(Marie Lafarge, verurtheilt als Giftmischerin und angeklagt als Diamantendiebin, Criminalgeschichte der neuesten Zeit)*, stories with ghosts, stories featuring the conventional roster of Italian bandits, and, quite unconventionally, a Polish bandit *(Malowksy, oder verschworenen Räuber in den polnischen Wäldern)*.[52]

The popularity of such stories declined somewhat after 1850, but until the end of the century, they were carried by many Colporteurs as sure sellers. As late as 1857–1858, the Matthes Publishing Company of Leipiz did a 10-volume series of these stories. Publishers in Reutlingen, Augsburg, and elsewhere issued many of them in the form of brief sections with illustrations throughout the period.[53]

## Selling reading matter to the masses

The ways in which books were sold to the masses were as old-fashioned, as timeless, as many of the books themselves. This not to say that these methods were not effective; on the contrary; it was their great effectiveness which insured that they did not have to be changed. Books were sold to lower-class Germans by teachers, government officials, binders, and, above all, by Colporteurs, just as they had been before 1820. The traditional taboo upon lower-class entry into retail book shops held strong throughout the 1820–1870 period.[54] In any event, their passive nature, and expensive operating procedures made book shops inherently unsuited for the mass trade. The peasant, artisan, or worker either had to be personally sought out and convinced of the value of a book before he would even consider purchasing it, or he had to be forced to buy it, as in the case of schoolbooks.

The number of teachers who sold schoolbooks and other mass-market items is unknown but probably considerable. Teachers were effective retail outlets because they held positions of authority towards which their potential customers were trained to be deferential. The same is true of government officials, who were used by mass-market publishers to sell calendars and other items. One of the main reasons for the high sales of the publisher Louis Schaefer's calendar *Der Veteran* in the late 1850s was that it was sold via various agencies of the Prussian bureaucracy. Prussian officials were not supposed to sell printed matter, but the law was vague and the profits from *Der Veteran* supposedly went to a foundation which supported old soldiers.[55]

## Book binders as booksellers

More important to the mass book trade than either teachers or bureaucrats were binders. They were second only to Colporteurs in the volume of books which they sold to the masses; in many urban areas, they may have outsold the Colporteurs. Binders were very numerous. In 1840 Dresden had 60 of them to its five full-scale book shops and Prussia at the same time had "at least 15,000 book-selling binders" to its 500 stationary book stores.[56] In general, binders were only permitted to sell mass-market books, and only a few types of those. Dresden's binders could sell only schoolbooks, prayer books, and songbooks, which sold for less than 1 *Reichsthaler*. A Prussian Cabinet Order of June 11, 1847, which remained in force at least through the 1860s, forbade binders to sell anything other than bound or unbound copies of schoolbooks, songbooks, and prayer and devotional books.[57]

## Colporteurs: stalwart of the mass book market

Binders sold enormous numbers of books. Despite this, however, and despite the many books sold to the masses by teachers and government employees, the mass book trade still rested largely upon the back of the Colporteur. As always, the Colporteur was restless, and loved to travel about; he might be "a tailor who cannot sit still, or an old cobbler who wants to enjoy once again the sweetness of his wandering journeyman years."[58] He was the most flexible of retailers. Wearing "black tails that look as if a schoolmaster had thrown them away (and) speaking like the books which he carries in his knapsack,"[59] he could go anywhere. Colporteurs hawked their wares from market places, taverns, open fields, and other public places. They went from village to village, and, if need be, from door to door. Traditionally the booksellers to rural areas, Colporteurs had little difficulty adapting to conditions in the large urban centers that were growing up in Germany. A report from Munich in 1860 tells of Colporteurs visiting factories, work sites, and barracks, using colored pictures as premiums to be sure that their books were snapped up.[60]

Colporteurs also adapted well to the shift by many mass-market publishers away from individual volumes and towards issuing books in series and in small, cheap sections.[61] Publishers preferred to sell such books by means of subscriptions so that they could know in advance if there was going to be a market for them. Thus, a new variety of Colporteur was needed. He was called a "subscription collector" or a "commission salesman" to differentiate him from the traditional Colporteur.[62] "Subscription collectors" generally dealt in only one or two books at a time, where Colporteurs carried a variety. The "subscription collector" carried samples, order forms, and books to be delivered; the Colporteur carried whatever books and other items he hoped to sell.

In the minds of the general public and even of the book trade, however, the distinction was never clear. There were good reasons for this: both traditional Colporteurs and "subscription collectors" were wandering peddlers who carried their goods on their backs. Both were normally free agents rather than employees of publishers. Both obtained their books or subscription forms from different publishers or, after 1857, from large wholesalers who catered to the Itinerant Trade. Moreover, the personal characteristics and sales techniques of the two were so similar that when reading contemporary accounts, it is frequently impossible to tell if they are referring to traditional Colporteurs or to "subscription collectors."[63]

## Sales techniques of itinerant booksellers

The sales techniques employed by both types of itinerant book peddler were varied. Sometimes they offered large "customer discounts"—those who sold

Reutlingen books were granting 50 percent off the selling price as a discount in the late 1820s; earlier they had granted 75 percent discounts. Colporteurs in Leipzig began staging lotteries to promote book sales in the late 1850s. When sweet reasonableness would not work, there was always the hard sell; from Hirschberg in Silesia (population 7,000) came the complaint in 1841 that: "a dozen so-called Colporteur-peddlers ... are sent down here practically every week from Berlin, Breslau, Glogau, and other cities ... they pester the inhabitants of our area until they get them to take their books, pictures, and so forth."[64]

Beyond the hard sell was the outright swindle, which was especially common in the realm of subscription collecting. One Georg Ramsperger of Freiburg (Breisgau) was sentenced to two and a half years in jail in 1863 for collecting subscriptions to non-existent works, then delivering packets of stones or waste paper.[65] He had also defrauded publishers by ordering books on credit in the name of fictitious firms. Fraudulent lotteries and premiums were attributed to numerous itinerant booksellers. One theory was that the business naturally attracted swindlers because the legal restrictions on it repelled decent men and made them unwilling to enter it.[66]

These legal restrictions were truly onerous—on paper. A Prussian law of March 10, 1838 placed restrictions on subscription collecting. Early in 1846 the law was made yet stronger, so that the only books which itinerant salesman—Colporteurs or "subscription collectors"—could legally sell were Bibles, other religious works, and (in some provinces) calendars. Every salesman had to have a peddler's permit, and these were to be granted as the exception, not as the rule. This legislation remained in effect after 1848.[67]

Most of the other German states had analogous laws. A Bavarian decree of June 11, 1824, for example, instructed all the police authorities of the Lower Main District that peddlers could sell subscriptions only to book dealers not to private persons. Of the larger states, only Saxony had laws which were relatively liberal in regard to wandering booksellers.[68] On the other hand, anti-Colporteur legislation was not consistently and systematically enforced, even in Prussia. Voigt never had difficulty in selling his *Neuer Schauplatz* in Prussia, although it contained neither religious books nor calendars. Moreover, even when and where the laws were strictly enforced, the peddlers often had enough skill and mobility to evade them. And frequent arrests did not deter them from making their rounds.[69]

Underlying the anti-Colporteur legislation was the fear that the adoption of reading by the masses could corrode the moral and political structure of society. "Through the collecting of subscriptions all manner of base and infamous writings could easily be distributed," it was argued in the Prussian law of March 10, 1838.[70] In imposing restrictions on itinerant salesmen, as well as in maintaining active censorship over all printed matter, Germany's governments were attempting to force the reading of the masses into limited and safe channels.

Respectable Germans of the middle and upper classes shared the fears and aspirations of their governments towards mass reading. Indeed, many of them were a good deal more fearful than the governments. The latent anxieties about the masses reading, which they had had since the eighteenth century, were aroused by the growth of the mass book market for folk literature and for Knight and Bandit stories:

> The latest so-called "folk literature," wrote the poet Eichendorff in the 1840s, aims at the corruption of the common people; in arguing away piety, morality, and rationality—in a word, all the higher things of life—it renders them [i.e., the masses] completely defenseless [against the mindless, anarchic dissolution of society].[71]

Many people feared that the glorification of bandits in the Knight and Robber stories would inspire the lower classes to emulation or worse—to individual criminality or to collective insurrection.[72] Among educated Catholics, such fears were joined by the fear that much of what the Catholic lower classes were reading, from schoolbooks to calendars, was laden with anti-Catholic propaganda.[73]

To a large extent, these fears were baseless. They were grounded in ignorance of both the extent of reading among the lower classes and its influence upon them. They were articulated by people whose ideas about the masses were gotten more from Aristotle's *Politics* or Plato's *Republic* than from actual observation. The masses read much less than the exponents of these fears believed; in particular, they read little fiction—at most several books in the course of a year—and were normally not at all influenced by it. Germany's masses were among the least revolutionary in Europe. Nevertheless, the fears about mass reading were strongly felt.[74]

## Notes

1 Probus (pseudonym), "Ueber die Eroeffnung neuer Absatzwege fuer den deutschen Buchhandel," *Börsenblatt* 1861, Nr. 98, p. 1630.
2 T. S. Hamerow, *The Social Foundations of German Unification 1858–1871, vol. I: Ideas and Institutions* Princeton, 1969, pp. 54–55; by the same author: *Restoration, Revolution Reaction* Princeton, 1958, p. 20.
3 Weinstein, *Die preußischen Volksschule*, pp. 53, 83.
4 Hamerow, *The Social Foundations of German Unification*, vol. I, p. 281; Schenda, *Volk ohne Buch*, p. 444.
5 Hamerow, *The Social Foundations of German Unification*, vol. I, p. 283.
6 Tews, *Ein Jahrhundert preussischer Schulegeschichte*, p. 105.
7 Quoted in Schenda, *Volk ohne Buch*, p. 447.
8 Ibid., pp. 454–456.
9 Quoted in Weinstein, *Die preußischen Volksschule*, p. 60.
10 Ibid., pp. 70–71.
11 Bischoff-Luithlen, *Auszuege*, pp. 198,199, 211, 233.
12 Ibid., see the chart on the inside front cover; see also: Neumann, *Der Buecherbesitz der Tuebinger Buerger*, pp. 39, 85, 86.
13 Schenda, *Volk ohne Buch*, pp. 264–265.
14 *Heinsius*: vol. IX, Part I, p. 32; vol. XI, Part I, pp. 36–37; vol. XIII, Part I, p. 43; vol. XIV, Part I, p. 51; vol. XV, Part I, p. 63.

15 Neumann, *Der Buecherbesitz der Tuebinger Buerger*, pp. 39, 85, 86; *Heinsius*: vol. X, Part 2, p. 297; vol. XIV, Part 2, p. 505; vol. IX, Part 2, p. 319; vol. XII, Part 2, p. 340.

16 Kunze, *Lieblings-Buecher*, p. 336; *Allgemeine Deutsche Biographie*, vol. I, p. 699, vol. XIX, pp. 116–119; *Viele Saaten–eine Ernte. Festschrift zum hundertjaehrigen Bestehen des Calwer Verlagsvereins 1833–1933* Stuttgart 1933, p. 106.

17 A. M. Weiss, *Benjamin Herder. Fuenfzig Jahre eines geistigen Befreiungskampfes* Freiburg im Breisgau 1889, pp. 68–69.

18 *Heinsius*: vol. VII, p. 418; vol. VIII, Part I, pp. 282, 435; vol. IX, Part I, p. 480, Part 2, pp. 212–214; vol. X, Part I, pp. 300, 432.

19 Meiner, *G. J. Manz*, p. 160; *Heinsius*: vol. VIII, Part I, pp. 386–387; vol. X, Part I, p. 403; vol. XII, Part I, p. 481.

20 *Heinsius*: vol. VII, p. 418; vol. IX, Part 2, pp. 367–368; vol. XI, Part 2, pp. 358–359; vol. XIII, Part 2, pp. 470–471; Kunze, *Lieblings-Buecher*, p. 336.

21 Kunze, *Lieblings-Buecher*, p. 335; Schenda, *Volk ohne Buch*, p. 315.

22 R. Gooeck, *Buecher fuer Millionen. Fritz Wixforth und die Geschichte des Hauses Bertelsmann*, Gutersloh 1968, p. 38.

23 Gaedicke, *Zur Statistik der deutschen Literatur*, pp. 30, 37; Kunze, *Lieblings-Bucher*, p. 408.

24 Gaedicke, *Zur Statistik der deutschen Literatur*, p. 44; Kunze, *Lieblings-Buecher*, pp. 408–409; *Heinsius*: vol. III, p. 407; vol. IV, p. 424.

25 *Börsenblatt* 1883, Nr. 257, p. 4986; T. Kellen, "Der Massenvertrieb der Volksliteratur," *Preussische Jahrbucher*, 98, Berlin, 1889, p. 80; *Heinsius*: vol. III, p. 830; vol. VIII, Part 2, p. 295; vol. X, Part 2, p. 303; vol. XI, Part 2, p. 321; *Deutsches Buecherverzeichnis. Eine Zusammenstellung der im deutschen Buchhandel erschienenen Buecher, Zeitschriften und Landkarten*, vol. 1 Leipzig, 1916, p. 527. Hereafter cited as "*D. B. V.*"

26 *Börsenblatt* 1855, Nr. 142, pp. 2012–2013.

27 Widmann, "Aus der Geschichte des Reutlinger Druck-und Verlagswesens," p. 101; *Börsenblatt* 1855, Nr. 6, pp. 68–69, Nr. 142, pp. 2012–2013: "Ein Kalender-Betrieb in Preussen," *Börsenblatt* 1858, Nr. 72, pp. 1003–1004.

28 *Heinsius*: vol. VII, pp. 422–423; vol. VIII, Part 2, p. 374; vol. X, Part 2, p. 385; vol. XII, Part 2, p. 523.

29 Schenda, *Volk ohne Buch*, pp. 271–277, 351–397, has excellent material on these fliers.

30 Titles from, respectively: J. U. Hebsacker, "Wie wird man Verleger? Statt einer Verlagsgeschichte," *Rueckblick fuer die Zukunft*, p. 16; Schenda, *Volk ohne Buch*, pp. 262, 358; *Heinsius* vol. XIII, Part 2, p. 126.

31 Hebsacker, "Wie wird man Verleger?," p. 18.

32 Schenda, *Volk ohne Buch*, p. 322.

33 K. Bernhardi, Ed., *Wegweiser durch die deutschen Volks-und Jugendschriften* Leipzig 1852, p. 81.

34 Ibid., p. 65.

35 "Das Conversationslexikon und seine Gruender," *Gartenlaube* (n.d.)—reprinted in the *Börsenblatt* 1873, Nr. 21, p. 327.

36 *Heinsius*, vol. XIV, Part I, P. 134.

37 Ibid., vol. III, P. 534.

38 Ibid., vol. XIV, Part I, p. 134.

39 Ibid., vol. III, p. 534.

40 R. Schmidt, *Deutsche Buchhaendler, deutsche Buchdrucker. Beitraege zu einer Firmengeschichte des deutschen Buchgewerbes*, 6 vols. Berlin and Eberswalde 1902–1908, vol. 6, pp. 990–995.

41 *Heinsius*, vol. X, Part 2, pp. 210–211.

42 *Heinsius*, vol. X, Part 2, pp. 210–211; vol. XI, Part 2, pp. 210–211.

43 *Heinsius*: vol. XII, Part 2, p. 477; vol. XIV, Part 2, p. 5737.

44 Ibid., vol. XIV, Part 2, p. 573, Part 2, p. 477.

45 Gaedicke, *Zur Statistik der deutschen Literatur*, p. 29.

46 Ibid., p. 151.

47 Ibid., p. 155; *Heinsius* vol. XII Part 2, p. 436.

48 Hebsacker, ed., *Ruckblick fuer die Zukunft* pp. 150–151; Schenda, *Volk ohne Buch*, pp. 299–305.

49 Appell, *Die Ritter-, Raeuber-und Schauerromantik*, p. 75.

50 Schenda, *Volk ohne Buch*, p. 469.

51 *Heinsius*, vol. IX, Part I, p. 92.

52 Ibid., vol. IX, Part I. p. 92.

53 Ibid., vol. XIII, Part 2, p. 272; Appell, *Die Ritter-, Raeuber-und Schauerromantik*, pp. 40–53, 76–78.

54 Probus, "Ueber die Eroeffnung neuer Absatzwege," *Börsenblatt* 1861, Nr. 98, pp. 1629–1631.

55 On sale of books by teachers see: *Börsenblatt* 1842, Nr. 85, p. 2293; Prinz, *Bausteine*, vol. V, pp. 7–8. On sale by government officials see: *Börsenblatt* 1855, Nr. 6, pp. 68–69, Nr. 13, p. 174, Nr. 17, pp. 225–226.

56 *Statistik des preussischen Staates*, 1845, p. 260; Richter, "Zur Vorgeschichte und Geschichte der … Walther'schen … Buchhandlung," p. 156.

57 Richter, "Zur Vorgeschichte und Geschichte der… Walther'schen … Buchhandlung," p. 156; "Aus der Provinz Westphalen," *Börsenblatt* 1865, Nr. 2, p. 21. On binders in general see: B., "Stimme eines reisenden Buchhaendlers," *Krieger'sche Wochenblatt* III, Nrs. 45–46, pp. 355–356.

58 *Suddeutsche Buchhaendler Zeitung* (n.d.)—reprinted in the *Börsenblatt* 1843, Nr. 105, p. 3718.

59 Ibid., p. 3718.

60 "Colporteur-Unfug," *Börsenblatt* 1860, Nr. 144, pp. 2414–2415. On the Colporteur and "subscription collecting" trade in general see: "Ist das Colportiren erlaubt oder nicht?" *Börsenblatt* 1841, Nr. 95, pp. 2369–2371, Nr. 102, pp. 2617–2620, the best by far of the contemporary articles.

61 Weinholz, "Fuegen die Kolporteure dem Sortiments-Buchhandel grossen Schaden zu?" *Börsenblatt* 1847, p. 248.

62 Drahn, *Geschichte des deutschen Buch-und Zeitschriftenhandels*, pp. 29–39.

63 "Ist das Colportiren erlaubt oder nicht?" *Börsenblatt* 1841, Nr. 102, pp. 2618–2619.

64 Schulze, *Der deutsche Buchhandel*, p. 173.

65 *Börsenblatt* 1841, Nr. 106, pp. 2740–2742.

66 *Börsenblatt* 1863, Nr. 62, p. 1030.

67 Probus, "Ueber die Eroeffnung neuer Absatzwege," *Börsenblatt* 1861, Nr. 98, p. 1630. This author is favorable towards itinerant booksellers, but flatly states that most of them were dishonest.

68 Ibid., Nr. 98 pp. 1629–1631.

69 *Krieger'sche Wochenblatt* IX, Nrs. 47–48, p. 371; Probus, "Ueber die Eroeffnung neuer Absatzwege," *Börsenblatt* 1861, Nr. 98, p. 1629.

70 *Börsenblatt* 1840, Nr. 34, pp. 888–889; *Börsenblatt* 1859, Nr. 132. pp. 2109–2110.

71 Quoted in Probus, "Ueber die Eroeffnung neuer Absatzwege," *Börsenblatt* 1861, Nr. 98, pp. 1629–1631.

72 J. Eichendorff, "Die deutsche Salon-Poesie der Frauen," *Neue Ausgabe der Werke und Schriften*, vol. IV Stuttgart 1958, p. 941.

73 There is a rich documentation of this point in Schenda, *Volk ohne Buch*, pp. 66–73, 87–88, 221–226.

74 Herz, Hermann, "Die Zeitlage bei der Gruendung des Borromaeusvereins," *Fuendundsiebzig Jahre Borromausvereins* Bonn 1920, pp. 168–171.

# 5 The decline and recovery of the regular trade, 1843–1866

By the middle of the 1840s, Germany's regular book trade and its market had been growing steadily for three decades. Its expansion unstopped by the depression of 1825, it quickly sloughed off the adverse effects of the 1830 revolutionary upheavals, the cholera epidemic of the early 1830s, and the depression in 1835. The boom years of the 1840s lasted longer for the book trade than for many other trades and industries. While the number of titles issued annually peaked in 1843, it declined but little during the next few years. Book dealerships continued to be established at a rapid clip: 1845 saw 102 new businesses set up, a record for the trade.[1]

During 1846, and even during 1847, the sales of books were still at a high level—which is certainly an indication that the comfortable classes still felt secure—and the *Börsenblatt* printed cheery articles on the future growth of the trade. In one of these articles, which appeared in 1846, Otto August Schulz, the editor of the trade's directory of members, wrote:

> Yes, our [German] presses have been given so much more to do recently that many small, relatively insignificant printers can no longer meet their obligations by using their old hand presses, but have had to install high-speed presses as well; while large printers [which already had high-speed presses] now have had to enlist the aid of steam power to get through their work.[2]

Of course printers did work for more than the book trade, but there is no doubt that much of their increased volume of work was due to the book trade.

## The Revolutions of 1848

Then the bottom fell out. The Revolutions of 1848 smashed the complacent prosperity of the book trade so brutally and so suddenly, that for half a decade thereafter it muddled about in a daze of stupefaction, and it was two full decades before anything like the vigorous confidence of the pre-Revolutionary years returned.

For many German book dealers, 1848 was the most dismal year of the entire century. Even dealers whose political views led them to favor the revolutions were faced with the problem that the book market had in large part evaporated. People did not buy books. As nobles fled, or prepared for siege, as wealthy farmers buried their money, as middle-class industrialists and merchants became swept up into the political maelstrom—who was there to buy books? "Wretched, everywhere wretched, in truth very wretched indeed, is how things look in our beloved book trade now," wrote a book dealer in the *Börsenblatt* in 1848.[3] The great Catholic publisher Benjamin Herder found 1848 the worst year of his career. On May 30, he wrote: "The wretched conditions of late have destroyed all trust among men and thus have sapped our powers horribly. All trade stagnates; no one pays the debts he owes; everyone demands money."[4] Publishers pressured retailers for payments, but retailers found it difficult to extract payments from their customers in return. Bankruptcies shut down scores of economically weaker dealers, while the specter of bankruptcy drove even the stronger ones to sell things like quack rheumatism cures to maintain solvency.

As if things were not bad enough already, the revolutionary governments abolished most legal barriers upon entry into trades, thus allowing anyone who desired to set himself up as a bookman. It is not known how many people took advantage of the new license to crash into the book trade, but in view of economic conditions then even a handful would have been too many: with the book market declining, the new dealers could only be parasites, stealing customers from existing dealers, not finding new ones.[5]

## Gradual but fitful improvement

1849 brought some improvement to the book trade, as the return of order made people somewhat more willing to spend money on books, but the old zest was gone from the market. Bookmen were still too shaken to do more than mark time, and so were their customers. The re-imposition of censorship, often in a harsher form than immediately before 1848, doomed the Liberal *Staatslexikon* of Welcker and Rotteck. Combined with the economic fatigue of the era, the mailed fist of the censor dropped the sales of Joseph Meyer's liberally-oriented encyclopedia to a pathetic segment of their former volume. Many dealers now believed that the market would remain stagnant, that it would never boom and grow again. This malaise lasted until about 1852. Prussia recorded a net loss of 11 book dealerships between 1849 and 1852—probably the first such drop since before 1815.[6]

Not until the boom years after 1851 did the book trade really begin to revive. The revival, however, was slowed by regional depressions like that in Silesia in 1854, and then ended abruptly by the Great Crash of 1858, which set off a wave of bankruptcies and general hard times among dealers all over Germany; bank credit evaporated, the fortunes of big book buyers disappeared, and even those with secure means hesitated to spend money on

*Table 5.1*  Number of titles published, 1841–1870

| Decade | Number of titles published |
| --- | --- |
| 1841–1850 | 111,386 |
| 1851–1860 | 88,784 |
| 1861–1870 | 108,999 |

Note
Figures are taken from J. Goldfriedrich, *Geschichte des deutschen Buchhandels vom Beginn der Frem-dherrschaft bis zur Reform des Boersenvereins im neuen deutschen Reiche, 1805–1889*, Leipzig 1913, pp. 199, 486–487.

books, which were considered to be luxury items. A few large publishers became so distraught in the panic atmosphere of the Crash, that they took the dramatic step of fleeing Germany, leaving behind large debts.[7]

The effects of the Crash were felt in the book market into 1859. But by the following year there had been a good recovery.[8] The early 1860s were good years for the regular trade. But these good years of rising sales lasted only until the middle of the decade.[9]

The frequent crises of these two and a third decades from 1844 to 1867 brought a mood of caution over the book trade; the contrast with the wild entrepreneurship of the 1820–1848 period is striking. Publishers were less ready to bring new books into print, more judicious in their choice of what to publish.[10] This was especially true of the 1850s. Where from 1838 to 1847 at least 10,000 titles (including reprints) had been issued each year, after 1847 the yearly production remained under 10,000 titles for slightly over two decades. The production of titles during the 1840s—despite the severe depression at the end of the decade—was greater than that of either of the following two decades (see Table 5.1).

To be sure, the number of titles issued is not synonymous with the total number of books printed: a year during which relatively few titles were brought out might have seen an unusually high number of books printed and sold. But generally speaking, the number of titles is a good gauge to the total volume of book production. The decade of the 1860s may have seen as many or more books printed and sold as the decade of the 1840s; the decade of the 1850s, however, most certainly did not.

## Market opportunities

For the book trade, however, there was a bright side to the political and economic upheavals of the time—books had to be written about these happenings, or because of them. The Munich publishing house of C. Beck got to publish the extensive revisions of Bavaria's laws (1849–1869), which were due to the Revolution. The upheavals, especially those of 1848–1849, provided exciting topics for books for decades—books about the leaders of 1848 were still saleable items half a century later. Books about the Austro-Prussian

War of 1866 made up a good proportion of the total titles published in 1866 and 1867: as of early 1867, 519 titles about the war were already in print.[11]

Another sign that things were not all bad was that many people were willing to establish new book dealerships. In fact, the dealer network grew. In 1855 there were 1,663 dealers in 555 cities, where in 1842 there had been only 1,274 dealers in 339 cities. There had been one dealer to roughly every 25,900 Germans in 1842, whereas there was one to every 19,677 in 1855. By 1865 the dealer network was larger still.[12]

Yet the growth in the number of dealers was hardly as rapid as it had been before 1842. The decade of the 1850s was one of sluggish growth, and many of the book dealerships which were founded then did not survive long. In the late 1840s and throughout the 1850s there were many complaints from established bookmen that too many new firms were being established, that the number of dealers was growing while the number of customers was not, and that the inevitable result would be gross misery and impoverishment for all book dealers. "The ever-increasing number of new establishments—a number which has risen rampantly in recent years—carries with it the seeds of the worsening of the book trade," wrote the contemporary publisher August Prinz in 1853.[13]

While such complaints were endemic to the book trade even in the best of times, they were more justified for this period than they had been earlier. Competition was fierce, bankruptcies common. Yet the fact that the growth in the number of bookmen could be sustained indicated that there was enough business to support both old and new dealers. How well they were supported, however, is another question. Until the boom years of the mid-1850s, they were not very well supported at all; the same was true of the depression periods of 1857–1859 and of 1866.

The growth of the dealer network did not alter the relative density of book dealers among Germany's various regions. The greatest density of bookshops and bookmen in general was still found in Central Germany and in parts of the Rhineland; the least density was still to be found in the far North, the far East, poorer parts of the West of Germany, and in Bavaria. Statistics gathered in 1855 showed that the Kingdom of Saxony had one book dealer to every 7,502 people; Prussia's Brandenburg Province (which included Berlin) had one to every 9,025 and Saxony-Coburg-Gotha one to every 10,000. By contrast, Hannover had one to each 30,932 souls, Oldenburg one to each 40,000 and Prussia's East Prussian Province one to each 76,500.[14]

## Progress in distribution institutions

As the dealer network was growing despite frequent bad times, so too was solid progress being made in bookmaking technology and in developing more efficient central institutions to handle the flow of books from Germany's hundreds of publishers to its thousands of retailers. In 1842 the Union of Leipzig Booksellers opened an "Order House" in which orders sent in by

*Table 5.2* The density of book dealerships in 1855

| State (or Prussian province) | Population | Book dealers | Inhabitants per dealer |
|---|---|---|---|
| Frankfurt/Main | 67,500 | 43 | 1,570 |
| Hamburg | 200,000 | 41 | 4,878 |
| Bremen | 79,050 | 11 | 7,186 |
| Kingdom of Saxony | 1,987,900 | 265 | 7,502 |
| Bradenburg (province) | 2,130,000 | 236 | 9,025 |
| Saxony-Coburg-Gotha | 150,000 | 15 | 10,000 |
| Luebeck | 53,000 | 5 | 10,600 |
| Anhalt–Dassau–Coethen | 112,000 | 10 | 11,200 |
| Saxony–Weimar | 262,000 | 22 | 11,909 |
| Brunswick | 265,000 | 22 | 22,045 |
| Hessen–Homburg | 26,000 | 2 | 13,000 |
| Mecklenburg–Strelitz | 100,000 | 6 | 16,667 |
| Wuerttemberg | 1,805,000 | 108 | 16,712 |
| Province of Saxony (Prussia) | 1,800,000 | 100 | 18,000 |
| Saxony-Meiningen-Hildburghausen | 163,500 | 9 | 18,167 |
| Schwarzburg–Sondershausen | 60,500 | 3 | 20,166 |
| Waldeck | 62,000 | 3 | 20,667 |
| Grand Duchy of Hessen | 853,000 | 41 | 20,805 |
| Holstein and Lauenburg | 527,000 | 25 | 21,081 |
| Saxony–Altenburg | 132,000 | 6 | 22,000 |
| Reuß (both lines) | 114,00 | 5 | 22,800 |
| Schwarzburg–Rudolstadt | 70,000 | 3 | 23,333 |
| Prussia (entire Kingdom) | 16,383,000 | 694 | 23,607 |
| Rhineland and Hohenzollern | 2,878,000 | 120 | 23,983 |
| Anhalt–Bernburg | 50,500 | 2 | 25,250 |
| Baden | 1,363,000 | 52 | 26,212 |
| Mechlenburg–Schwerin | 537,000 | 20 | 26,850 |
| Westphalia (Prussia) | 1,465,000 | 53 | 27,642 |
| Hannover | 1,825,000 | 59 | 30,932 |
| Bavaria | 4,520,750 | 146 | 30,964 |
| Electoral Hessen | 760,000 | 24 | 31,667 |
| Schaumburg–Lippe | 32,000 | 1 | 32,000 |
| Silesia (Prussia) | 3,062,000 | 90 | 34,022 |
| Pomerania (Prussia) | 1,198,000 | 33 | 36,303 |
| Oldenburg | 280,000 | 7 | 40,000 |
| Nassau | 428,000 | 10 | 42,800 |
| Lippe-Detmold | 104,800 | 2 | 52,400 |
| West Prussia (Prussia) | 960,000 | 18 | 53,333 |
| Posen (Prussia) | 1,360,000 | 24 | 56,667 |
| East Prussia (Prussia) | 1,530,000 | 20 | 76,500 |

Source: *Börsenblatt*, 1855, p. 205.

Note

* Dealers included both publishers and retailers.

retail book shops were sorted out and forwarded to the correct publishers. In 1852 a Leipziger named Louis Zander made life easier for retail shop owners when he established the first "Wholesale Book Shop". It featured a large stock of pre-bound popular books which Zander had ordered from myriad publishers and had had bound. By ordering from Zander, a book shop owner could spare himself the difficulty of dealing with scores of separate publishers. The books which Zander had in stock were the ones which practically any book shop would want to have on its shelves.[15]

The "Wholesale Book Shop" and the "Order House" helped Leipzig to maintain itself as the center of the book trade at a time when it seemed to many that the development of railroads and of the telegraph, by making possible rapid communication between retailers and publishers anywhere in the country, would end the need for central storage and forwarding institutions like those in Leipzig. In the 1850s it seemed to August Prinz, for example, that "the old ways of doing business have been totally annihilated."[16] Prinz echoed another common view when he said that few retail shops would bother to keep books on hand anymore because they would be able to order and receive them so quickly via the new communications wonders.[17] The expected revolution did not materialize, however. The railroads did cut freight costs a great deal and did speed up transport, but the telegraph proved too expensive to be used for routine ordering. Leipzig (and to a much less degree Stuttgart) remained the institutional and distributional center of the German regular book trade.[18]

## Advances in printing technology

More important to the book trade than the railroad or telegraph were the significant advances in bookmaking technology which occurred during this period. In 1844 a Saxon binder named F. G. Keller discovered a way to use wood chips to make paper; although not as good as rag paper, wood pulp paper was far cheaper, especially as the techniques for making it were continually refined over the next few decades. Type-casting machines, invented in the USA and in Denmark in the 1830s, were introduced to Germany during the following decade. The 1840s and 1850s also saw the development of machines which could bind books—a cost-saving blessing for the country's book buyers (but also another blow to Germany's artisans). The first large-sized steam-powered bindery was opened in Leipzig in 1866. A few years earlier the firms of Schreiber in Esslingen and Röder in Leipzig had put into operation high-speed lithograph presses, which made possible truly inexpensive illustrated books.[19]

Some older technological advances which Germany's bookmen had at first spurned came increasingly into use during this period. In 1845 the publisher Leonard Schwamm in Neuss became the first German publisher to use a steam-powered König Rapid Press to print books; earlier, such presses had been used only for newspapers. The Reutlingen firm of Johann Conrad

Mäcken, Inc. and the Berlin publishing house of E. S. Mittler installed similar presses in 1853 and 1857, respectively. More widespread was the use of the stereotype reproductive process, which allowed the same printing plates to be used again and again. By the 1850s it was employed by scores of publishers who wished to issue large, cheap editions of the same books repeatedly; classics, schoolbooks, and new books which were likely to have a large sale were commonly done by stereotype. The publishing houses of Philip Reclam in Leipzig and Heinrich Bertelsmann in Gütersloh owed much of their success in the marketplace to the skillful use of this process.[20]

## Increasing specialization

The book trade was becoming more modern, less afraid to use the new technological advances. One sees the trend towards modernization in the increasing specialization by publishers during this time, too. Many limited themselves to the publication of one or two types of book for which they knew the market very well. This tendency was furthered by the growth of specialization in the sciences and academic disciplines. By the late 1840s, A. Hirschwald in Berlin specialized in medical works, C. Heymann of Berlin specialized in jurisprudence, E. S. Mittler (Berlin) in military books, Julius Springer (Berlin) in works on forestry, F. Riegel (Potsdam) in works on building technology, K. Wiegand (Berlin) in pedagogy, and Justus Perthes of Gotha in maps and atlases. Many other examples could be given.[21]

To be sure, there were scores of publishing firms which resisted the trend towards specialization. They included some of the biggest houses in Germany—for example, Cotta, Brockhaus, and Reimer (Berlin). But even publishers who did not specialize came increasingly to give up their lending libraries and retail shops in order to concentrate on publishing alone. By this time there was little if anything left of the old Barter System which had once made it imperative that publishers retail and that retailers publish books. There was some opposition to the abandonment of the old ways; however, as late as 1858, the city government of Munich insisted that bookmen there do both publishing and retailing. But few other places were so traditionally-minded as Munich in this respect. The Heidelberg publisher J. C. B. Möhr had no difficulty in giving up his retail shop to his son in 1842 so that he could do publishing exclusively. The Ruprechts in Göttingen separated their publishing and retail operations in 1853. In Leipzig, Philip Reclam gave up his lending library. Those who were publishers exclusively issued the bulk of Germany's book production by the end of this period. Nonetheless, a numerical majority of the country's dealers continued to do both publishing and retailing, but most of these dealers were in smaller cities and published mainly works of limited, local circulation.[22]

The era saw no new publishing-marketing geniuses of the caliber of Brockhaus or Joseph Meyer emerge, and none of its publishers achieved the commanding stature and prestige within the trade which Perthes and Cotta had earlier. The firms founded by these four men carried on ably, but without breaking any new ground, under the leadership of sons and relatives of the founders. The Brockhaus Company continued to issue a wide range of books in addition to successive—and successful—editions of the *Conversations-Lexikon*, Joseph Meyer led his Bibliographisches Institut until his death in 1856, but did not originate any important ventures after beginning his encyclopedia in 1839 (46 volumes 1839–1852, six supplementary volumes 1853–1855) He was succeeded by his highly competent but more cautious son Hermann, who applied and refined his father's methods with great skill, while shying away from significant innovation. Of a similar temperament was Georg Cotta, who headed what was still Germany's most prestigious publishing house for three decades after his father's death in 1832.[23]

## Publishers—initiators of books

But if the era lacked geniuses, it did have a good many very capable and energetic publishers who made the role of the publisher as the initiator, the ultimate creator, of books an increasingly important one. Although it was unrecognized by either the reading public or by copyright legislation, it was (and still is) a fact that publishers, not authors, were responsible for the creation of much of what appeared in print. Considering all the categories of writing, only three were due more to the initiative of their actual authors than of their publishers: (1) the more serious creative fiction, (2) scholarly monographs, and (3) autobiographies and memoirs. Even in these realms, however, publishers were sometimes creative figures. The publisher Julius Campe's generous encouragement of the "Young Germany" School doubtless helped lubricate the creativity of its writers.[24]

Countless books of all types came into being because a publisher felt that there was a need for them and contacted people to write them. Hack fiction, encyclopedias, dictionaries and other reference works, periodicals, biographies, translations of all types, as well as new editions of the classics and other older works–all these usually owed their inception to their publishers, and not to the people who actually wrote them.[25]

Examples of publishers' initiative in creating books during these years are legion. The famous dictionary of Jakob and Wilhelm Grimm was the idea of the publisher Karl Reimer, who asked the Grimms to do it in 1837. Later Reimer and his partner Salomon Hirzel asked Theodore Mommsen (who was Reimer's son-in-law) to write a general history of Rome, and thus Mommsen wrote his great *History of Rome (Römische Geschichte)*. Hirzel inspired Gustav Freytag to write the immensely popular *Pictures from Germany's Past (Bilder aus der deutschen Vergangenheit)*. Gustav Langenscheidt (1832–1895) originated the plans for, and worked actively in the execution of, his firm's dictionaries and foreign-language instruction manuals. Ernst Rohmer, a high employee of the C. H. Beck publishing house in Munich, personally initiated two of the firm's large works on Bavarian laws. The beloved *Brehm's Animals (Brehms Tierleben)* by Alfred Brehm (1st edition 1864–1869, 6 volumes) is said to have been largely due to the initiative of Hermann Meyer.[26] Ulrich Hendschel, an employee of the Thurn and Taxis Postal Service, compiled and published on his own the first comprehensive book of railroad and post coach timetables for all of Germany; this was in 1845. The venture met a growing need so well that Hendschel kept issuing new, up-to-date editions. Called *Hendschel's Telegraph* after 1847, this time-table had no competition until the advent of the *Reichskursbuch* in 1872.

The publishing firm Velhagen and Klasing had enormous good fortune over two decades with Henriette Davidis' famous cookbook (1844–1860s), which in its peak sales year, 1858, produced 2,762 Thaler of profit. Velhagen and Klasing took over the cookbook after three other publishers had passed on it. In the 1850s and 1860s Davidis wrote popular non-fiction books with great appeal for young women, for example *The Maiden. Words of Advice Preparing Her for her Role (Die Jungfrau. Worte des Rathes zur Vorbereitung auf ihrer Beruf)* in 1857.[27]

The publisher Benjamin Herder originated the idea for his *Kirchenlexikon* (1856, 2nd edition revised 1876), a famous encyclopedia of Catholic theology. Like many other publishers, Herder found it a difficult task to keep rein upon the scholars whom he had contracted to write the work:

> Learned collaborators are the least punctual (of writers). If they feel that their assigned tasks are too trifling, they will not take them seriously; conversely, they may pile all their learning into what was to have been a brief essay, distorting all measure and bursting, the set bounds of the book.[28]

Series, or collections, of books which occupied an important place in the book market normally owed their existence to publishers. Examples included Franckh's *Das belletristische Ausland* (8 volumes, 1843–1865) a series of foreign novels, plays, and stories, and Christian Bernhard Tauchnitz' (1816–1895) *Collection of British Authors* (volume 1, 1841; volume 4,312, 1912), which included popular British (and some American) fiction and non-fiction, all of which was published in English. It is true that the books which were included in these two series were entirely their authors' creations, but their inclusion in the series—which greatly increased their circulation—was a creative act by the series' publishers. In series made up of reference and handbooks, on the other hand, the individual volumes themselves were usually done at a publisher's request, and every aspect of the series was due to the publisher.[29]

The books thus far cited were successful. Sometimes, however, a publisher could devote considerable effort to shaping a work only to see it fail in the marketplace. As always, publishing was a gamble. From 1860 to 1865, for example, the Bockhaus Company originated and published a work known as the *Illustrated Lexikon for Home and Family: a Handbook for the Practical Life (Illustrierte Haus-und Familien Lexikon, ein Handbuch für das praktische Leben* 10 volumes). Anyone familiar with the German book market would have considered this work a certain success: it had a topic of broad appeal, it was issued in small, inexpensive segments, it had over 2,000 illustrations, and its publisher's marketing skills were among the best in the trade. Yet it failed. The public did not buy it. There is no explaining why.[30]

## Imitation

Had the book been avidly snapped up, on the other hand, the Brockhaus Company would have faced another kind of problem—imitation. Any number of other publishers would have quickly hit the market with books scarcely distinguishable from that of Brockhaus. August Prinz, whose *Bausteine zu einer späteren Geschichte des Buchhandels* is the best contemporary account of the 1840s and 1850s, asserted that by the 1850s, imitation of successful works was as much or more of a problem as outright piracy had been in its heyday.[31] A series of books for travelers published by a publisher named Yorck was quickly copied by three other publishers, one of them Brockhaus. The situation was even more competitive when it came to translations of popular foreign novels. In the mid-1840s no less than 20 publishers were doing translations of books by the Frenchman Eugene Sue; there were seven editions of the *Mysteries of Paris* on the market, and nine of the *Wandering Jew*. Of course, Sue was unusually popular. A mania of similar intensity did not strike the German book trade again until 1859–1860, when a ridiculously large number of publishers rushed out translations of *Uncle Tom's Cabin*. But even a moderately popular British, French, or American novel was likely to appear in two or three different German translations, all of them done too quickly to be very good.[32]

Publishing was a rough and tumble business. Competition was intense. The public was fickle and mysterious. The publisher had not only to come up with ideas for books, once they were written he had to do most of the task of marketing them; the traditions of the trade dictated that the publisher play the active role in marketing, while the retailer could loll about as a passive intermediary between the producer and the public.

Generally speaking, publishers marketed books in this period with techniques which had been developed or refined during the years 1820–1843. Some of these were further developed from 1844 to 1867, but there were no great innovations in marketing. Publishers experimented with the appearance of books in some instances to bolster sales, but the idea that the physical form of a book might influence its sales was, as we have seen, nothing new. As his father had pioneered with the "pocket editions" of the 1820s, so in the 1840s and 1850s Georg von Cotta originated the most enticing new shape for a book in his time, the "miniature edition"; it was about as large as the earlier "pocket editions," but was elegantly bound (gold lettering graced the covers) by the publisher, one of the first cases in which German books were sold prebound. Cotta found these editions the ideal way to sell the popular sentimental poetry of which he published a great deal—works like Zedlitz' *Waldfraülein* (1843) and Kinkel's *Otto der Schütz* (1843). Such books became the desirable gift items for educated women which almanacs had been earlier.[33]

Cotta's new format was soon imitated by other publishers, as could be expected. After mid-century it was common for publishers to issue books which seemed likely to have a large sale in elegant bindings. Some of these books were in the "miniature" size, others more traditional octavo sizes. The "Cash Booksellers" who purchased large lots of books from publishers for resale to retailers also had books bound. Book shop owners found that a good stock of bound books helped encourage sales. Book jackets had yet to make their appearance on German books, however.[34]

## Advertising

Advertising, which had become an important part of publishers' marketing campaigns before 1843, remained so afterward. A handful of publishers did enjoy large sales without advertising, but few could realistically hope to be so fortunate.[35] Most publishers assumed advertising was a necessary burden. During the 1860s some publishers began to make use of the advertising agencies then springing up, but most continued to do their own promotional work.[36] The flamboyant, often ludicrous, phrasing which characterized much of the more ambitious book advertising of earlier periods was still much favored. Joseph Mayer, for example, never altered his hyperbolic style, and after he died his son Hermann imitated him perfectly.

While the literary style of advertising remained largely unchanged, the form in which advertisements were put did change. Direct recommendations and admonitions went out of style in newspaper adverts, replaced by pseudo "dispatches to the editor." Of course we today would recognize these efforts as public relations. The "dispatches" were designed to look like genuine news articles. Typically, they opened with some chatter about the high price of bread or meat, then casually mentioned how cheap by comparison the book being advertised was. Here is a "dispatch to the editor" used in 1857 by the Kayser'sche Book Company of Erfurt:

> (To the editor:) Christmas draws near, that wonderful time of apples and nuts... of Christmas trees and happy faces;—but also a time of ANXIETY for those who would like to give gifts but who are uncertain of what to give.—I too, fellow sufferers, have found myself in this predicament, hurrying from shop to shop, growing more rather than less confused and indecisive by the many, many attractive things I saw, and in the end hardly more certain of what to choose than I was at the beginning.
>
> Poor dear fellow sufferers! You who appreciate my dilemma will also appreciate my great joy as in the Kayser Book Shop I at last found something which ended my restless search...[37]

Of course, not every bookseller would descend to such a level of insipid absurdity. Some opined that "dispatches to the editor" were the worst book advertisements that had ever appeared.[38]

There were practitioners of a more blunt style. The Metzler'schen Book Company of Stuttgart advertised its translation of Macaulay's work in 1850 by asserting that the rival translation published by T. D. Weigel of Leipzig was no good.[39]

As before, advertisements for books were placed in a variety of media, depending upon the type of book and its expected market. Publishers were consciously matching audiences with media vehicles. For books which would appeal to a general audience, advertisements in newspapers, general-interest periodicals, trade papers, and notices in catalogs continued to be the mainstays of the publisher's promotional campaign; circulars sent to retailers and adverts on the wrappings of books were also commonly used for such books. Ambitious publishing ventures were occasionally advertised by means of direct letters to prospective customers. Specialized books such as scholarly monographs or medical writings were publicized in the appropriate learned journals and periodicals. As the *Börsenblatt* became the predominant trade paper, advertisements in it became more effective and important. Although it was not read by the general public, retailers read it carefully, and retailers made recommendations to their customers.[40]

According to August Prinz, notices in the larger newspapers, which were circulated over wide areas, always generated some book sales.[41] Local newspapers also could be effective advertising media, but publishers complained that they charged too much for advertising space. Moreover, publishers suspected that retail booksellers, who were given money by publishers in order to put ads in their local papers, took kickbacks from editors greedy for advertising revenue. Worse, some booksellers were said to take the publishers money and pocket it without placing any advertisements at all. For these reasons advertising in local newspapers was not favored by publishers, but it was not abandoned. The editors of periodicals and journals were also rabid for revenue from book advertisements, besieging publishers with requests for adverts and making inflated claims of their periodicals' circulation and readership.[42]

Most of the major publishers, as well as some of the lesser ones, owned one or more of their own journals and periodicals, which gave them a reliable medium through which to publicize their own books. They also found that these periodicals were a good means of attracting authors. A few of these periodicals had no other justification than as advertising media for their owners. From 1862 to 1867, for example, the Brockhaus Company published something called *Announcements for Friends of Literature (Central Anzeiger für Freunde der Literatur)*; issued twice a month, it contained a modicum of literary chit-chat, a listing of the new books on the market, and detailed description of some new books. Most of the latter were Brockhaus' own books, though other publishers could also have their books described if they paid Brockhaus a fee.[43]

The volume of book advertising put out by Germany's publishers fluctuated with the rhythms of the marketing seasons, rising to a peak before Easter, when sales were high, ebbing as the summer sales doldrums set in, and ending the year with very heavy advertising for the Christmas market, the busiest of the year for the book trade. Indeed, so heavy, so intense, was the book advertising before Christmas, that some people both within and without the trade came to suspect that it was not only costly, but also self-defeating—that the great welter of advertisement in newspapers, periodicals, circulars, and other places merely confused the public and made selection difficult. A Berlin newspaper correspondent wrote in 1855 that Christmas advertising was "a risky lottery [for the publisher] since the greatest possible profit could not cover the high cost [of the ads]. It is practically proven that of all the books advertised only a tiny fraction will sell."[44]

## Advertising for the Christmas season

Fortunately, for both the reading public and publishers a better method of Christmas book advertising began to develop in the mid-1840s—the Christmas catalog. These catalogs were intended for the general public; they were sold for a low price or distributed gratis to the public, with the publishers and retailers bearing the costs. They listed the books of many different publishers; publishers normally had to pay to have their books listed.

The first of the Christmas catalogs was the publisher A. Hoffmann's *Illustrated Christmas Catalogue (Illustrierter Weihnachtskatalog)*, which contained few illustrations despite its title (publishers had to provide their own and few did) and a failure to include worthwhile books of publishers who had not paid Hoffmann, proved astonishingly popular with the public. Sixty thousand copies of the 1847 edition were required to meet the need; over 50 publishers were smart enough to have paid Hoffmann to list their works in it. About two-thirds of the copies were distributed through newspapers in Berlin and other Prussian cities, the remainder through booksellers. It cost the reading public nothing.[45]

Soon analogous catalogs were being issued by other publishers, among them Louis Zander and the J. C. Hinrichs Book Company, both of Leipzig. Zander's catalog was entitled the *Bibliographischer Hausschatz*. Unlike Hoffmann's, it cost five Groschen a copy, but its contents were more carefully screened and selected. At first, Zander even listed books by publishers who had not paid him to have them listed, a burst of charity which soon ended. Many copies of both Zander's and Hinrichs' catalogs were bought in large lots by enterprising book stores and distributed gratis to customers. Hinrichs, for example, revealed in August of 1861 that 9,580 copies of its catalog for that year had already been ordered by book stores.[46]

Many publishers considered book reviews to be as valuable a source of publicity as formal advertising. By 1864, decades before the first public relations agencies, at least one publisher was reported to be sending ready-made reviews to newspapers (all the paper had to do was set the type and print them), a practice which grew in popularity during succeeding decades.[47] It was already common to send out piles of review copies to numerous news-papers and periodicals, hoping that the books would be reviewed. Odd as it may appear, publishers seemed to have been far more concerned that a book be reviewed than that it be favorably reviewed. It was a considerable expense to send out all those review copies, especially since most of them were never returned, but publishers considered it a necessary business expense.[48]

There was more to a publisher's marketing campaign than placing advert-ising and scheming to get his books reviewed. If the book had the potential to be very popular he might set the price unusually low to get sales off to a fast start. Today we call this penetration pricing. The publisher might issue the book in numerous inexpensive sections and/or at subscription prices. He might offer premiums to either the retailers or their customers if they bought the book. Probably he would send the book on approval to as many book-shops as would accept it. If sales were poor despite all, he might lower the price or, less frequently, change the book's title.

All of these techniques of marketing had of course been developed before this period, before 1843. The 1844–1866 period was not one of significant innovative marketing by publishers. The single really new marketing gimmick of the era—trade-in allowances on old books—was used only by two pub-lishers and only for encyclopedias. The two publishers were Brockhaus and the Bibliographisches Institut, the latter accepting not only older editions of its encyclopedia as trade-ins for the 1857 version, but also older editions of the Pierer and Brockhaus encyclopedias.[49]

But although the marketing of this era lacked innovation, it was quite vigorous. The sense of competition in the book market was as keen as it had been during the two decades of explosive growth after 1820. One young publisher is said to have gone so far as to have his friends order many copies of his books from book stores to make retailers think these were hot items; when the books arrived, the friends were not around to actually purchase them, which enraged the gulled book store owners.[50] Other publishers let loose an ever-swelling flood of approval books on Germany's bookshops: "The mass of new approval books is fearful!" wrote a retailer in 1860: "It grows from week to week! The bookseller is crushed—it is positively imposs-ible to maintain order and control over these masses of books."[51] Teachers were sent free copies of books to induce them to adopt the books as texts. The offering of premiums and gifts—usually "free" pictures—reportedly increased markedly after 1848, as publishers strove to overcome the lethargic book sales which were the Revolutions' immediate legacy to the trade.[52] Some publishers put enticing new titles on old books they had never been able to sell, hoping that sales would thus be fired up. This type of cosmetic alteration, however, was considered disgraceful and unethical by a majority of bookmen, no matter how ambitious they were.[53]

It was, on the other hand, considered ethical to lower the prices of books which had not been selling satisfactorily, and many publishers did so: catalogs listing books which had been thus reduced in price were more common than they had been before 1843. The era's most successful publishers were men who knew that it was best to set prices low from the outset, who knew that a book should appear inexpensive when it first entered the marketplace. Publishing ventures like Bernhard Tauchnitz' *Collection of British Authors* and Philip Reclam's stereotype edition of Shakespeare (1858, 15th printing 1867) owed much of their success to their publishers' foresight in selling them at relatively low prices—0.5 Reichsthaler per volume for the *Collection* (about half the usual price for novels) and 1.5 Reichsthaler for all 12 volumes of the Shakespeare.[54]

The old marketing standbys of subscription deals and the issuing of large works in myriad small sections continued to be much employed by publishers in this period, especially for large works. Both among bookmen and subscribers, however, there was an increasing intolerance of the problems which arose with subscriptions and installments. The main difficulty was that publishers were often unable to get out a large work as rapidly, and in the size, that they had promised subscribers. Subscribers to Joseph Meyer's encyclopedia, for example, were told in the early 1840s that the work would have 252 sections and would cost a total of 56 Reichsthaler when it was completed in the mid-1840s. As things worked out, about 200 sections were required to cover the first four letters of the alphabet, the work was not completed until after 1848, and its final cost was more than 300 Reichsthaler; none of this was Meyer's intention, but it angered his subscribers nonetheless. The second edition of Pierer's encyclopedia was projected to be 25 volumes. When completed, it filled 34, and those who had originally subscribed had to pay more than they had intended. Pierer's subscribers grew angrier yet when it was revealed that a few used-book stores were selling new copies of the book for less than the supposedly rock-bottom subscription price.[55] Subscribers always had the option to take their complaints before the courts, and some did so with success, which did nothing good for the reputation of the book trade.[56] Small wonder then that a writer in the *Börsenblatt* in 1845 referred to the whole business of subscriptions and of issuing books in sections as a "swindle" upon the public and a disgrace to the trade.[57]

There is no indication, however, that such hostility chilled any publisher's readiness to offer subscriptions or sections. No German publisher was daring enough to issue a large multi-volume work without the assurance given by advance subscriptions. To gather subscriptions, they relied upon far more than retail book shops alone, a good indication of the fact that the trend towards the circumvention and supplementation of conventional book shops with other retail outlets was continuing unabated from the pre-1843 years. Ambitious publishers continued to find too many retailers to be listless, excessively conservative businessmen who were actually afraid of large sales. Hermann Meyer's marketing strategy for a deluxe version of the Bibliographisches Institut's encyclopedia (second edition), for example, assumed that there were only 50 book shops in all of Germany capable of dealing with this work in a suitable manner. And yet the work was intended for the very wealthy, supposedly the group with whom conventional book shops had the strongest rapport.[58]

Travelling salesmen, government officials, Modern Second-Hand dealers, and direct sales to the public by the publisher—these were the principle retail outlets used by publishers who believed that conventional book stores were not enough. All had been developed before 1843. Thus in the early 1850s, a Stuttgart publisher named Heinrich Köhler offered Zimmermann's *History of the Peasant's War (Geschichte des Bauernkriegs)* directly to the public, postage paid, at a lower price than the book stores were to charge—and threw in a premium as well. The Gebauer'sche Book Company of Berlin allowed Prussian government officials to collect subscriptions for the second edition of Rauer's *Criminal Laws and Ordinances (Polizei-Gesetze und Verordnungen)* in 1853; the subscription price was half that charged by book stores. According to articles in the *Börsenblatt*, this type of deal was common all over Germany, especially for the sale of general books on government and of books of wide appeal.[59]

Travelling salesmen were used by more and more publishers of the regular trade. In addition, some were employed by aggressive book shop owners. Salesmen were found to be extremely effective at getting subscriptions for such large works as the editions of the classics published by Cotta, and also for encyclopedias. Moreover, some bookmen believed that travelling salesmen stirred up new strata of customers for the regular trade; a Berlin dealer wrote in 1859 that they were able to "cultivate ... fields which have been completely neglected by the retail bookshops and thus [they] open up new, very significant markets for the [regular] trade."[60]

To be sure, these views on travelling salesmen were not unanimously accepted in the regular trade. Some traditionalists were certain that the obstreperousness and uncouth manners of many travelling salesmen drove away more customers than they attracted. Others would grant that salesmen might sell a few books which otherwise might not have been sold, but found it "contrary to the dignity of the book trade to sell books from door to, door like eggs and butter."[61] Travelling salesmen degraded all booksellers "into the class of common food vendors," in this view.[62]

## The Modern Second-Hand book shop

The Modern Second-Hand, or Modern Antiquarian, book shops which had first developed in the decades before 1843 also had their vociferous supporters and detractors, the former made up of the buying public and many publishers, the latter composed of retail book store owners who felt threatened by Modern Antiquarian competition. Compared to the number of conventional book stores, the number of Modern Second-Hand operations was and remained small—at no time did it exceed 50 or 60 in number. These operations continued to be found only in the larger cities. But their sales and influence extended far beyond the borders of the cities in which they were located. Ironically, they were more of a threat to provincial book shops than to most big city shops because the big city shops tended to specialize in types of books which never got into the hands of Modern Antiquarian dealers. Provincial book stores, on the other hand, relied upon the sales of precisely those general, popular books which did get into the hands of Modern Antiquarian dealers.

The most talked-about Modern Second-Hand Shop of the period, the Gsellius Book Company, founded by F. W. Linde in Berlin in 1842, sold many books to customers in small towns and cities—and even to book shops in such places. The firm advertised a great deal in small city newspapers as well as in Berlin and national newspapers; most Modern Antiquarian firms did make lavish use of newspaper advertising, which they themselves rather than book publishers paid for. Gsellius also sent letters making offers directly to potential customers, especially those who did not live in Berlin.[63]

The basic reason for the success of the Gsellius and other such firms was, however, due less to advertising and hullabaloo and more to genuinely low prices. These firms could afford to grant low prices because they bought in volume and neither gave books on approval nor extended credit to customers. In the grand tradition of the Modern Antiquarian trade, the Gsellius Company never, ever sold books at the publishers' prices: it always sold them for less. When a few conventional book shops in Berlin attempted to undersell Gsellius, they learned that much of the book-buying public simply refused to believe that their prices were lower.

While the Gsellius Company thrilled Berlin, in Frankfurt the pioneering Modern Antiquarian dealers M. L. St. Goat and Joseph Baer were growing in prosperity too. Baer managed to gain an enviable reputation as well by building a stock of rare and scholarly works which became known to scholars all over Europe. In 1859 he crowned his career with the opening of an immense book shop in the Rossmarkt. The *Allgemeine Zeitung* described it as "an establishment as tasteful as it is magnificent, an establishment that is more like a palace of world literature than the shop of a single German book dealer."[64] Here, scholars might mingle with common bargain hunters amidst several floors of displays and reading rooms.[65]

The esteem in which Baer, M. Veit of Berlin, and a handful of other Modern Antiquarian dealers came to be held by even the most serious book buyers (and by publishers) was not typical. As a group, the Modern Second-Hand book dealers were vilified by much of the trade—by publishers as well as conventional retailers—and were disdained by the snobbier elements among the public (who bought books from these places anyway). Since most Modern Antiquarians were Jewish, they were felt to be a source of shame to Jewish bookmen anxious to be assimilated into respectable anonymity in the trade. An 1845 article in the Jewish periodical *Orient* is the strongest denunciation of the Modern Second-Hand Trade I have seen: "You can see them, like vultures drawn by the stench of corpses, hovering about the dying and unfortunate products of publishers' speculations, dead books which they will drag to life in the market again."[66] The denunciation by gentile book shop owners were not as vividly worded, but expressed just as much hatred. The old story that Modern Antiquarian book dealers obtained much of their stock from thieves was repeated endlessly. In Leipzig, the Rhineland, Westphalia, and Munich conventional retailers petitioned the governments to legislate the Modern Second-Hand Trade out of existence. The governments did not heed their anguished pleas, however. Attempts by retailers to boycott publishers who sold books to Modern Antiquarian dealers were equally futile.[67]

## Conventional book shops

It seemed to the book shop owners that they were being ground down by undignified and unfair competition from every side: not just from the Modern Second-Hand vultures, venal government officials, greedy publishers, and travelling salesmen, but also by binders, book hawkers who carried their wares about on their backs, and religious organizations which sold books—for example the Catholic Borromäus Society.[68] From the 1840s there was serious talk that all this competition would doom the conventional book shop, especially the general small city shop, to extinction.[69]

Could the retail shop fight back? Many were doubtful. Its operating procedures, above all the approval system, seemed too clumsy, too inefficient, too out-of-line with the aggressive retail practices of the mid-nineteenth century. A contributor to the *Börsenblatt*, wrote in 1866:

> The basic problem is that most retail booksellers are mired in old-fashioned, now inadequate business methods. When they have trouble they blame it on the publishers ... instead of recognizing their own practices as the problem and adopting rational business methods.[70] Many observers felt that book stores extended credit too easily to people who were all too likely to be very slow in actually paying. But customers demanded such treatment, notably in the small cities and towns, where it was normal that a customer take one to two years to pay, and where some paid in kind rather than in cash. Then there was the problem of approval books: if a shop accepted all of them, which publishers sent unrequested, they were overwhelmed with paper work. But it had long been a usage of the trade that retail shops would accept such books. To be sure, a growing number would accept only those books which they had requested.[71]

To make matters worse for the conventional retailers it often seemed that when they did demonstrate some vigor by selling books below the publishers' prices or by granting "customer discounts," the main result was to hurt other book shops in the area rather than the hated travelling salesmen or Modern Antiquarians. The other shops very often expressed their anger by dropping prices even lower, and driving "customer discounts" even higher. Competition among book shops sometimes reached a pitch of viciousness that would have cheered any Social Darwinist.

Sometimes retailers openly advertised that they intended to undersell all the other book shops in the region. A bookseller named Ehlers in the city of Einbeck, for example, proclaimed in the mid-1850s his resolve to sell every single book advertised by other book stores in his area at a lower price.[72] In December 1865, a Berlin retailer named Oskar Rolaff had street corners plastered with signs proclaiming that he gave a high— 20 percent—"customer discount" on top of the already reduced prices of books which he sold.[73] In view of such goings-on some members of the trade questioned if the retailers themselves, and not the Modern Antiquarians, book-selling government officials, etc. were the principle cause of their economic woes.[74]

Whoever their main enemies, however, there was a consensus in the regular book trade that, as August Prinz articulated it in the late 1850s:

> For years now the greater number of retailers have had a destiny which is not to be envied: they eke out a meager living, pining away, and many and sundry vanish from the trade without a trace; or they are hounded, often mercilessly hounded [by their publisher-creditors], until their last little bit of property is squeezed out of them; while many others are kept indefinitely on tenterhooks by their publisher-creditors.[75]

There were many bankruptcies among the conventional retailers during these years. Statistics for 1856, for instance, show that 120 firms expired that year, most of them retail book stores. Not all of them expired because of financial problems—in some cases the owners died and so forth—but most of them did. In 1858, 56 bookshops closed for various reasons.[76]

Yet in both 1856 and 1858, as well as in almost every other year from 1853 to 1866, more new book shops were founded than old ones closed. This was shown earlier in this chapter. In 1858, 73 new book shops were founded and 18 more than had shut down. Thus despite the very real difficulties which many book shops experienced, the total number of book shops increased—certainly an indication that the conventional retail trade was healthier than contemporaries knew or were willing to admit. The rhetoric of gloom and doom employed by Prinz and others exaggerates. If there was a high risk of failure in establishing a new book shop, there was a greater chance of success. During this period hundreds and hundreds of people were optimistic enough about the prospects of the book shop, that they each invested from anything from one to several thousand *Reichsthaler* to found one of their own.[77] Would so many people enter a dying business? The competition from travelling salesmen, bureaucrats, Modern Antiquarians, as well as from other book stores, was less chilling than contemporaries said it was. Moreover, there were clear signs that the business practices of many book shop operators were more intelligent, dynamic, and abreast of contemporary retailing practices than was commonly supposed. Display windows, which came into use by stores in general after mid-century, were installed by a good many booksellers. They were installed because these booksellers knew that show windows helped lure people into the shop. Many of these same book-sellers worked to make the exteriors of their establishments more elegant looking, since it had been observed that an elegant-looking exterior was another great aid in attracting people inside.[78] To be sure, there were other retailers who proudly resisted all such new trends, but fewer of them than most people thought.

Conventional retailers began to find ways to counter the threat of the Modern Second-Hand stores too. In some cities several retailers would pool resources to buy large lots of books at advantageous prices, then sell these books more cheaply than the Modern Antiquarians. As we have seen, this was less successful than hoped for in Berlin when used against the Gsellius Book Company; elsewhere, however, the results were more pleasing. A more common tactic used by book stores was to themselves deal in popular used books. This tactic proved an effective way to win back customers from the Modern Antiquarians. Neither of these two tactics are known to have driven any Modern Second-Hand shops into bankruptcy, but they were a sign of energy by old-line book shops.[79]

Other developments helped the retail book shops too; for example the growing availability of pre-bound books, which stores could get either from the publisher or from wholesalers like the Zander Book Company. All trade experts agreed that a stock of bound popular books—classics, beloved works of contemporary fiction, well-known cookbooks and handbooks, school-books, prayer books, and works of local interest—could not but increase a store's business. "The richer the stock of books on hand, the more it will arouse the buying urges of those who come in," wrote a contributor to the *Börsenblatt* in 1859.[80] Customers liked to have books to browse among; often they bought some of those they saw.

Then too, the traditional strong points of the retail book store were undiminished by time. The store could obtain through the approval system a wide variety of material for its customers to examine and could extend credit to enable them to purchase books; the other retail outlets, on the other hand, normally sold only a narrow selection of the most popular books and neither offered anything on approval nor extended credit. To its customers, a well-run book store was the center of their cultural lives; it was not just another mercantile establishment. It was a genteel place where one could commune with the muses for hours. Its operator and staff, well-versed in German and European book production, were able to give literary counsel and advice when asked. The recommendations of such booksellers were very important factors in determining what many people bought.[81]

A description of the Hamburg Book Shop originally established by Perthes and owned by the Mauke family in the mid-1850s illustrates the appeal of the traditional book store very well. Settled in an excellent location on the corner of the *Jungfernstieg* and the *Große Bleiche*, the shop's appearance was that of an old, solid establishment. Like most book stores in Germany then, it was open from nine in the morning until nine at night. During the day its interior was illuminated by light pouring through a large window; there were also three display windows, but little calculated use was made of these. The shop's large stock of books was set up on shelves of old, rubbed mahogany. Near the windows were comfortable arm-chairs where customers could relax and peruse whatever books they felt might be of interest. What a contrast to the crass bustle of a Modern Antiquarian book shop—how much more dignified an atmosphere. Here one would not hesitate to ask for advice—but who of the respectable classes would want to rely upon the literary counsel of a travelling salesman or bureaucrat?[82]

Of course, numerous book stores were operated by fools, and some by knaves. There were those who were lethargic, who kept poor records, who insulted customers, who kept few books in stock—who were, in other words, incompetent businessmen. There were retailers who insisted on establishing themselves in towns or in areas of cities which could not possibly support their businesses. There were unstable types, swindlers, and con-men who set themselves up as book shop operators, probably because it was relatively easy to get the required government license for book shops; according to Prinz, Berlin swarmed with such men.[83] In the Prussian capital, Berlin, in November of 1852, for example, there opened the fancy book store of one Constantin Breuer on *Unter den Linden*. Breuer had financed the shop with borrowed money. A slothful man, he did not bother to keep written records; but merely kept on ordering more and more and more books from publishers. He had a penchant for ordering bound copies of costly luxury editions. Breuer sold very few of the books he received, and paid none of his bills. So in March of 1853 the bill collectors closed in upon him; Breuer fled, rumor had it to Paris. A binder named Bachmann, a ghoul who thrived upon dead businesses, bought up the store's stock.[84]

All over Germany, insisted the contemporary publisher August Prinz, ambitious but foolish young men rushed to set up book shops, even in the most insignificant and culturally barren little towns. They would hardly have established themselves when they plunged into publishing as well, fancying themselves as the new Cottas, Brockhauses, and Perthes. Most went bankrupt, quickly.[85]

It would be too easy, however, to exaggerate the prevalence of incompetents and frauds in the retail book trade of that time. Most German book store operators were neither fools nor knaves. On balance, they were competent businessmen who made out, who in some cases even prospered, from their trade. If in the smaller towns many book shops had to sell non-book items ranging from cigars to stationary to provide a living for their owners, this was nothing new. What is significant is that more and more book stores were able to do well selling books alone.[86]

# Notes

1 In neither the *Krieger'sche Wochenblatt* nor the *Börsenblatt* could I find mention of any serious adverse effects of the depressions of 1825 and 1835. Berger, "Der deutsche Buchhandel," pp. 136–138, implies that the 1830 revolutions were more invigorating than depressing to the trade, as does Prinz, *Bausteine*, vol. I, p. 22. See also: H. F. Meyer, "Mittheilungen zur inneren Geschichte des Deutschen Buchhandels von 1811–1848," *Arichi fuer Geschichte des deutschen Buchandels*, Leipzig 1884, p. 178.

2 O. A. Schulze, "Vergleichende Statistik," *Börsenblatt* 1846, Nr. 19, p. 256. See also Berger, "Der deutsche Buchhandel," p. 149.

3 Ein Verlags und Sortimentsbuchhaendler, "Einige Worte ueber den jetzigen Zustand des Buchhandels," *Börsenblatt* 1848, Nr. 47, pp. 555–556.

4 Quoted in Weiss, *Benjamin Herder*, p. 35.

5 On the 1848 Revolutions and the book trade see: *Börsenblatt* 1848, Nr. 40, p. 517; "Einige Worte," *Börsenblatt* 1848, Nr. 47, pp. 555–556; Prinz, *Bausteine*, vol. II, pp. 29–31, 37–42; Berger, "Der deutsche Buchhandel," p. 149; Meyer, "Mittheilungen zur inneren Geschichte des Deutschen Buchhandels," p. 178; Crous & Falter, *Festschrift der J. A. Mayer'schen Buchhandlung*, pp. 112–116.

6 "Zur Statistik des preussischen Buchhandels," *Börsenblatt* 1855, Nr. 157, p. 2299.

7 "Aus Breslau," *Börsenblatt* 1855, Nr. 76, pp. 1008–1009; Prinz, *Bausteine*, vol. II, pp. 37–43, vol. III, pp. 70–71, vol V, pp. 70–71.

8 Goldfriedrich, *Geschichte*, p. 467.

9 "Der Buchhandel in den Jahren 1865 und 1866," *Börsenblatt* 1868, Nr. 101, pp. 1158–1160.

10 C. A. Seemann, *Fingerzeige zur Abschatzung von Sortiments-(Antiquariats) und Verlagsgeschiften*, Leipzig 1863, p. 25.

11 Goldfriedrich, *Geschichte*, pp. 199, 486–487.

12 Muehlbrecht, "Die politisch-historische Literatur des Jahres 1866," *Börsenblatt* 1867, Nr. 18, pp. 169–172, Nr. 19, pp. 181–185.

13 *Börsenblatt* 1855, p. 205. Goldfriedrich, *Geschichte*, p. 457, gives figures on the number of German book dealers and the number of cities with dealers—all over Europe and in the New World as well.

14 Prinz, *Bausteine*, vol. II, p. 65.

15 *Börsenblatt* 1855, p. 205.

16 Uhlig, *Geschichte des Buches und des Buchhandels*, p. 50.

17 Prinz, *Bausteine*, vol. II, p. 61.

18 Ibid., pp. 61–62.

19 Widmann, *Der deutsche Buchhandel in Urkunden und Quellen*, vol. I, p. 113.

20 Uhlig, *Geschichte des Buches und des Buchhandels*, p. 64.

21 A. Meiner, *Reclam. Geschichte eines Verlages*, Stuttgart 1958, p. 10.

22 O. Hase, *Development of the Book Industries of Leipzig*, Leipzig 1887, p. 50.

23 *Werden und Wesen des Hauses R. Oldenbourg Muenchen. Ein Geschichtlicher Ueberblick 1858–1958* Munich 1958, p. 19.

24 Hohlfeld, *Das Bibliograehische Institut*, pp. 167–240; Lohrer, Cotta, pp. 95–125.

25 Schuermann, *Organisation und Rechtsgewohnheiten des deutschen Buchhandels*, vol. I, pp. 261–267.

26 See Hiller, *Zur Sozialgeschichte von Buch und Buchhandel*, pp. 7–45.

27 This is according to Hohlfeld, *Das Bibliographische Institut*, pp. 211–212. But Hiller, *Zur Sozialgeschichte von Buch und Buchhandel*, pp. 42–43, maintains that Meyer's role may not have been so important. Similarly, Hiller's assessment of Reimer's role in inspiring the Grimm brothers to produce their famous dictionary is not corroborated by H. Gerstner's article "Hundert Jahre Deutsches Woerterbuch der Brueder Grimm 1854–1934," *Imprimatur*, vol. XII (1954/1955), pp. 202–207.

28 Tabaczek, *Kulturelle Kommercializsierung*, pp. 151–155; Hiller, *Zur sozialgeschichte von Buch und Buchhandel*, pp. 29–32; *Bruecken zu fremden Volkern. 100 Jahre Langenscheidt*, Berlin 1956, pp. 4–15.

29 Quoted in Weiss, *Benjamin Herder*, p. 25. Pages 15 to 34 of this book give the best description of the making of a large collaborative work that I have seen.

30 Christian Bernhard Tauchnitz should not be confused with his uncle, Karl Tauchnitz, (1761–1836), who is mentioned earlier.

31 Huebscher, *Hundertfuenfzig Jahre F. A. Brockhaus*, pp. 215–216.

32 Prinz, Bausteine, vol. III, pp. 70–73, vol. IV, p. 37.

33 Ibid., vol. III, pp. 70–73; *Heinsius*, X, 2, pp. 316–317.

34 Lohrer, *Cotta*, p. 116.

35 Berger, "Der deutsche Buchhandel," pp. 153–155. 104; Schulze, *Der deutsche Buchhandel*, p. 101.

36 The Chelius Publishing Company and the firm of Winckelmann and Son were said to sell many books without advertising; see N., "Ueber Weihnachtsinserate und deren Nutzen," *Börsenblatt* 1866, Nr. 140, p. 2472.

37 e, "Die Annoncen-Bureaus," *Börsenblatt* 1866, Nr.74, p. 1355.

38 *Börsenblatt* 1858, Nr. 8, p. 103.

39 See: X, "Das Anzeigewesen und die Reclame," *Börsenblatt* 1857, pp. 2559–2560.

40 *Börsenblatt* 1850, Nr. 8, p. 99, Nr. 11, pp. 140–141.

41 H. Bethmann, "Ueber die Nichtbeachtung der buchhaendlerischen Circularen," *Börsenblatt* 1848, Nr. 105, p. 1283.

42 Prinz, *Bausteine*, vol. II, pp. 57–58.

43 Ibid., vol. II, p. 38. Also: *Börsenblatt* 1852 Nr. 36, p. 578; "Die Inseraten-Jagd," *Börsenblatt* 1863, Nr. 142, p. 2494.

44 *Central Anzeiger fuer Freunde der Literatur, passim.*

45 "Aus Berlin," *Börsenblatt* 1856, Nr. 18, p. 256.

46 *Börsenblatt* 1847, Nr. 72, p. 971, Nr. 76, p. 1031.

47 *Börsenblatt* 1861 Nr. 99, p. 1662, 1863, Nr. 106, p. 1784, Nr. 142, p. 1494.

48 See "Zum Recensionswesen," *Börsenblatt* 1864, Nr. 156, p. 2872.

49 Periodical and newspaper editors were supposed to return review copies to the publisher whether they had reviewed the book or not, but few did. Many review copies supposedly fell into the hands of used-book and Modern Antiquarian dealers: see "Missrauch und Unfug mit 'Recensionsexemplaren'," *Börsenblatt* 1855, Nr. 31, p. 427.

50 There was a fixed trade-in allowance of 14 *Reichsthaler* for the customer's old set. See *Börsenblatt* 1844, Nr. 31, p. 1038.

51 "Neue, bisher unerhoerte Manipulation eines Verlegers," *Börsenblatt* 1854, Nr. 149, p. 2075.

52 "Ein Schmerzenschrei aus dem Sortimentshandel," *Börsenblatt* 1860, Nr. 143, p. 2392.

53 *Börsenblatt* 1862, Nr. 70, p. 1170.

54 Spiritus asper (pseudonym), "Zur Geschichte der 'neuen wohlfeilen' Ausgaben," *Börsenblatt* 1850, Nr. 99, p. 1400, which is the best single article on this phenomenon.

55 *Reclam.*, pp. 13–14.

56 Pierer had sold the work to many book stores, but they were not supposed to sell it for less than the subscription price. Unfortunately a few of these shops went bankrupt; their stocks were sold off to used-book dealers, who felt no compunction about selling the books for less than the subscription price.

57 *Börsenblatt* 1849, Nr. 7, p. 77.

58 H. Fluegge, "Buchhindler-Schwindelerein," *Börsenblatt* 1845, Nr. 50, p. 537.

59 Hohlfeld, *Das Bibliographische Institut*, p. 217; Probus, "Ueber die Eroeffnung neuer Absatzwege fuer den deutschen Buchhandel," *Börsenblatt* 1861, Nr. 98, p. 1629.

60 On the Gebauer deal see the *Börsenblatt* 1853, Nr. 51, p. 615.

61 *Börsenblatt* 1844, Nr. 105, pp. 3677–3678.

62 Ibid., pp. 3677–3678.
63 On the Gsellius Book Company, see: –r, "Vom Berliner Buchhandel," *Börsenblatt* 1852, Nr. 5, pp. 59–60. On Modern Antiquarian practices in general use see Seemann, *Fingerzeige zur Abschitzung von Sortiments-(Antiquariats) und Verlagsgeschiften*, p. 7.
64 Quoted in the *Börsenblatt* 1859, Nr. 153, pp. 2508–2509.
65 "Eines Mannes Rede ist halbe Rede, man soll sie hoeren alle Beede," *Börsenblatt* 1865, Nr. 16, pp. 274–275.
66 "Ueber die juedischen Buchhaendler," *Orient*, reprinted in the *Börsenblatt* 1845, Nr. 16, p. 183. The Orient article emphasized that "Jewish book dealers do not want to know anything about Jews and Jewishness; they simply want to be German book dealers." (p. 183). The Berlin dealer M. Veit disagreed: "Erwiderung," *Börsenblatt* 1845, Nr. 19, p. 225. Nr. 154, p. 2244.
67 "Von den 'Neuen Etablissements'," *Börsenblatt* 1853, Nr. 132, p. 1688.
68 For complaints against book hawkers see: A. Weinholz, "Fuegen die Kolporteure dem Sortiments-Buchhandel grossen Schaden zu?," *Börsenblatt* 1847, Nr. 20, p. 248. For complaints against binders see, for example: "Aus der Provinz Westphalen," *Börsenblatt* 1865, Nr. 2, p. 21. Nr. 22, pp. 300–302.
69 Prinz, *Bausteine*, vol. V, pp. 3–12.
70 "Nachlaßgesuch," *Börsenblatt* 1866, Nr. 110, pp. 1841–1842.
71 "Wie ein Sortimenter den Zorn seiner Kunden verwirkt," *Börsenblatt* 1849, Nr. 79, p. 915; –n–, "Die grosse Misere des Sortimentsbuchhandels," *Börsenblatt* 1860, Nr. 128, p. 2088.
72 A. Eggeling, "Ueber Schleuderei im Sortiments-Buchhandel," *Börsenblatt* 1855, Nr. 6, p. 69.
73 "Es kommt immer besser," *Börsenblatt* 1866, Nr. 4, p. 67.
74 See, for example: "Wer zerstoert mehr das Sortimentsgeschaft, die Sortimenter oder die modernen Antiquare?," *Börsenblatt* 1864, Nr. 151, p. 2778.
75 Prinz, *Bausteine*, vol. V, pp. 4–5.
76 *Börsenblatt* 1857, Nr. 5, p. 57.
77 Seemann, *Fingerzeige zur Abschatzung von Sortiments-(Antiquariats) und Verlagsgeschiften*, pp. 9–10, says that it cost between 1,200 and 2,100 *Reichsthaler* to establish a new book shop with a good stock of books. Additional capital was needed to cover operating expenses during the first few years. It was somewhat less costly to purchase an already-established shop.
78 Berger, "Der deutsche Buchhandel," pp. 149–150.
79 Seemann, *Fingerzeige zur Abschatzung von Sortiments (Antiquariats) und Verlagsgeschiften*, p. 7.
80 W. J., "Das Prinzip der Association," *Börsenblatt*, 1859, Nr. 37, pp. 619–621, Nr. 38, pp. 635–636.
81 "Weihnachtsgedanken," *Börsenblatt* 1863, Nr. 11, pp. 175–178.
82 From a description of the store by Lucas Graefe, who had worked as an apprentice and then as an employee from 1855 to 1870, in Bertheau, *Geschichte der Buchhandlung W. Mauke Soehne*, pp. 96–99.
83 Prinz, *Bausteine*, vol. VII, pp. 4–75, and vol. III, pp. 30–40.
84 Ibid., vol. VII, pp. 42–45.
85 Ibid., vol. III, pp. 30–40.
86 Examples of prosperous book stores in this period include the academic book store of Friedrich Cohen in Bonn and the Munich store of Carl Beck, for which see, repectively, Hundert Jahre Friedrich Cohen Bonn Bonn 1929, pp. 12–13, and *Festschrift des Verlages C. H. Beck*, p. 33.

# 6   The book market of the regular trade at mid-century, 1843–1866

In the middle decades of the nineteenth century, the book market serviced by the regular trade was far larger than it had been at the close of the Napoleonic Wars. Yet its basic structure had changed little: the social groups and institutions which bought books were the same ones which had done so earlier; buying patterns were much the same as earlier. There was much talk that the tastes of the reading public had become completely degenerate and mindless, obsessively following one idiotic sensation after another, but if actual book sales are any indication, these tastes can best be characterized as conservative and practical.

## Segmenting the market

The public of the regular trade still included many titled nobles, hardly surprising in view of the continued wealth and high social stature of the German nobility. The Mauke Book Shop in Hamburg was proud to have as customers: "the old Duke of Augustenberg, the Duke of Glücksberg, [and] many nobles with estates in Holstein."[1] Hermann Meyer judged that "the thousand members of the ruling families ... the ten thousands of the noble houses, and in addition holders of high orders from State and Court"[2] would constitute a lucrative market for a deluxe edition of his firm's encyclopedia. Part of his sales program for this work involved doing research on genealogical calendars and other works on nobility to determine exactly who the real nobles were—the earliest example that I have found of formal market research. Among the nobility, Meyer believed, the tradition of the large private personal library was still alive and such libraries would of course be stocked with deluxe editions.

Pursuing his thinking about appropriate segments, Meyer also realized that an even greater market for the luxury edition would be found among "the Plutocracy ... [i.e.,] big industrialists, ... the founders of successful businesses, bankers, large [non-noble] property owners, [and] wealthy retired merchants."[3] Meyer knew that such people were obsessed with "vanity," with the desire "to procure for themselves the attributes of cultivation and the appearance of refinement. They certainly need such a work far less than [the nobility] but love to appear as if they need it [more]."[4]

Less affluent members of the middle classes could not afford luxury editions, but they too were enslaved to the need to appear educated and genteel. As Annemarie Meiner, one of the best modern historians of the German book trade, put it:

> The upward-striving middle class, which despite the failure of the 1848 movements believed itself the bearer of the future, was obsessed with the desire to be considered "cultivated" *(gebildet)*. It availed itself of every means which would bring this about: literary journals and circulating libraries, ... series of "miniature", "pocket" and *"Groschen"* books, then of mutual exchanges of books among acquaintances.[5]

Its urge towards "cultivation" made the middle class, from plutocrats to low-level bureaucrats, by far the largest single segment of the book market of the regular trade, a phenomenon already apparent by 1820 and one which grew ever-stronger after 1820.

## Middle-class taste in books

A valuable look at the relationship of the middle class to the book is provided by a popular etiquette manual of the time, August Lewald's 1847 *Society: the Book for those who wish to become People of the World (Das Buch der Gesellschaft. Fur angehende Weltleute)*. To acquire the requisite "cultivation," counseled Lewald, one began by getting an overview of German literature. This could be acquired either from a hired teacher or from one of several handbooks on German literature. Ideally, one then read a great deal of German literature, especially the works of classic authors such as Lessing, Goethe, Schiller, and Jean Paul; a smattering (no more was necessary) of Herder, Klopstock, Wieland, Voss, and Bürger was also useful. Of non-fictional works, those "on history are highly recommended," [6] The nineteenth-century writers to read were: Uhland, Friedrich Schlegel, Tieck, Novalis, Grillparzer, Chamisso, Heine *(Das Buch der Lieder)*, Rückert, Lenau, Herwegh, and such beloved singers of the sweet muse as Freiligrath and Emanuel Geibel. It is no wonder that collections of the German classics were such steady selling items; being able to show that one owned them was the true test of cultivated respectability.

But it was not especially necessary to read them very much, according to Lewald. For many people the appearance, rather than the substance, of "cultivation" was adequate: "To be accepted in society as a person well-versed in literature, it generally suffices to have a familiarity with the immortal authors and with a few much-discussed contemporary novels."[7] By scanning during the day books they were going to chatter about in the evening, people could present the maximum impression with the minimum of effort. In the large cities there were "conversation teachers" who gave lessons about currently fashionable books.[8]

Still, for all this sham and pretense about reading, middle-class Germans did read a great deal—if not always of the best literature. Children learned to read young and were expected to read voraciously. The evening family gatherings at which one member read aloud to the others remained a revered and widespread custom throughout the entire nineteenth century. The middle-class woman spent a large part of her day reading, impelled to do so by the advances in female education which had given her literacy, by the availability of servants which gave her free time, and by the powerful social mores which dictated that she should read.[9]

In fact, middle-class women probably made up the largest single segment of the regular book trade's reading public. This was deplored by Eichendorff and others on the grounds that so many of these women had neither intelligence nor taste. The perceived boorishness of such women—as well as of many male readers—increasingly upset the refined sensibilities of serious authors, who in reaction began that trend to aloofness from, and scorn towards, the general reading public, which has culminated in the petulant obscurity of much twentieth-century "literature".[10]

Even more upsetting than the public's lack of good taste, however, was its frugality. Serious authors were joined by middle-brow authors, hacks, publishers, and booksellers in anger at the continuing, relentless parsimony of the reading public, which supposedly purchased less than its counterparts in England, France, and the USA.[11]

True, there were some big individual book buyers in Germany, like the instant millionaires who in the heady years before the 1857 Crash snapped up "luxury editions" as fast as they were put on the market, or the Berlin clerk who embezzled 20,000 *Reichsthaler* from his employer and spent nearly all of it on books. There still were a few scholars who assembled large personal research and reference libraries: the geographer Karl Ritter had 25,000 volumes, the historian Heinrich Leo about 6,000 titles.[12]

But these were exceptions to the long-term general trend away from large-scale book buying by a wealthy elite of individual Germans. "The older book buyers, who emphasized building up their own personal libraries, are dying out more and more," ran a typical lament in the *Börsenblatt* in 1853.[13] In the 1840s Heinrich Hoffmann v. Fallersleben, who was a university librarian as well as a patriotic songwriter, had observed that:

> The learned and scholarly are no longer as able as they once were to buy all the books which they need for their studies ... because the growth in the number of books has outpaced the growth of their salaries.[14]

## Borrowing rather than buying reading matter

Most of the books which Germans read were not those they had purchased, but rather those they had borrowed from a lending institution. The reasons for this were partly economic and partly cultural. The economic reason lay in the relatively high cost of German books; aside from the low-priced speculative ventures the more ambitious publishers put on the market. Most German books were far from cheap, particularly in comparison with books in France, England, or the United States. For most of the German middle classes, and even some of the nobles, book purchases were therefore a luxury, and remained so until after 1870. In the 1843–1866 period it was common for even institutional buyers like lending libraries to complain about the high cost of German books. The lending library operators were glad that so many of their customers liked French novels, which were far cheaper to buy. The high cost of books forced most scholars to abandon any thought of creating large personal research libraries, a trend which had been underway even before 1820.[15]

The cultural reasons for borrowing rather than buying books were in part an outgrowth of economic necessity. In Germany there was absolutely no stigma attached to borrowing books—even to borrowing greasy and tattered books from circulating libraries. No less an arbiter of decorum than August Lewald enthusiastically recommended patronizing lending libraries.[16] Of course, it was socially desirable to own copies of classics, encyclopedias, and other works considered to be of substance and enduring value, and many people purchased such books for their home libraries, but there was nothing wrong with borrowing even these books. To buy anything but classics, indispensable reference works and the like was considered an unnecessary, indeed profligate and foolish, expenditure. An essayist wrote in 1859:

> In Germany it has become a down-right act of immodesty and indecency to buy rather than borrow even those books which are necessary. Nobody considers it a luxury to buy jewelry, or costly woolens and furs (in addition to the many they already have!), or expensive furniture; but to spend a few *Gulden* per year for books, that is considered the height of prodigality.[17]

While this essayist did assume a more widespread affluence than was actually the case in Germany then, there is a good deal of validity to his observation.

Thus, the non-scholarly reading public cheerfully flocked to get much of its reading matter from the circulating libraries and reading circles, making these the principle market for fiction and general non-fiction. Actually the same was true in Great Britain. Specialized and scholarly German readers depended upon the libraries of learned and of fraternal societies, and upon royal, state, municipal, and university libraries (all of which catered to scholars only and kept the general public out), thus making these libraries, considered together, the principle domestic market for learned books. (There was also an important export market for German scholarly works, which grew as the prestige of German scholarship and science did.)[18]

Enough information on the growth and acquisitions' budgets of Germany's libraries has survived to give a good indication of the size of the market for scholarly works within Germany. Even municipal libraries, then, were basically research or archival institutions, purchasing only learned works and works concerning local matters—pleasure reading was left to the circulating libraries. The acquisitions' budgets of public libraries varied considerably: around 1850, for example, they ranged from nothing in Ulm, Danzig, and Konigsberg (which had to rely entirely upon gifts), to 50 Reichsthaler annually in Trier, 1,200 Reichsthaler in Mainz, 3,600 Marks in Hamburg, and 5,660 Marks in Frankfurt/Main. The great Royal Library in Berlin had a yearly budget of 10,000 Reichsthaler after 1848, to which were added gifts from the King. From 1836, Munich's Royal Library got 17,500 Gulden per year in order to buy books. The acquisitions' budgets of the smaller princely libraries at mid-century ranged from 400 Reichsthaler a year in Wolfenbuttel to 2,000 Reichsthaler in Oldenberg and 10,000 Florins in Darmstadt.[19]

Germany's university libraries also presented large markets for books. Between 1822 and 1853 the library of Göttingen University enjoyed an average annual growth rate of 4,840 volumes, that of Tübingen 4,510, Heidelberg 3,390, Landshut-Munich 3,900, Bonn 2,600, and Leipzig 2,260.[20]

In all of these cases, as well as in the cases of royal, state, and municipal libraries, it does have to be kept in mind that not all books acquired were contemporary German works purchased on the market. Some were foreign works, others were used and out-of-print books, and still others were "compulsory copies," which publishers had had to give the libraries free of charge.[21] Even so, the libraries were purchasing large numbers of new German books.

Private scholarly associations were a smaller market, but they did in some cases buy up large numbers of books for their libraries. In the 1850s the Upper Lusatia Society in Gorlitz had 32,000 volumes in its library, the Silesian Society for the Culture of the Fatherland in Breslau had over 20,000 and the Historical Society of Lower Saxony in Hannover had 8,000. In Hamburg there were private libraries operated by and for local historians, doctors, lawyers, and mathematicians; the Patriotic Society for the Advancement of the Arts and Sciences there owned over 40,000 volumes as of 1852.[22]

Some government agencies absorbed large numbers of books in stocking their reference libraries. In 1866, for example, the Bavarian Justice Ministry authorized the expenditure of 30,000 Gulden to build a new law library for itself. A consortium of three Munich bookshops won the contract to provide these books, a rich plum indeed.[23]

What university, royal and other government, and learned societies' libraries were to the scholarly book market, was what circulating libraries were to the market for works of general interest—for novels, dramas, collections of stories, poetry, and for popular works in history, biography, politics, and the sciences. More general works were sold to lending libraries than to individual buyers. Only very famous, classic or near-classic, novels, for example, were ever bought by private individuals, and, even so, more were purchased by lending libraries.[24]

The number of these libraries increased from about 600 in 1842 to about 780 in 1865 and 961 in 1870. The size of individual lending libraries varied greatly, some having as few as 1,500 to 2,000 books, a handful having over 100,000. Some lending libraries specialized: Stuttgart in the late 1840s had one especially for children, another for workers, and one operated by a Lutheran religious group. In 1863, a Berliner named Fritz Borstell ushered in a new era in German lending libraries when he established one modeled after the enormous Mudies' Library in London. Borstell's was the first major city lending library to service outlying areas, including even isolated military garrisons. This idea was quickly imitated by large Leipzig libraries. Borstell was also unusual in buying books so lavishly that there was always a plentiful supply of fresh, clean copies of the books people wanted; the conventional thing in German lending libraries was to hold off purchases of new copies until absolutely necessary, until the existing ones had become so smashed up, cut up, smudged, shredded, and otherwise defaced by patrons and their unruly children that they were no longer in one piece. Among Borstell's patrons were Bismarck and the historian Mommsen.[25]

Because of the notorious reluctance of most lending libraries to replace worn and decrepit books, publishers, retailers, and authors believed that these institutions existed only to rob them of sales and income. They pointed to Britain, France, and the USA as wonderful places where books sold infinitely better and where bookmen and authors were justly remunerated, even though in Britain lending libraries had a major presence.[26]

It certainly was true that the sales of individual books, especially novels, were much higher in these three countries than in Germany, even though Germans read at least as much. The most successful novel of the first six decades of the nineteenth century in Germany was Wilhelm Hauff's *Lichtenstein*, of which 50,000 copies were sold between its publication in 1826 and the late 1850s. The most successful German novel of the 1850s was Gustav Freyteg's *Soll und Haben*, with sales of 22,000 copies between 1855 and 1859. During a single year in that decade in the United States, by contrast, 180,000 copies of three novels by Fanny Fern were sold; the greatest best seller of the decade, Mrs. Stowe's *Uncle Tom's Cabin*, registered an incredible sale of 300,000 copies during its first year in print (March 1852–March 1853). A single book store in Chicago sold 10,000 copies of Alfred, Lord Tennyson's *Enoch Arden*. One need but imagine what the combined Anglo-American sales figures for Dickens' works were then. In Germany, Friedrich Stolle's historical novel *1813* was considered a great success because 10,000 copies of it were sold in the two decades after its publication in 1838, but in France, innumerable novels sold as well in much less time.[27]

The only way in which German publishers could have radically increased their sales, however, would have been to have radically lowered the prices of their books—and even this, in view of the social respectability of borrowing books, would not have pushed sales up to the levels achieved in England, France, or the United States. The adventurous Franckh Brothers of Stuttgart sold a series of translations of popular foreign novels called *Das belletristische Ausland* (3,618 volumes, 1843–1865) at prices that were "lower than the fees of a circulating library,"[28] and managed to garner 15,000 subscribers for it. That was an impressive figure by German standards; it included private individual buyers as well as lending libraries. But, it would have impressed no one in the English, French, or American book trades. In addition to *Das belletristische Ausland* there were other low-priced books on the German regular book market. But most of the time, the majority of German publishers were simply too conservative, or too afraid of financial disaster, to risk selling books at unusually low prices.

Actually, publishers and authors should have been grateful for the lending libraries, for without them the market for general books would have been much smaller. In spite of their unwillingness to buy any more books than they absolutely had to, circulating libraries did absorb a great many books. For one thing, they could not stay in business unless they bought whatever was in fashion, and fashions changed more and more quickly as the century went on. In the late 1850s it was estimated that the average lending library had six copies of *Soll und Haben* in stock.[29] Big libraries would have had more. Since *Soll und Haben* remained popular for decades, from time to time libraries had to buy new copies to replace those which had fallen apart from use. The same applied to any popular book.[30]

For much of the 1843–1866 period, the most frequently purchased, most popular, fiction continued to be foreign novels, usually in translation. In other words, the rage for English, French, American, and other foreign novels, begun in the 1820s with the Scott mania, retained its strength. In the 1840s the chief foreign novelists on the German book market were the Englishmen Bulwer-Lytton, Marryat, and Dickens; the Swede Frederike Bremer; and the French authors Dumas, Georges Sand, and Eugene Sue. Around 1845, requests for Dumas' *The Count of Monte Cristo* could have been heard daily in almost any lending library. The single most popular foreign author of the 1840s was Sue, translations of whose works were marketed by 20 different German publishers between 1842 and 1846. *The Wandering Jew* and the *Mysteries of Paris* were the most popular of Sue's novels with German readers. Eleven translations of the former appeared in 1844, while the latter inspired not only several translations but also several German imitations, like *Secrets of Berlin—from the Papers of a Berlin Law Enforcer* (*Die Geheimnissse von Berlin. Aus den Papieren eines Berliner Criminalbeamten*) Mayer and Hoffman Publishing Company,1844. The literary historian J. W. Appell reported with disgust that "ladies of the highest class" read Sue's *Mysteries of Paris* with "hot hunger."[31]

Sue's popularity faded after a few years. The 1850s found German publishers at each other's throats in order to get out the most successful translation of Harriet Beecher Stowe's *Uncle Tom's Cabin*. In 1853, in an attempt to scare away all the competition from producing editions of the novel, the Freiherz Brothers Publishing Company of Leipzig announced the most grandiose scheme in the history of nineteenth-century German publishing: there would be translations of Mrs. Stowe's novel into all of the nearly 200 German dialects used in Europe; each translation would be available in single-volume, multi-volume, and elegant miniature editions; to these would be added "editions for teenagers, editions for children up to age 13, and editions for sincere young virgins."[32] But that was not all—the entire "magnificent undertaking"[33] would be crowned "by the secret which we are now revealing: that ... the entire text is to be set to music, for which we have already engaged the services of the most highly-praised and highly-paid composers of both hemispheres."[34]

For unknown reasons, however, the Freiherz Brothers were unable to get a single volume onto the market. In any event, unveiling their plans had not deterred other publishers, 16 of whom had done editions of *Uncle Tom's Cabin* by 1856; these editions ranged in price from 18 New Groschen *(Neu-Groschen)* to one Reichsthaler 12 New Groschen. The Verlags Comptoir of Hamburg, a major producer of fodder for lending libraries, did a children's edition. Most of the 16 editions probably failed to repay their publishing costs—the novel market was vicious, and had far more losers than winners. Just as had been the case since the 1820s, the most successful edition of a foreign novel was often that which appeared first, because the public could not wait to read the latest fashionable thing. For its impatience the public was rewarded with shoddy, hastily done translations.[35]

Since many Germans could read French, and some could read English, novels in those languages were often read in the originals rather than in translation. French and Belgian publishers sold novels so cheaply that they had the French-language market in Germany to themselves; the market for English-language books in Germany (and the entire Continent), on the other hand, was in the hands of the Leipzig publisher Bernhard Tauchnitz, the originator of the great *Collection of British Authors*. Tauchnitz paid generous royalties to British and American authors to obtain the exclusive rights to publish and market their works on the Continent. It is difficult to say exactly how many of the readers of the *Collection* were German, since it was often stocked primarily for English and American travelers. The set now owned by the library of Johannes Gutenberg University in Mainz was acquired originally by a lending library in the small Taunus Mountain health resort of Schlangenbad, which had English-speaking as well as German visitors.[36]

## Erotic books

For those readers whose tastes ran to more stimulating matter than original language works by Bulwer or Dumas, Germany's publishers provided, and lending libraries purchased, erotic literature, most of it French in origin. The works of Paul de Kock, for example, were extremely popular, although hardly very titillating by present-day standards. De Kock's books were available in either French or German translations. Enterprising German publishers periodically reprinted the novels of Choderclos de Laclos and other erotic writers of the eighteenth century; the demand for such books was steady. In the late 1840s and early 1850s, a Stuttgart publisher produced a reprint of the 1775 *The Voluptuous Life of Capucin Monks and Nuns … (La Vie voluptueuse des Capucins et des Nonnes tirée de la confession d'un frère de cet ordre).* De Sade's *Justine* was also reprinted in Stuttgart; it had the high price—30 *Reichsthaler*— which signified really hot stuff. Presumably, the circulating libraries which acquired the book financed it by imposing a surcharge on those who wanted to borrow it. A. P. Reclam of Leipzig, later famous as the founder of the *Universalbibliothek*, in his younger and less responsible days, published a 61-volume series of piquant and erotic books called the *Bargain Entertainment Library for Cultured Readers (Wohlfeile Unterhaltungsbibliothek für die gebildete Lesewelt).* Even such prosperous and respectable houses as those of Brockhaus and Duncker and Humblot published erotic books.[37]

In the 1850s a few German publishers began to challenge the hegemony of the French erotic literature with pseudo-scientific analyses of prostitution and analogous topics. The leading publishers of such material were Edward Moses Heilbutt of Altona and August Prinz of Hamburg. Prinz' firm was located in St. Pauli, close to the action. A characteristic production was Heilbutt's 1859 *Prostitution in Hamburg or Secrets of the Dammthorwalle and the Schweiger Street (Die Hamburger Prostitution oder die Geheimnisse des Dammthorwalles und der Schwiegerstraße),* the fourth installment of which covered such matters as "the latest happenings in the realm of prostitution and immorality."[38] Outcries from within the trade against this and other erotic literature were frequent but ineffectual.[39]

There is no evidence that the native erotica produced by Heilbutt and Prinz ended reader interest in foreign erotica, but its success did show that German writers could appeal to a larger body of readers than previously. In the 1860s, as the great popular writers of England and the USA were growing old or dying, German novelists and poets began to dominate the popular book market and the shelves of the lending libraries for the first time in over 40 years. To be sure, there had always been some German authors of great general popularity, like Wilhelm Hauff, the Austrian Ludwig Donin (1810–1876), Carl Postl, Charles Sealsfield (1793–1864), and Countess Ida von Hahn-Hahn. Such novels as Friedrich Wilhelm Hackländer's (1816–1877) *Bilder aus dem Soldatenleben* (1840, 8th printing 1873), Karl Gutzkow's (1811–1878) *Die Ritter vom Geiste* (Leipzig 1850–1851, reprinted five times despite its great length of nine volumes), Luise Mühlbach's *Friedrich der Große und sein Hof* (1853), Ludwig Rellstab's (1853) *1812: Ein Historischer Roman* (1834, 6th printing 1891) had long been lending library staples. But ever since the Scott mania, one foreign author after another had been the chief rage in Germany.[40]

## German writers increase in popularity

Now, in the 1860s, native writers became supreme in the popular book market, although none of them had much appeal outside of the German-speaking countries. The most popular writers of the 1860s were Berthold

Auerbach (1812–1882) with his *Schwarzwälder Dorfgeschichten* and his other stories, and Josef Viktor von Scheffel, whose *Ekkehard Historischer Roman aus dem Jahre 1000* (1855) was easily the most popular novel of the entire second half of the nineteenth century, with 375,000 copies in print by 1910. Scheffel was also an extremely popular poet. Auerbach had first published his *Schwarzwälder Dorfgeschichten* in 1842. With each succeeding decade, the sales of these stories rose; by 1870, 75,000 copies of each volume had been sold, and sales were still rising. Auerbach's publisher, Georg von Cotta, paid him higher royalties for his collected works than the original Cotta had paid Goethe for the *Ausgabe letzter Hand*. Every reprinting of one of Auerbach's books was of 7,500 copies, several times the size of a normal reprinting. Slightly less popular than Scheffel and Auerbach were the adventure writers Friedrich Gerstäcker (1816–1872) and Gottfried Keller, whose best-loved works were *Der grüne Heinrich* (1854–1855) and *Die Leute von Seldwyla* (1856). Like Scheffel and Auerbach, these writers remained popular throughout the remainder of the century.[41]

While novels and stories were purchased almost exclusively by circulating libraries, several other types of book were purchased both by libraries and by individuals. These were: poetry, classics, children's literature, and popularizations of scientific and scholarly themes.

Until about 1840, most poetry had sold poorly. After that date, however, it grew rapidly in popularity, and the works of the most popular poets came to outsell every other type of fiction. Ferdinand Freiligrath's first book of poetry (it was non-political) was issued to the tune of 35,000 copies between 1837 and 1868. Twent-thousand copies of Klaus Groth's *Quickborn*, a book of low German poems about everyday life, were sold between its publication in 1852 and 1870. Emanuel Geibel's folksy *Gedichte* was so popular that it was reprinted almost 50 times between 1840 and 1860—and 80 times after 1860 (130th, 1903). More exotic but equally popular were the poems in Friedrich Bodenstedt's *Die Lieder des Mirza Schaffy*; they purported to be translations of folk songs of the Caucasus (Berlin 1851, 110th printing 1884, 161st printing 1902). Karl Gerok's *Palmbätter* (Stuttgart 1857, 130th printing 1900) was "one of the standard items in every middle-class home library and above all a beloved (if not always read) gift book."[42] Its main appeal was to women, as was that of the very popular anthology of poetry edited by Elise Polko, *Dichtergrüsse* (1860, 300th printing 1900).[43]

The most popular single type of poetry was the sentimental, pseudo-Gothic verse epic, which appealed to women who found novels too crude and realistic. Gottfried Kinkel's *Otto der Schütz* (Stuttgart and Tübingen 1846) first showed the female public how thrilling pseudo-Gothic epics could be; the work was reprinted 79 times by 1900. Three years later, Oscar v. Redwitz released his *Amaranth* (35th printing 1884, 44th printing 1904); five years later came Otto Roquette's *Waldmeisters Brautfahrt* (100th printing 1924), and eight years after this appeared the most widely circulated volume of poetry in the history of nineteenth century Germany, Joseph Viktor von Scheffel's *Der*

*Trompeter von Säckingen* (Stuttgart 1854, 100th printing 1882, 300th printing 1914). Scheffel was the greatest master of popular writing the German book trade had yet seen.[44]

Little of the most-read poetry of that era is read today. Some of the poets of that time, now considered classic, were fairly popular then however; others were not. The poetry of Mörike and Droste-Hülshoff sold very slowly. That of Rückert, Lenau, Heine, and above all Uhland did much better in the marketplace. Uhland's *Gedichte* had to be reprinted annually in the 1850s and 1860s; at first the reprinting amounted to 1,000 to 2,000 copies, later it was larger.[45]

The market for the German classics, growing ever since the early 1820s, was by now quite large. At mid-century, Goethe and Schiller were the most popular of the German classic writers, thousands of copies of their works being sold yearly in a variety of editions by the Cotta Publishing Company. The works of Jean Paul, Lessing, and Körner sold well, too, but those of Hölderlin had little popular appeal. Of non-German classics, the plays of Shakespeare were by far the most often purchased works, rivalling Goethe and Schiller in sales. The classics of Antiquity still had a large market as school texts.[46]

## Children's books

Children's books commanded a very large market, especially at Christmas and Easter. In Germany's middle class were many people who would rarely buy books for themselves but often got books for their progeny, hoping to inspire the children with that love of culture's higher endeavors which separated respectable people from the beer-sodden canaille. These people were confronted with an "almost unbelievable number" of books.[47] A Nurnberg teacher named G. W. Hopf, author of a critical guide to children's literature, observed in 1849 that:

> The mass of children's literature has already grown gigantic. From all sides flood in entertaining stories for children; ... then there are calendars for children, cheap magazines translated from English, ...encyclopedias and fliers, and other books with enticing titles ... good, mediocre, and bad in motley variety.[48]

Hopf's guide was intended to help parents and friends confused by the large volume of available works. As of about 1850 there were approximately nine other such critical guides on the market, too—some indication of the number of people who were anxious to buy children's books.[49]

In the maelstrom of books for children, some of the older, classic children's literature continued to hold its own in popularity. This was true above all of Campe's *Robinson der Jüngere* (1779–1780, 102nd printing 1881). The most beloved of the contemporary children's authors were Gustav Nieritz,

Christoph Schmid, Johann Wilhelm Hey, and Heinrich Hoffmann. Their stories "deeply influenced the attitudes and opinions of middle-class and rural children."[50] At least one million copies of works by each of the four were sold by the end of the century.

Both Nieritz and Schmid were extremely prolific writers and well-known public figures. Nieritz, for example, was "the most famous secular author" in Germany at that time.[51] Schmid, whose life was considered a model for children to follow, was the most honored and beloved Catholic children's author of his time. All of Augsburg turned out to celebrate his eighty-fifth birthday in 1848. The best known of Schmid's stories were "*Die Ostereier*" and "*Weihnachtsabend*"; these and other stories were issued in a variety of editions by the publisher Georg Josef Manz. Nieritz was a more controversial character than Schmid; some accused him of writing un-Christian stories that were unfit for children to read. But his 117 stories had literally millions of admirers; among them two little Hannoverian princesses who wrote him in 1860 to

> express our sincere thankfulness to you for the many happy hours your books have given us.... We hope that dear God will allow you yet many more vigorous years and a joyful old age, because you have given children so much joy.[52]

Hey and Hoffmann wrote far less than Nieritz and Schmid and were not as well-known as individuals. Nonetheless, their few works were enormously popular. Hey, a preacher had his *50 Fables for Children (50 Fabeln for Kinder)* published by Perthes in 1833; the books were illustrated with woodcuts and line drawings by Otto Specter. A few years later Hey and Specter again collaborated to produce the *Noch Fünfzig Fabeln in Bildern*. According to Horst Kunze, the two works "can without exaggeration be called one of the greatest book successes of the 19th Century."[53] Hoffmann's *Struwelpeter* has been an enormous success from its publication by Rütten and Loening of Frankfurt/Main in 1845 down to the present day. The first edition, of 1,500 copies, was sold out in four weeks. Hoffmann himself was not even a writer, but rather a nerve doctor who wrote the book because he did not think there were suitable books available for his child.[54]

German children—and adults—read a great deal of non-fiction as well as works of imagination. There was a great appetite for books which would explain natural history, for example. The Ensslin and Laiblin Publishing Company of Reutlingen did very well with its *Wunderbuch für die Jugend* by J. E. Gailer and its *Naturhistorisches ABC und Bilderbuches* by Friedrich Hoffmann, both published after 1850. Countless thousands of adults read W. F. A. Zimmermann's *Die Wunder der Urwelt* (Berlin 1855) and Friedrich Schoedler's *Das Buch der Natur* (2 volumes, Brunswick 1846).[55] Published by Gustav Hempel of Berlin, Zimmermann's book went through 10 printings in its first year and 24 additional ones by 1898, while his other popularizations of natural science did very well too. His background was not scientific—he had begun his writing career with mediocre lascivious novels—but the public certainly liked the ways in which he interpreted science. Schoedler had more impressive credentials as a scientific writer, having had been an assistant to Justus Liebig for several years and having participated in major scientific expeditions. His *Das Buch der Natur* was re-issued 23 times before the century ended and was translated into six other European languages.[56]

## Humboldt's *Kosmos*

The greatest scientific book of the age, both in sales and in the estimation of contemporaries, was Alexander von Humboldt's *Kosmos* (5 volumes 1845–1862), a cosmology based upon physics, laid down to an awe-stricken world by a man whose cultural standing at that time rivalled Goethe's, a man who the *Allgemeine deutsche Biographie* called the "crowned monarch of science."[57] Humboldt was paid the highest royalties of any German author of the nineteenth century by his publisher, Georg v. Cotta. Cotta's generosity was rewarded: although each volume cost more than three Reichsthaler, Cotta sold 37,000 copies of volume I and 35,000 of volume II; volumes III, IV, and V were more technical and difficult, yet 15,000 copies of each were sold. Contemporaries believed that at mid-century, only the Bible was read more. When the book first appeared, demand was so great that shipments destined to be sent abroad were plundered instead. People employed fisticuffs to get copies.[58]

Although the popularity of works explaining science was high, the market for religious books among the middle class had hardly dried up. Zschokke's *Stunden der Andacht* was as popular as ever, and was displayed proudly in home libraries and on the shelves of circulating libraries alike.[59] More than 80,000 copies of individual volumes of H. A. W. Meyer's scholarly 17-volume critical commentary on the *New Testament* were published in the 1850s and 1860s by a Göttingen publisher. One of the best-selling authors of the 1850s was Christian Bunsen (1791–1860), scholar, advisor to the Prussian court, friend of Alexander v. Humboldt, and author of hymnals and of books which reassured the faithful that their beliefs were still strong and valid, like *God in History, or the Progress of Faith in the Moral World Order* (*Gott in der Geschichte, oder der Fortschritt des Glaubens an die sittliche Weltordnung*, 3 volumes, Leipzig, 1857–1858). Bunsen's *Die Zeichen der Zeit. Briefe an Freunde über die Gewissensfreiheit und das Recht der christlichen Gemeinde* (2 volumes, Leipzig 1855) criticized both Ultramontanes and Protestant divines who were opposed to German unification. It spun rapidly through three editions.[60]

While interest in religious works was holding its own, interest in historical works was rising. After 1850, historical novels were increasingly popular. The historian Leopold von Ranke's books sold unusually well for scholarly works. The old standard general histories by Becker, Kohlrausch, and Rotteck continued to sell steadily, although the censors gave Rotteck's publishers difficulties in the aftermath of the 1848 Revolutions. (The conservative counterpart to Rotteck's work, Heinrich Leo's *Lehrbuch der Universalgeschichte* [1839–1841] did not sell nearly as well as Rotteck's book). Of popular histories written during that time, Gustav Freytag's *Pictures from the German Past (Bilder aus der deutschen Vergangenheit)*, published by Solomon Hirzel in 1859, was the most successful in the marketplace; it became, and long remained, the most beloved of all works on German history. Friedrich Föster's *Prussia's Heroes in War and Peace (Preußens Helden in Krieg und Frieden* 7 volumes, finished 1861) made its way onto so many bookshelves in Prussia that it went through seven large printings by 1877. Its publisher, Gustav Hempel had issued it in three different formats to appeal to different pockets and tastes.[61]

## Influences on popular tastes

As always, contemporary interests and issues influenced the public's taste in books about the past, and astute publishers made sure that there were books to meet these tastes. Growing social and political unrest during the 1840s, for example, was one reason why Dahlmann's *Geschichte der englischen Revolution* went through four printings in three years (1843–1846). Two decades later, when Louis Napoleon was successfully masquerading as Europe's mightiest statesman, intense interest built up in the book trade and among the public when it was learned that the French Emperor had written a biography of Julius Caesar. From the moment the word of this book's existence leaked out of Paris; through the agonies of the German publishers who vied with one another for the rights to an exclusive German translation, through the news that the Sultan had ordered it translated into Turkish, through the attempt by a Berlin publisher to issue a cheap unauthorized edition— through all this, as event piled upon event, the suspense and excitement grew to an unbearable pitch. Neither the public nor the trade could have withstood it much longer.

Fortunately, events moved rapidly forward. Having won the right to produce the German-language translation, the Gerold Publishing Company of Vienna shipped six tons of copies of the book, *Das Leben Caesars*, by rail from the Austrian capitol to Leipzig to prime the German trade for official publication day. This was barely enough: on publication day, March 9, 1865, 14,000 copies were sold between 7 a.m. and 10 a.m. Within a few months, 10,000 copies of an expensive luxury edition had been sold in Germany (in addition to 6,000 copies of French-language editions); for those of slender means the publisher released the book in cheap sections as well, 20,000 copies of each section every week. Some booksellers became so intoxicated by the furor that they ordered far more copies of the book than they could sell, but sales were high until the popularity of the book burned itself out about a year later. Had France triumphed in 1870–1871, the biography might have enjoyed a revival; as it was, however, it was quickly forgotten, like the reputation of its author.[62]

History books were, then, popular. So too were travel books, whether guides for those intending to travel or descriptions of exotic places and journeys intended to be read in comfortable chairs at home. Actually, both types were read for diversion, though some readers did use the guidebooks on their own travels. The most famous travel guides of the era were those written by Karl Baedeker, who died in 1859. Baedeker's guides sold very well, but it is impossible to determine how many were purchased by Germans and how many by other Europeans, especially in the case of the guide to the Rhine's wonders. Felix Mendelssohn-Bartholdy's *Reisebriefe* was a popular travel description issued in numerous editions by the Leipzig house of Avenarius and Mendelssohn. The most successful travel description of the era, however, was Karl v. Scherzer's *The Voyage of the Austrian Frigate Novara 1857 until 1859 (Reise der oesterreichischen Fregatte Novara 1857 bis 1859)*, an account of the first expedition to circumnavigate the globe made by Germans (Austrians). The expedition had aroused the interest and pride of all Germans, no matter whether they lived in Austria or in one of the other German states, and it is certain that most of the 28,000 copies of Scherzer's book sold by 1864 were purchased in Germany, the Austrian book market being too small to have absorbed anywhere near that many.[63]

## Practical information books: bulwark of the German book trade

Finally we come to one of the great bulwarks of the German book trade: the practical information books found in home, office, and workshop libraries, the books which were purchased by people who otherwise never bought books—the handbooks, encyclopedias, and reference books which so many would not do without. This was the only category of secular books that were sold to more individuals than lending institutions. Hundreds were published. Quite a few became great successes on the market. Ninety-thousand copies of Carl Ernest Bock's health care manual *Das Buch vom gesunden und kranken Menschen* were sold between 1854 and 1870, despite its price of nearly two Reichsthaler. Baron Ernst von Feuchtersleben's guide to mental health *Zur Diätetik der Seele*, went through 42 printings, between 1844 and 1874. Few books could equal the sales of successful dictionaries like the German–French, French–German dictionaries of Thibaut and Mole. Between its publication early in the century and 1873, 365,000 copies of the Thibaut were sold; Mole's competitive work did nearly as well. Thousands and thousands of copies of books on such topics as how to write letters, how to run various businesses, how to compliment and flatter people, and related subjects were sold year in and year out.

Year-in-and-year-out encyclopedias continued to fill the coffers of their publishers with Florins and Reichsthaler as they filled the minds of middle- and upper-class Germans with the rudiments of respectable knowledge.

Joseph Meyer's *Konversationslexikon* (1839–1855) had 70,000 subscribers in the mid-1840s, though censorship and other problems reduced that number after 1848. Coming out with a de-liberalized encyclopedia the censors could not fault, Meyer's son Hermann was able to sell almost 40,000 sets in the 1860s, while the Brockhaus Company continued to do very well selling both the longer and the shorter versions of its encyclopedia.[64]

## Notes

1 Bertheau, *Geschichte der Buchhandlung W. Mauke Soehne*, p. 98.
2 From Meyer's "Program zur Vertrieb," quoted in Hohlfeld, *Das Bibliographische Institut*, p. 217.
3 Quoted in ibid., p. 217.
4 Ibid., p. 217.
5 August Lewald, *Das Buch der Gesellschaft. Fuer angehende Weltleute*, Stuttgart 1847, p. 47.
6 Ibid., p. 45.
7 Ibid., pp. 45–46.
8 Wolfgang Langenbucher, "Das Publikum im literarischen Leben des 19. Jahrhunderts," in: *Der Leser als Tell des literarischen Lebens*, Bonn 1971, pp. 65–66.
9 Langenbucher, "Das Publikum im literarischen Leben," p. 61; Magill, "The German Author and his Public in the Mid-Nineteenth Century," entire.
10 Magill, "The German Author and his Public in the Mid-Nineteenth Century," pp. 494–495.
11 Prinz, *Bausteine*, vol. VII, pp. 71–74.
12 *Börsenblatt*, 1853, p. 2021.
13 Widmann, *Der deutsche Buchhandel in Urkunden und Quellen*, vol. I, p. 103.
14 *Börsenblatt*, 1876, Nr. 263, p. 4173.
15 Lewald, *Das Buch der Gesellschaft*, pp. 50–52. He did caution against allowing children to visit lending libraries alone, as they might be corrupted by the racy material these libraries often stocked.
16 *Börsenblatt*, 1860, Nr. 11, p. Ib5.
17 Recognizing the importance of libraries as markets for scholarly books, both the *Börsenblatt* and the *Bibliopolisches Jahrbuch* printed lists of libraries, giving addresses, holdings, and so forth; the aim was to make publishers and booksellers aware of the library market.
18 Leyh, "Die deutschen Bibliotheken von der Aufklaerung bis zur Gegenwart," pp. 194, 221, 225.
19 Ibid., pp. 243–244.
20 Figures from Heidelberg show that, of 4,248 volumes acquired between 1836 and 1839, 470 were "compulsory copies" and 324 were gifts. The rest were purchased, but there is no record of how many of them were foreign or used books.
21 *Bibliopolisches Jahrbuch*, 1841, pp. 69–70.
22 "Aus Bayern," *Börsenblatt*, 1866, Nr. 39, p. 791.
23 E. R., "Die Leihbibliothek," *Börsenblatt*, 1858, Nr. 145, pp. 2259–2261.
24 E. R., "Die Leihbibliothek," *Börsenblatt*, 1858, Nr. 145, pp. 2259–2261, maintains that one "Prince X" threw lending library books at his dogs during frequent fits of temper; although facetious, the story has a ring of truth.
25 "Fuer und wider die Leihbibliotheken in frueheren Tagen." pp. 581–582; R. Altick, *The English Common Reader*, Oxford 1957.
26 On the German best-sellers see: "Buecherabsatz in Deutschland," *Börsenblatt*, 1859, pp. 588–589.

27 On book sales in Great Britain, France, and the USA, see: *Börsenblatt*, 1853, Nr. 17, p. 207. On sales of popular American books during the nineteenth century, see J. D. Hart, *The Popular Book: A History of America's Literary Taste*, New York 1950, pp. 67–200.

28 So screamed one of their prospects in the 1840s; quoted in Hiller, *Zur Sozialgeschichte von Buch und Buchhandel*, p. 42.

29 E. R. "Die Leihbibliothek," *Börsenblatt*, 1858, Nr. 145, pp. 2259–2261.

30 Nutz, *Der Trivialroman*, pp. 100–101.

31 Appell, *Die Ritter-, Raeuber- und Schauerromantik*, p. 79; Appell considered Sue to be a deranged opium-eater and a wicked influence; see pp. 79–81.

32 *Börsenblatt*, 1853, Nr. 39, p. 1388.

33 *Börsenblatt*, 1853, Nr. 7, p. 76.

34 Ibid., p. 76.

35 Ibid., p. 76.

36 Prinz, *Bausteine*, vol. III, pp. 70–71.

37 Tauchnitz established a good reputation among British and American authors by paying royalties before there was any international copyright compelling him to do so. See *Fuenfzig Jahre der Verlagshandlung Bernhard Tauchnitz*, pp. 16–29.

38 Appell, *Die Ritter-, Raeuber- und Schauerromantik*, pp. 87–88.

39 *Börsenblatt*, 1859, Nr. 2, p. 23.

40 *Börsenblatt*, 1859, Nr. 7, p. 92, Nr. 14, p. 203, Nr. 23, pp. 363–364.

41 Kunze, *Lieblings-Buecher*, pp. 212–213, 222, 231, 233, 235; Schenda, *Volk ohne Buch*, pp. 147, 457.

42 *Börsenblatt*, 1870, Nr. 273, p. 3704; *Deutsches Buecherverzeichnis. Eine Zusammenstellung der imdeutschen Buchhandel erschienenen Buecher, Zeitschriften und Landkarten*, vol. I Leipzig 1916, p. 1407—hereafter known as *DBV*.

43 Kunze, *Lieblings-Buecher*, p. 297.

44 Ibid., pp. 238, 291–292, 297.

45 In 1882 Scheffel wrote his thanks to: "Women and Children all, who year in and year out order new copies of The Trumpeter" ("Den Frauen und Jungfrauen all/ Und all den guten Gesellen,/Die in der Heimat jahraus, jahrein/Sich neu den Trompeter bestellen."). Quoted in Schulze, *Der deutsche Buchhandel*, p. 121.

46 Krieg, *Materialien zu einer Entwicklungsgeschichte der Buecher-Preise*, pp. 128–129.

47 Meiner, *Reclam*, p. 13.

48 So exclaimed a Hamburg educator in 1844; quoted in Schenda, *Volk ohne Buch*, p. 83.

49 G. W. Hopf, quoted in Schenda, *Volk ohne Buch*, p. 84.

50 Bernhardi, *Wegweiser durch die deutschen Volks- und Jugendschriften*, pp. 121–122, lists and evaluates these guides, and finds Hopf's the best.

51 Schenda, *Volk ohne Buch*, p. 163.

52 Ibid., p. 170.

53 Letter of Princesses Frederike and Mary, June 5, 1860; reprinted in G. Nieritz, *Selbstbioraphie* (Leipzig 1872), pp. 456–457.

54 Kunze, *Lieblings-Buecher*, p. 424.

55 A. Frommhold, "Ruetten & Loening. Ein Rueckblick auf 125 Jahre Verlagsgeschichte," pp. 9–89 of *Hundert-fuenfundzwanzg Jahre Ruetten & Loening 1844–1969. Ein Almanach*, Berlin 1969, p. 33.

56 The sub-title of Zimmermann's book was: *Eine populaere Darstellung der Geschichte der Schopefung und des Urzustandes unseres Weltkoerpers sowie der verschieden Entwicklungsperioden seiner Oberfliche, seiner Vegetation und seine Bewohner bis auf die Jetztzeit. Begruendet auf die Resultate der Forschung und Wissenschaft.*

57 On Zimmermann, see: *Börsenblatt* 1864, Nr. 135, p. 2408.

58 *Allgemeine Deutsche Biographie*, vol. XIII, p. 382.

59 Lohrer, *Cotta*, pp. 102.

60 *Börsenblatt* 1866, Nr. 148, p. 2654.

61 Ruprecht, *Vaeter und Soehne*, pp. 142, 178, 184.
62 These formats were: (1) a seven-volume set, (2) a one-volume edition, (3) an edition which appeared in the form of many small, individually inexpensive segments; see Sabell, ed. (*sic*), "Gustav Hempel," *Börsenblatt* 1877, Nr. 29, p. 472.
63 The whole story is in the *Börsenblatt*: 1865, Nr. 22, pp. 395–96, Nr. 25, p. 460, Nr. 26, p. 480.
64 Of the 28,000 copies, 21,000 were of a cheap edition, 2,000 of a luxury edition and 5,000 of a conventionally-priced edition. See "Die Volksausgabe von K. V. Scherzers 'Reise der Novara'" *Börsenblatt* 1864, p. 1082.

# 7 Good times, 1867–1888
## The middle- and upper-class book market after mid-century

Without great drama, without any spectacular innovations in marketing or luminescent personalities among bookmen, the regular trade had, by 1866, made a thorough recovery from its mid-century decline. Its growth during the next two decades was to be explosive, as a happy combination of historical and other circumstances served to stimulate the second great era of expansion of the nineteenth century.

### "Freeing" the German classics—1867

Things got off to a vigorous start in 1867 with one of the most dramatic events in the history of the German book trade, the "freeing" of the German classics into the public domain on November 9 of that year. This touched off the biggest buying boom ever experienced by the trade. The decision to free the classics in 1867 had been made by the Bundestag of the German Confederation 11 years before—a fine example of how earlier events contributed to the economic boom of the Founding Years. The only firm which had much to lose by the decision was the Cotta Publishing Company, which for decades had enjoyed a near-monopoly on the German classics of the late eighteenth and early nineteenth centuries. Cotta's impending plight engendered little sympathy, since it was generally believed that the firm had forfeited its right to custodianship of the national classics by issuing too many sloppily printed, inadequately annotated, poorly edited, and over-priced editions.[1]

For most bookmen, for the reading public and for cultural leaders, the end of Cotta's dominance over the national classics was a joyous event. A typical reaction was the wild enthusiasm expressed by a writer in the *National Zeitung*:

> The year 1867 will … mark an important phase, not only in the development of the German book trade, but also in the entire development of our cultural life. With joyous expectation one sees the time nearing when hundreds and thousands of canals will carry the works of their heroes to the German people, when the hand of the worker will reach for his copy … of Schiller, of Lessing.[2]

Some of that was, of course, only wishful thinking. In 1867, as in any other year, the "hand of the worker" would more likely be reaching for a beer or brandy glass; when it did reach for something to read, it certainly was not for a classic, but more likely for a dream or prayer book or a violent and sensationalistic pamphlet.

The hand of the middle- or upper-class German, though, would reach eagerly for its own copies of the classics—if it could afford them. We have seen repeatedly that the classics were among that small group of books which Germans would actually consider purchasing for their home bookshelves rather than borrowing from a circulating library. Prior to 1867, many middle-class Germans had been unable to afford their own copies of the classics—even the cheap editions of Schiller and Goethe by Cotta, and the pirated editions by men like Spitz and Meyer, had been too costly for them. Now, however, these people would get editions they could afford, truly inexpensive editions. A. P. Reclam's *Universal-Bibliothek*, for example, offered both parts of Goethe's *Faust* for four Groschen, or entire plays by Schiller for two Groschen. In a last attempt to salvage something of its classics trade, Cotta offered a 12-volume edition of Schiller's complete works for one Reichsthaler, a quarter of the price of the immensely successful Schiller edition of the late 1830s, only two-tenths the price of the "pocket" edition of the 1820s.[3]

So great was the demand for such cheap classics, that printers in Leipzig and Berlin were busy stamping them out in quantity for almost two years before they could be sold. When the Cotta monopoly finally did end, book stores were thronged as never before. An employee in a Berlin book shop happily observed that:

> The book trade has brought much that is new and elegant to the Christmas table, and for the first time there are things for those of moderate means. It is truly heartening to see the undreamed of enormity of sales of the classics. We alone always order copies of Schiller, Goethe, and Lessing by the hundreds and can sell them using only a simple display in our show window. Several publishers of cheap editions of the classics have sold out printings of 500,000 copies in a matter of days.[4]

The market for classics in late 1867 and early 1868 was the largest market for any one type of book ever seen in Germany.

## The boom keeps going

The boom touched off by the liberation of the classics kept going even after the first great wave of classics buying was over. In 1868, 10,563 titles were published in Germany, the first time in two decades that the 10,000 level had been exceeded. By 1877, 13,925 titles appeared—a figure which was greater than for the previous record year of 1843. After 1877 production climbed still more (see Table 7.1).

*Table 7.1* Number of titles published, 1879–1888

| Year | Number of titles published (including reprints) |
|------|--------------------------------------------------|
| 1879 | 14,179 |
| 1881 | 15,191 |
| 1885 | 16,305 |
| 1888 | 17,016 |

Note
Figures are from J. Goldfriedrich, *Geschichte des deutschen Buchhandels vom Beginn der Fremdher rschaft bis zur Reform des Boersenvereins im neuen deutschen Reiche, 1805–1889*, Leipzig 1913, p. 487.

Thus the number of titles published annually had increased by 62 percent between 1868 and 1888.[5]

It is true that an increase in the number of titles did not necessarily indicate a corresponding rise in the sales of books. But a fullness of evidence indicates that the number of books sold did rise dramatically after 1867. In 1865, for example, German book retailers ordered approximately 16,000,000 Marks worth of books from Leipzig publishers' agents, those middlemen between publishers and retail book sellers. A decade later they ordered 30,000,000 Marks worth; since the average price of books declined slightly between 1865 and 1875, the number of books ordered must have more than doubled. Gerhard Menz, one of the most intelligent historians of the German book trade, estimates that the trade's total sales rose from 25,000,000 Marks in 1865 to 55,000,000 Marks in 1875, then continued to rise further. As personal incomes rose, asserts Menz, per capita expenditures on books rose: where each German spent 64 Pfennig per year for books in the late 1860s, he or she was spending nearly double that (1.20 Marks per year) in 1875.[6]

The steady growth in the number of book dealers, both publishers and retailers, is another reflection of rising book sales, because this growth could only have been sustained by a growing market. The number of book dealers in the German book trade increased by 105 percent during the two decades from 1865 to 1885, from 3,079 to 6,304.[7] These figures include dealers located outside Germany itself, who amounted to about one-fifth of the total.[8]

Equally impressive was the growth in the number of dealers solely within Germany itself. In the Kingdom of Saxony, for example, the number of retail book shops more than doubled between 1867–1868 and 1890–1891.[9] For the rest of Germany too, growth was the order of the day. The number of dealers rose, and so did the number of cities and towns which had book dealers—from 786 municipalities with book dealers in 1875 to 1,140 in 1888.[10]

The book trade had grown faster than the population of the German Empire. Where there had been one regular book dealer to every 19,677 Germans in 1855, there was one to every 8,080 in 1888. (This included Alsace-Lorraine. In Germany outside of Alsace-Lorraine there was one regular book dealer to every 7,919 people in 1888.) As it always had been, the distribution of book dealers was uneven, being most dense in Central Germany and in large cities. In fact, over half of Germany's book dealers in 1888 were located in cities whose population was 50,000 and greater, although these cities contained only about one-eighth of the Empire's population. Yet there were 517 dealers located in towns of 5,000 and fewer people—something which could be said of few if any other countries, and there were impressive concentrations of dealers in medium-sized cities with universities or active cultural lives.

The reasons for the rapid growth of the book trade and its market after 1867 are many. In addition to the freeing of the classics, which had an exhilarating effect upon both bookmen and their customers, a rush of favorable political, social, and economic developments fueled the boom. These were:

1   the abolition of state and guild restrictions on entry into trades by the North German Confederation in 1868, which allowed dynamic new blood (as well as every other kind of blood) to enter the book trade;[11]
2   the weakening of state censorship, most notably by the Reich Press Law of 1874, which gave bookmen a rousing sensation of freedom;
3   the development of a national postal service by the new Empire, which made it possible for both publishers and retailers to mail books much more cheaply and to have to rely less on slow freight service;
4   the growth of the universities, and of academic education in general, which provided a larger pool of educated readers;[12]
5   the growth of cities, especially large cities, whose population had more potential book buyers and readers per capita than smaller cities, towns, and rural areas;[13] and
6   the general economic boom of the Founding Years, which gave more people greater means with which to acquire such luxuries as books.[14]

Technological advances were another booster for the book market at that time. The introduction of the rotary press to Germany in 1873, the use of the wood cellulose process in paper making in the 1870s, and, the invention of an effective binding machine in 1878 made it easier and cheaper than ever for publishers to do large editions of inexpensive books. The cellulose process, for example, made it possible to produce wood pulp paper which was reasonably decent in quality yet low in price. Advances in binding technology encouraged more and more publishers to issue their books already bound.[15]

## The key to growth: aggressive marketing

Yet these developments in themselves could not have caused the book market to expand as much as it did; they were less the causes of the market's growth than a series of opportunities, of potentialities, which were exploited by energetic bookmen to cause growth. As had been true in all the eras surveyed in this essay, the crucial factor in the market's growth in the era after 1867 was the response of book dealers—especially publishers—to the opportunities they were presented with. Had the conservative attitudes of the immediate post-Napoleonic period still dominated the trade in 1867–1888, most bookmen would have considered it beneath their dignity to exploit the potentialities for growth which economic, technological, and political trends had brought about; they would have scorned a growing book market as degrading to the trade. But by 1867, these traditional attitudes were nearly extinct. To be sure, the *Börsenblatt* still ran crotchety articles lamenting the "misery" of the German book trade, which was attributed to the influx of people from other fields into the book trade and to aggressive modern business practices. Often reading as if they had been lifted verbatim from the pages of the *Krieger'sche Wochenblatt* of 50 and 60 years before, these articles did not reflect the general attitude of the trade—few desired to go back to the "good old days" idyllically depicted in them. They were merely indications of a lachrymose nostalgia which infected some German bookmen when they became old and confused.[16]

By 1867 the vigorous entrepreneurship pioneered by Brockhaus, Meyer, the Franckhs, and others in the earlier decades of the century was accepted by an overwhelming majority of German book dealers, especially publishers, as the essence of modern business practice, and modern business practice was what the trade wanted to follow. Low prices, huge editions, showy advertising, premiums, and gimmicks—things once reviled by the trade were now enthusiastically practiced by it. From the radical creed of a daring few, modern business practice had picked up adherents during every decade since the 1820s, and by 1867 was the dominant creed of Germany's regular book trade.

It was modern business practice to stimulate the market, attempting to make it larger than it would otherwise have been. The history of the German book trade from 1867 to 1888 is rich in examples of market stimulation, and of publishers seizing upon and exploiting opportunities. Much of the demand for classics in 1867 and 1868, for example, could have been met with lackluster editions priced a bit lower than Cotta's editions had been. Many people would have purchased editions even lethargically, and thousands did buy the uninspired but relatively inexpensive editions of the classics put out in 1867 by such houses as the Bibliographisches Institut and the Hendel Publishing Company of Halle.[17]

Other publishers, however, excited the public with innovative editions of the classics marketed with flair and fervor. The Brockhaus Company's *Library of German Literature of the 18th and 19th Centuries (Bibliothek der Deutschen Nationalliteratur des 18. und 19. Jahrhunderts)* had very carefully edited texts and good explanatory notes, two features which Cotta editions had not had. The *Hausbibliothek Deutscher Klassiker* published by the young Hamm publisher Carl Müller-Grote had illustrations, yet was priced at only eight Groschen per volume. The initial printings of 8,000 copies per volume were sold out in a few months. Gustav Hempel's *Nationalbibliothek*, one of the largest series issued by a German publisher in the nineteenth century (232 volumes in 600 sections appeared between 1867 and 1877), had neither explanatory notes nor illustrations, but its selling price of 25 Pfennig per section was very low. Hempel himself did much of the editing of texts of the earlier volumes, often working until midnight, because he knew that the series' initial volumes would determine its reputation with the public.[18]

## A big marketing campaign—Gustav Hempel

To sell the *Nationalbibliothek*, Hempel mounted one of the most massive marketing campaigns ever seen in Germany. Four million prospects and 300,000 letters were printed up for distribution to the public via retailers and by the publisher's own direct mailings. Several hundred thousand copies of Installment One of the series' first volume were distributed as samples to show people what the *Nationalbibliothek* would look like. Retailers were motivated to push the series because Hempel guaranteed them a 33.3 percent margin, larger than was common for popular books in those years. Hempel's earlier success with books like Förster's *PreuBens Helden* and Zimmermann's *Wunder der Urwelt* had convinced many retailers that any book published by Hempel was likely to sell well. Hempel's promotional efforts for the *Nationalbibliothek* generated so much excitement among bookmen and the reading public that mad rumors began to gather about the series months before its first volume was actually published. There were stories that it would eventually grow to 7,000 volumes, that it would take 280 years to be completed, that it had 100,000 subscribers—these and other wild conjectures filled the air. Forty-thousand people had actually subscribed to the series by March of 1867, eight months before the publication date of the first volume.

## Reclam's *Universal Library*

The greatest series to come out of the freeing of the classics was not Hempel's, however; it was Anton Philipp Reclam's *Universal-Bibliothek*, which is still being published today. Reclam (1807–1896) had been a bookman for nearly 40 years when he unveiled this series with Goethe's *Faust* in 1867. Reclam's idea had come from France, based on the *Bibliothek Charpentier*, which had been founded in Paris in 1838.[19] After early careers as a lending library operator and publisher of frivolous and erotic literature, he had turned to the speculative publishing of serious literature in the 1860s. In 1865–1867, for example, he produced an edition of Shakespeare. Reclam himself grew more serious and concerned with the state of culture as he aged; the *Universal-Bibliothek* was the great work of his maturity. The 100 volumes were issued before the end of 1868 and were heavily weighted towards the classics. Works by Shakespeare, Goethe, and Schiller comprised fully half of them; there were also works by Jean Paul, Lessing, Körner, Kleist, Hebel, Kotzebue, and E. T. A Hoffmann. In this respect the *Universal-Bibliothek* was no different than other series which began then. But it was soon broadened to include classics of world literature—ancient and modern—(in translation), new editions of forgotten but worthwhile books, and respectable light reading.

The *Universal-Bibliothek* had a physical format of such appeal that it was not changed at all for half a century and has never been fundamentally modified. Small, austerely printed, and covered with red paper, the volumes were inspired by and were a refinement of the "pocket" and "miniature" editions which various publishers had been issuing since the 1820s. The price of the volumes, two Groschen apiece, was amazingly low. Even more amazing, the volumes were sold individually: one did not have to subscribe to the whole series, or even part of it, which is why Reclam subtitled the series a "collection of *individual;* editions of universally beloved works" (italics mine). His advertising proudly stressed the advantage this had over all other German series:

> Since the volumes may be purchased individually, everyone is in a position to create a [personal] library according to his own taste and requirements, without being forced to take books he cares nothing about in order to get those which he does want.[20]

For the book buyer, a burden was removed; for the publisher, however, the security offered by subscriptions was gone. No other German publisher, not even Joseph Meyer, had ever dared to sell a large series as individual volumes. Reclam gambled that sales of the most popular works in the *Universal-Bibliothek* would more than cover the losses incurred by those which few people bought.

He further gambled that he could launch the series with only a moderate amount of advertising, with a few newspaper advertisements and a few circulars which were sent to booksellers. Reclam believed that high publicity costs could only be met by increasing the selling price of the books, something which he wanted to avoid. He met with some resistance from traditionalist booksellers, who questioned whether anything so cheap as the *Universal-Bibliothek* could have any value, or bring any profit; Reclam's response was to keep issuing new titles and to let the sales speak for themselves. They did. Despite modest advertising, the public quickly learned about the *Universal-Bibliothek*, and supported it so enthusiastically that Reclam was able to enlarge it constantly: to 120 titles by the end of 1868, then at a rate of 80 new titles per year until 1877, and 140 per year in the 1880s. Buyers included public libraries, Good Literature societies, theaters, and schools, but above all individual purchasers, who bought them either for themselves or to give as gifts.[21]

## The gift book market

Reclam's were not the only books to be purchased as gifts. Indeed, such purchases played an increasingly important role for many publishers and came to comprise an increasingly important segment of the book market in this period. Not that giving books as gifts was anything new; it was not. And publishers had long issued books which were intended to be gifts, such as the almanacs of the years before 1830 and the "miniature" editions of the 1850s. "Luxury editions," in which large size combined with lavish illustrations and such to offer subtle testimonial to good taste, had often been created and marketed as gift items by publishers.

Now, however, rising prosperity had vastly enlarged the potential of the gift book market; affluence had given the German middle class the means to indulge its long-repressed love of luxury and display, and since Germany was as afflicted as Britain and the USA with the general decline of taste of the last three decades of the century, practically any grotesque and ostentatious thing could satisfy the public's urge for luxury. Germany's publishers moved quickly and deftly to exploit this potential. A careful analysis of book-buying patterns in 1884 revealed that more general books—both fiction and non-fiction—were sold for gifts than for any other reason.[22]

Even novels and works of light fiction were now frequently purchased as gifts, where once they had been bought almost exclusively by lending libraries. To be sure, not all novels could be sold as gifts, only ones by popular and highly regarded authors; first novels and the works of lesser-known novelists were still sold only to circulating libraries. During the four months between October 1883 and January 1884, for example, a single Leipzig book store sold, mainly for gift purposes: 81 copies of novels by Felix Dahn, 101 novels by Georg Ebers, 55 novels by Conrad Ferdinand Meyer, and 186 novels by Gustav Freytag; it also sold 111 copies of books by the humorist Ernst Eckstein and 60 copies of J. V. v. Scheffel's *Ekkehard*. The recipients of these books were mainly women, the principal readers of novels in Germany (as elsewhere in Europe) at that time. Women also delighted to receive pretty editions of the poetry of Kinkel, Scheffel, Geibel, and other masters of the pseudo-Gothic epic.[23]

Women and children were the principal recipients of gift books. Their tastes must have been broad, since the gift book market included far more than novels, sugared epics, and children's books: publishers tried to cater to many tastes and to have gift books in many price ranges. Vandenhoeck and Ruprecht sold many copies of translations of books by Charles Kingsley, Frederick W. Robertson, and other English Christian Socialists in the 1880s as gifts. These authors appealed to the growing interest in social questions among educated Lutherans. Vandenhoeck and Ruprecht also published gift editions of Thomas Carlyle's *Memoirs* and his other books, all in German translation. Carl Müller-Grote's moderately priced *Hausbibliothek Deutscher Klassiker* was intended to be sold for gift purposes, as were most of the other editions of the classics (both ancient and modern) published at this time; the classics were believed to have a salutary effect on women and children.[24]

## "Luxury" editions

The success of the *Hausbibliothek* inspired (and financed) Müller-Grote's next major venture, costly "luxury" books. Following the hallowed conventions for such books, these were physically big—large quarto and folio sizes—and richly illustrated; some were made up entirely of illustrations. Examples include Bodenstedt's *Album deutscher Kunst und Dichtung*, an edition of Tennyson's *Enoch Arden* with illustrations by Thumann, an illustrated Goethe's *Faust*, Fritz Reuter's stories, and Shakespeare's plays. Most of these books, as most "luxury" and gift books in general, were done at the initiative of the publisher. Müller-Grote commissioned such noted artists of the time as Gabriel Max, Eduard Grützner, and the brothers Ferdinand and Carl v. Pilotz to illustrate his "luxury" editions. The most successful such work that he published was the artist Arthur v. Ramberg's book of illustrations of scenes from Goethe's *Hermann und Dorothea*.[25]

Other publishers found a ready market for fancy gift books, too. Bernhard Tauchnitz' display editions of the Greek and Latin classics were purchased to adorn the homes of many upper-middle-class Germans. Alphons Dürr of Leipzig published a lavish edition of the *Odyssey* illustrated by Preller in 1870; a third printing was required by 1876. Another Leipzig publisher, T. O. Weigel, issued many "luxury books", one of the Förster's *Monuments of German Architecture, Drawing, and Painting (Denkmale deutscher Baukunst, Bilderei und Malerei)*, which had over 600 plates and cost 150,000 Marks to produce. Eduard Hallberger of Stuttgart published the popular author Georg Ebers' *Egypt in Word and Picture (Aegypten in Wort und Bild)*, a fine example of conspicuous consumption which had 700 illustrations spread across its large folio pages. It cost 72 Marks, yet still sold well. Elaborate Bibles, a staple of the book market for centuries, still found many buyers in the Age of Blood and Iron. Typical was the five-volume "Illustrated Display Edition" of the Vulgate (in German translation) published by G. J. Manz from 1883 to 1885. Enriched with about 900 illustrations, it proved very popular even though the great Catholic scholar Döllinger pronounced the translation to be wretched. Literary value was the least important attribute of a "luxury" edition.[26]

In the 1880s, as "luxury" editions were more popular every year, the other end of the gift book spectrum began to be developed for the first time with the publication of large series of inexpensive books expressly designed to be given as gifts; earlier cheap series like Reclam's were not specifically designed as gift items, although they had often served that purpose. The cheap gift books were due to the initiative of a few publishers who saw that there would be a huge market for such items and who utilized the technological advances which made it possible to produce cheap yet very attractive books.

The first low-cost gift books were in the *Collection Spemann*, which the publisher Wilhelm Spemann began to publish on April 1, 1881. The first volume contained two stories by Louise von François; other volumes followed rapidly, as the *Collection* expanded to include novels, short stories (*Novellen*), travel descriptions, ancient and modern classics, and books on politics, history, and natural science. Each volume had about 250 pages and was bound in blue cloth with gold lettering on it—quite a bargain at a selling price of one Mark. It was Spemann's intention to keep the price so low that it was scarcely more than the cost of borrowing a book from a circulating library. The *Collection* was sold by subscription, with subscribers receiving a copy of the Goethe–Schiller correspondence as a premium.[27]

That Spemann had uncovered a strongly felt need was quickly shown by the *Collection's* high sales. In 1883 alone 550,000 copies of 81 titles were sold. Unfortunately for Spemann, his success inspired imitation by some able and powerful houses. In 1882 the house of Cotta, still the most prestigious name in German publishing, unveiled its *Bibliothek der Weltliteratur*. Although the books in Cotta's series were not completely identical to those in Spemann's, Cotta's having more classics, the physical appearance and price of the two were identical. Even the type used was the same.[28] In 1884 the Engelhorn Publishing Company of Stuttgart began publishing its *Allgemeine Romanbibliothek*, which was obviously inspired by the success of Cotta's and Spemann's gift series. Engelhorn's volumes were shorter than those in the earlier two series, averaging about 160 pages in length, but they were also cheaper, the volumes being available in paper covers at 50 Pfennig and in red cloth covers at 75 Pfennig apiece. Engelhorn was very fortunate in its choice of Georges Ohnet's *Der Hüttenbesitzer* as the first volume of the *Romanbibliothek*: the public's enthusiastic reception for this book got the series off to a fast start.[29]

Engelhorn's series became one of the great publishing successes of the later nineteenth century. Cotta's *Bibliothek der Weltliteratur* also achieved a "gigantic circulation."[30] Both owed some of their success to the customers they drew from the *Collection Spemann*, whose sales went into a tailspin. There is no doubt that many buyers preferred to have the prestigious Cotta name stamped on the books which they gave as gifts rather than the unknown name Spemann; in the world of gift books, appearances were everything. Moreover, Spemann's choice of books was not as gifted as those of Engelhorn and Cotta. Spemann attempted to win back customers by upgrading the contents of the series, even including in it 16 volumes of Bismarck's speeches, but by the late 1880s the decline of the *Collection* had proven to be irreversible. Allowed to die in 1891, its fate was indicative of the intense competition among bookmen in this period, when the public was cajoled, exhorted, and enticed more than ever before by rival publishers to buy their books as gifts.

## Christmas catalogs

A great deal of this cajoling, exhortation, and enticement was done by publishers in the profusion of Christmas catalogs, which were issued during these
years and in which anywhere from one to scores of publishers advertised their
wares for the Christmas market. They had been developed and used earlier,
but in the two decades after 1867 their number and the use of them by publishers increased considerably, until by 1888 there were complaints from
bookmen that there were too many of them and that it cost too much to
place advertising in all of them. The older catalogs published by Hinrichs and
Volckmar continued to be published, joined now by many others.

In the 1880s three religiously-oriented Christmas catalogs were instituted,
two for Catholics and one for Protestants. They were reactions to what the
pious perceived as inadequate coverage of religious works as well as too much
coverage of anti-religious literature in the existing Christmas catalogs. The
Protestant entry was entitled *Treasury of Books for Christians (Der Bücherschatz
für das christliche Volk).*[31]

Of the secular, non-sectarian Christmas catalogs, F. Volckmar's basic
appeal lay in its high standard of illustrations, while Hinrich's lay in the best
coverage of gift books; it was very popular with retailers as a source of
information. The most successful of the new catalogs was the *Illustrated Christmas Catalog (Illustrierter Weihnachtskatalog)* published by Elert Arthur Seemann,
a Leipzig publisher who specialized in art books. This catalog first appeared in
1871, when Seemann pooled resources with the publishing firms of Alphons
Dürr and G. Grote.[32]

Unlike the older catalogs of Volckmar and Hinrichs, that of Seemann was
pitched exclusively at the potential book buyer rather than at both the buyer
and the retail shop owner; Seemann intended it to be "a means of arousing
the buying impulses"[33] of the public, not a systematic reference work for the
book shop owner. The "buying impulses" were to be activated—or at the
very least titillated—by a carefully chosen list of popular books likely to
appeal to the educated public, by illustrations, and by a descriptive bibliographical report on those of the year's new books that were deemed to be of
interest to the discriminating and tasteful reader. Seemann's was the first
catalog to have such a bibliographical report.[34] However, some retailers, sunk
deep in the proud and invincible stupidity which characterized some of them,
missed the point of the *Illustrierter Weihnachtskatalog* completely, complaining
that it was a poor reference work. The discriminating public for whom it was
intended, however, took to it enthusiastically. In 1872 Seemann decided to
print up 30,000 copies each year. That may seem like a small number for
such a popular item, but Seemann's like all the other catalogs then, was
usually distributed to book shops and read by people there rather than taken
home. As the number of titles published annually grew far too great for any
non-bookmen to master and comprehend, and as the Christmas catalogs
proved a reliable guide to gifts people would like, the public came to rely

more and more upon Seemann's and other catalogs to guide it towards the most suitable purchases. Publishers complained of the cost involved in placing listings and advertisements in the catalogs, but there was no doubt that the cost was justified: given its warm and trusting attitude towards catalogs, the public was much more likely to believe and act upon an advertisement in a catalog than upon one in a newspaper.

## Book reviews as sales aids

Similarly, the public was impressed by good reviews—a good review was the best publicity a book could receive. Publishers therefore devoted more and more effort to getting good reviews of their books. They deluged newspapers with review copies of their new works, hoping for favorable notices; most books so sent were neither reviewed nor returned.[35] Undaunted, publishers tried new tacks. More and more of them drew up "wash tickets," or ready-made reviews, and sent them to newspapers editors along with free copies of the books in question. There are no exact figures on how many editors printed these "wash tickets" as genuine reviews, but since the ready-made reviews continued to be sent by publishers for decades, some newspapers must have used them. Small, struggling newspapers were treated far less deferentially than large and prosperous ones: they were often told to publish good reviews or get no book advertising.[36]

That was a serious threat, because book advertising could be an important source of revenue. Despite the greater effectiveness of Christmas catalogs and book reviews, much newspaper advertising was still placed by Germany's publishers. In the early 1870s, and perhaps later, publishers delighted to place advertisements which masqueraded as newspaper articles, although some in the trade found these quite tasteless.[37] Along with newspapers, such other long-used advertising media as printed circulars and form letters continued to be employed extensively by publishers.

The total volume of advertising increased markedly during these years. The use of illustrations and eye-catching lettering escalated. Yet the literary style of book advertising, especially that of books intended for large sale, showed little change from earlier decades. The phrasing used by Wilhelm Spemann to announce a lavishly illustrated history of Germany in 1876 could well have been cast by Joseph Meyer half a century before:

> With the most rigorous historical accuracy and exactitude of description, yet at the same time with color and vivid animation, this book depicts how Germans of all classes and all levels of society have lived and striven, suffered and quarreled, planned and achieved from the beginning of their history down to the present. The founding and development of the Fatherland's material and intellectual culture, the work of our forefathers in the home and in the field, in war and in peace, in State and in Church, in art and in science; the agricultural, industrial, religious, political, social,

scientific, literary, and artistic development of the nation; all the changes in morals and custom, in rural and in urban life, in the existence of the peasant, the townsman; and the noble; German poetry and tracts, love and yearning, knowledge and desire—all of this will find both a place and appreciation in a ... description of scientific reliability and of a form which will attract, edify, and delight alike young and old, man and woman. The work takes as its conclusion the founding of the new German Empire in the year 1871.[38]

The physical appearance of the book would be as magnificent a tribute to German greatness as its content, according to Spemann:

For the leading men of the German artistic world have worked joyfully together to create a work which in every sense deserves to be called A NATIONAL DISPLAY EDITION and which will be an ornament to every educated household—a family book of the most noble type, designed to awaken and nourish patriotic thoughts and feelings, to make clear the spirit of German history, to cleanse the soul of partisan passion, and to ignite in all hearts the holy fire of true patriotism.[39]

Spemann's words were presented to the German public in circulars which he sent to book stores for distribution.

Silly as such an announcement may appear to us, at the time it was quite effective. It appealed to the middle-class German's desire to be considered educated and to belong to a nation which was looked up to by the rest of the world. The lush rhetoric impressed people; it did not strike them as superannuated nonsense. There was, however, another school of advertising rhetoric also in vogue then. It was the blunt approach, usually consisting of the blunt assertion that the bookseller who commissioned it had lower prices than any other. It was used much more by retail booksellers than by publishers, however.

Like the flowery approach, it was nothing new, having been used by the infamous Spitz and other pirates early in the century. In fact, it was not until the Wilhelmine period that there were really significant changes in book advertising. The principal advances in marketing which publishers made during this period were not in advertising but in making their books more physically attractive and in pricing books to maximize sales.

## Book design improves to increase sales

Reclam, Müller-Grote, and other successful publishers of broad-appeal works made book design a part of their overall marketing strategy. Reclam had actually experimented for a few years to find a dye for the covers of his *Universal-Bibliothek* which would not fade even if the books were exposed to the sun in store display windows.[40] Müller-Grote was one of the first German publishers to issue bound copies of fictional works, beginning in 1874 with a series of inexpensive books by contemporary authors. The pains which he took to make the bindings attractive were one reason why two million copies of books from the series were sold by 1913.[41]

By the 1880s, even the publishers of scientific and scholarly works were conscious that the outward appearance of a book—its paper, the type used to print it, the number and quality of its illustrations, and its covers or binding (more and more publishers had their books bound)—contributed to its fate in the marketplace. Publishing houses such as Westermann in Brunswick strove to make their learned books more attractive.[42] Not all of Germany's publishers got the message, however. Cotta was faulted by both literary critics and the literary public for continuing to issue drab-looking books; the firm's editions of the German classics were considered especially unforgiveable. Many publishers had their books printed on low-grade wood pulp paper, which disintegrated at a touch after a few years—hardly contributing to the idea that books were an enduring investment.[43]

## Low-priced books

The most important development in book marketing to take place in the regular trade during this period was the advent of the truly low-priced book. The trade historian Walter Krieg speaks of a "new era of inexpensive books."[44] There had of course been cheap books on the regular book market before 1867, but nowhere near so many as after; furthermore, the "cheap" books of the post-1867 years were cheaper than the "cheap" books of the pre-1867 years. Technology had made inexpensive books possible, aggressive publishers showed that they could be very profitable. The success of the low-priced editions of the classics put on the market in 1867 led to such low-priced series as the *Collection Spemann* and the *Bibliothek der Weltliteratur*, and to low-priced individual books. Even novels were sometimes priced low.[45]

Statistics on German book prices show how common low-priced books became in this period. In 1875, 33.3 percent of all the titles published had a selling price of under one Mark; a decade later 42.5 percent did. True, some of these inexpensive titles were intended for the mass market, but many were for the regular book market.[46] Thus the percentage of books costing five Marks or more remained almost constant, while that of books costing between one and five Marks—medium-priced books, in other words—decreased. The gain in the percentage of low-priced books came at the expense of the medium-priced ones.[47]

Most of the books which sold for under one Mark were so priced when they were first published. Some, however, were books originally priced higher but reduced in price by their publishers in an effort to stimulate lagging sales. This was an old practice: Frommann and others had published whole catalogs listing reduced-price books before 1850. In the 1870s, the *Catalog of Reduced-Price Books (Katalog im Preise herabgesetzte Bücher)* published by L. M. Glogau of Hamburg, which had a press run of 40,000 copies in 1867, was only one of several catalogs listing books whose publishers had reduced their prices.[48] There were those in the trade who argued that to reduce the price of a book was to cheapen not only it, but all other books in the eyes of the public, a process which would destroy the public's belief in the book as an investment. This traditionalist argument seems not to have deterred many publishers from lowering prices, however.[49]

Despite the fact that so many books were reduced in price, and despite the fact that a growing number of books were very low in price from the outset, there was a widespread conviction in the book trade that German book prices were too high and were tending to go ever higher. Along with this conviction went the belief that the German book trade had a long way to go before it achieved the low-price, high-volume conditions found in the more modern British and French book trades.[50]

Although these beliefs exaggerated, and did not take into account the growing number of inexpensive books, there was some truth to them. Many German publishers kept to the old ways, issuing small editions with high prices; it would be a mistake to think that the dynamic bookmen so often discussed in these pages were representative of all German publishers. Publishers of scholarly and scientific works usually had no alternative to small editions: even with the growing export trade and the expansion of the German universities there was not likely to be demand for more than a thousand copies of most scientific and scholarly books. Small editions, rising printing costs, and rising royalties pushed the prices of these books steadily upward during the decades after 1867.[51]

Novels and other fiction were frequently high in price, too, with the exception of cheap speculative editions of very popular and famous works of fiction. Novels by authors like Spielhagen and Freytag often cost from 12 to 15 Marks in substantial-looking editions, although cheaper, flimsier editions were normally available too. Fontaine's 285-page novel *Petösy* cost 7.50 Marks when it was published in 1884. In 1881, the German translation of a novel by A. Daudet cost three times as much as the original French version and 10 times as much as the Italian translation. The reason why novels, plays, and stories published in Germany were so costly was simply that most of them were intended for sale only to circulating libraries, and thus were printed up in small editions. Most publishers of fiction did not believe that things could be otherwise. Although it was evident in this period that private individuals would buy popular books of fiction by highly regarded authors, most publishers were skeptical that anything, even low prices, would induce private individuals to purchase run-of-the-mill fiction. Some publishers disagreed with this analysis, but they were unable to convince their colleagues.[52]

In Germany it was the accepted truth that even the wealthiest nobles preferred to borrow greasy and battered circulating library copies of fiction rather than buy them. In Germany, authors and bookmen alike related with weary anger stories like that of the wealthy admirer of Berthold Auerbach who held a salon party at his home to honor Auerbach, yet owned not one book by the author. This noble, the story went on, was quite embarrassed during the festivities when his young daughter brought out and laid upon the damask tablecloth the only copy of a book by Auerbach to be found in the house—a circulating library copy so fouled with use that it stained the tablecloth.[53]

In Germany it was believed that the British, French, and North Americans treated their authors with infinitely more consideration. It was believed that publishers in these countries could get rich by producing novels and plays. And there is no doubt that in France, Britain, and North America the market for fiction was larger than in Germany. To give an example: Scheffel's *Ekke-hard* was the most popular novel of the second half of the century in Germany, with 114,000 copies being sold between the years 1854 and 1887 alone. But in Britain almost every single novel written by the prolific Miss Braddon (Mary Elizabeth Braddon, 1837–1915) in the 1870s and 1880s, sold at least 200,000 copies.[54]

Yet such comparisons with the book markets in what were the wealthiest countries in the world at that time should not be taken to minimize or obscure the German achievement. The German book market had grown impressively. Not only were more general books sold as gifts and for personal libraries, but also the number of circulating libraries, those traditionally voracious consumers of books, rose dramatically.[55] In the mid-1870s, it was estimated that the average provincial lending library had from 7,000 to 9,000 volumes and spent from 1,000 Marks to 1,200 Marks each year replenishing its stock, while the average big city library had 25,000 to 30,000 volumes and spent about 3,000 Marks annually on new books.[56]

The German market for fiction, as for non-fiction, was vastly larger in 1888 than it had been in 1867—the evidence is overwhelming. The market had grown faster than the German population. While some of the old buying (or non-buying) habits of the German reading public, and some of the conservative marketing habits of the German publishers, had not died out by the late 1880s, they were on the wane. The tenor of the time was set by dynamic publishers and retailers, who induced the public to buy more books than ever before.

In the years 1867–1888, the retail branch of the regular book trade entered into the most dramatic phase of its history. Opportunities were great, growth was fast, competition was vicious, and change was bewilderingly rapid. The newer, energetic segments of the retail trade asserted themselves so forcefully that they had grabbed a very considerable portion of the total retail sales by the mid-1880s. These newer segments were: (1) the high-volume, price-cutting dealers in the big cities; (2) the Modern Antiquarian dealers, and (3) the various itinerant book dealers. Of the three, the Itinerant Book Trade boomed the most spectacularly.

## The "Itinerant Book Trade"

The number of firms engaging in the itinerant retail trade increased from about 200 in 1869, to 589 in 1875, 697 in 1885, and 988 in 1890—a fivefold increase. In 1869 there was roughly one itinerant retail firm to every 10 book stores; in 1890 there was one to every four and a half.[57]

In its rapid growth, the Itinerant Trade developed four distinct branches, which differed in their methods and also in what they sold and to whom they sold it. One branch was composed of the traditional book peddlers who carried their wares upon their backs, selling complete books and calendars for cash. Although they sometimes carried books from Reclam's *Universal-Bibliothek* and analogous cheap series, and included clergymen and teachers among their customers, their principal business lay in selling devotional books and other mass-market items to the lower classes in rural areas. Originally known as "Colporteurs," they came to be called merely "peddlers" to differentiate them from the newer types of itinerant booksellers. A second branch of the Itinerant Trade was the so-called "flying book trade" *(fliegende Buchandel)* whose members hawked periodicals, newspapers, and postcards on street corners.[58]

Most significant, dynamic and self-important was the third branch, which by the 1870s had arrogated to itself the name "The Colporteur Book Trade." Its vigor and exuberance were reflected in the great claims which it made for itself, such as: "That the Colporteur Trade is the future and the salvation of the book trade is truer, and more universally acknowledged, every day."[59]

The Colporteur Book Trade was made up of firms which employed salesmen to sell subscriptions to books and magazines (magazines made half of its volume) from door to door. These firms operated mainly in large and medium-sized cities, but were found "even in many little places," according to a trade manual published in 1878.[60] Two were established in the small (population 5,900) Lusatian city of Löbau in the early 1870s, for example. Estimates as to how many Colporteur firms were established in the 1870s and 1880s vary wildly, but everyone agreed that many more were established than failed.[61] As to the number of salesmen employed by the Colporteur Trade, a conservative estimate would be that they had from 15,000 to 20,000 working during the peak sales period of the autumn and winter months during the 1880s.[62]

No segment of the book trade benefitted more from the introduction of freedom to enter any occupation than this one. To establish a Colporteur firm required much less capital than to establish a book shop or publishing operation, hence practically anybody with a bit of money could get into the business. "One hears almost daily of the establishment of new firms of this type,"[63] wrote an enthusiast in 1876; he observed that these firms were being founded by shop owners, binders, merchants of all types, and brokers, among others. The only real initial expense these people had was in purchasing stock from the large wholesalers who catered to the Colporteur Trade.[64] The headquarters of a Colporteur operation could literally be a hole in the wall. The salesmen worked for commissions, not salaries.[65]

The Colporteur Book Trade sold both to the masses and the middle and upper classes. However, it did not sell the same things to these two very different groups. To the middle and upper classes were sold: popular magazines like the *Gartenlaube*, display editions of classics and other popular works, books on popular science, small encyclopedias, handbooks and other popular non-fictional books, some novels, and cheap editions of the classics. Almost all of these books were sold in installments rather than as complete volumes.[66] Orders for books and magazines were taken by salesmen; the goods were delivered either by the salesmen themselves or by messenger boys. Deliveries were usually made once a month. In the 1860s and 1870s, subscribers had to pay in cash for each magazine or each section of a book as it was received. But by the late 1880s, competition among rival firms had heated up, and they tried to lure each other's customers away with generous extensions of credit, premiums, and the like. Novels were frequently offered as premiums.[67]

But however great the competition, no Colporteur firm would reduce prices.[68] This refusal spared the Colporteur Book Trade some of the miseries that afflicted other branches of book retailing.

The basic sales tools of the Colporteur salesman were sample issues of periodicals and sample installments of books. Each firm ordered masses of samples from publishers or, more frequently, from large "Colporteur wholesalers" who acted as middlemen. Most salesmen went from door to door leaving samples, then returned a few hours later to collect them and attempt to talk people into subscribing. A gifted minority of salesmen relied more upon their own persuasive powers than upon the charms of the samples: they simply went from house to house enchanting people into signing up for subscriptions, waving the samples about occasionally to give some idea of what they were selling.[69]

Most Colporteur-salesmen were not so gifted, in fact, a good number were incompetent, or stupid, or dishonest; some were all three. Colporteur-salesmen regularly swindled both their employers and their customers, acquiring subscriptions under false pretexts, falsifying order forms, and making extravagant claims that could not be fulfilled.[70] An 1878 manual on the Colporteur Trade advised employers to take a deposit from newly hired salesmen before giving them any sample copies or order forms.[71]

Actually, it was a wonder that there was not more difficulty with salesmen. Colporteur-salesmen were usually recruited by newspaper advertisements worded along the following lines: "Desire immediately 50 subscription-collectors for an easy-to-sell product" or "Respectable gentlemen will make good earnings through the sale of books." Most of the men who answered these notices were unstable types unable to stay with any occupation very long. The North German Confederation's Occupations Law of June 21, 1869, which became the basis for the Empire's Occupations Law a few years later, did bar from the Itinerant Trade: those who had served jail sentences of more than six weeks for crimes against morality and/or property, those under police surveillance, those with infectious or disfiguring diseases, those under 21 years of age, and those who were notorious beggars and drunkards. There is no certainty, however, that the law was always strictly enforced. Every itinerant book salesman who sold printed matter outside of his home district had to have a license. But this requirement was so loosely enforced in some areas that salesmen did not bother to apply for the licenses. On the other hand, there were areas where the licensing law was strictly enforced.[72]

The moral failings of many of its salesmen helped give the Colporteur Book Trade a disreputable image among both the public and the book trade in general.[73] The more respectable kinds of book retailers sometimes wondered, angrily and jealously, why the middle- and upper-class public did not automatically bar its homes to Colporteur salesmen.[74]

More and more publishers observed that the respectable public, far from barring its homes to Colporteur salesmen, was perfectly willing to deal with them. The publishing house of Velhagen and Klasing, one of the most reputable in Germany, sold two-thirds of its production of Lutheran works and patriotic literature through Colporteur salesmen in the 1870s and 1880s. Records kept by the company indicate how effective these salesmen were in dealing with the middle and upper class public. Of those who purchased Velhagen and Klasing books from Colporteur salesmen:

- 17 percent were merchants
- 15 percent were officers and other military personnel
- 15 percent were teachers
- 20 percent were transportation officials (*Verkehrsbeamte*)
- 9 percent were owners and white-collar employees in the construction business
- 6 percent were government administrative officials
- 5 percent were estate owners
- 3 percent were judicial officials
- 3 percent were artists
- 2 percent were innkeepers
- 3 percent were listed merely as "retired persons"
- 1.5 percent were medical doctors
- 1.5 percent were students
- 1 percent were lawyers[75]

A Stuttgart publishing firm, the Ferdinand Carl Company, found in the 1880s that it could sell children's literature all year round by means of Colporteur salesmen; the usual selling season was before Christmas. The Carl Company hired its own salesmen.[76]

## Why was the "Colporteur Book Trade" successful?

How can the success of the Colporteur Book Trade in selling books to the upper social strata be explained? These social strata were obsessed with "respectability" and with getting bargains. The Colporteur Trade offered neither. The books which the trade sold could frequently be had for less in big city book stores; they could be had for the same amounts the trade charged in book stores anywhere, and any book store was more "respectable" than a Colporteur salesman. The middle and upper class public tolerated in the Colporteur Trade things which it would not tolerate in conventional book stores.

There were two main reasons for the success of the Colporteur Trade in the regular book market. The first was that it went directly to the customers in their homes, where it was able to play upon and draw out book needs which were latent. An 1883 publication of the General Union of Colporteur Book Dealers colorfully contrasted the active bookselling of Colporteur salesmen with the passive bookselling of conventional book stores:

> By the sweat of his brow the Colporteur salesman makes his offers door to door, house to house, in every kind of wind and weather. [He thus achieves] more than the stationary retailer, who sits and waits, and waits for such people as are so interested in buying books that they will exert themselves to come to his shop and place their orders.[77]

Book shops were not equipped to deal with latent needs, Colporteur salesmen were.

The second reason for its success was that the Colporteur Trade sold only popular books or new books that seemed strongly destined to become popular. Taking no chances, it sold only those books which people were most prone to buy in any event. Only a relative handful of the thousands of titles published in Germany every year were sold by Colporteur salesmen. Friedrich Streissler's *Der Kolportagehandel*, an 1887 trade manual, advised stocking as few titles as possible, and only titles which were easy to sell.[78] These titles included: *Brehms Tierleben*, published by the Bibliographisches Institut, *The Book of Discoveries (Das Buch der Erfindungen)* and *The Housewife's Book (Das Buch der Hausfrau)*, which were published by Otto Spamer of Leipzig, the R. Schultz' Publishing Company's *Illustrated Lexikon for Good Health (Illustriertes Gesundheits-Lexikon)*, and Weiss' *Picture Atlas of the Heavens (Bilderatlas der Sternenwelt)*, which was published by J. F. Schreiber of Esslingen. Other recommended titles included the popular non-fictional works issued in sections by the Ferdinand Dümmler Publishing Comapny of Berlin, the Julius Maier Company of Stuttgart and the G. A. Gloeckner Company of Leipzig. Editions of the German classics, Shakespeare, and of such small encyclopedias as the Bibliographisches Institut's *Kleine Konversationslexikon* were also recommended by Streissler. Both cheap (50 Pfennig per section) and expensive editions of the German classics sold well. Firms which knew their customers well, according to Streissler, could sell works of restricted geographical interest, manuals for various trades, and fiction; but most firms were advised not to gamble on selling such books.[79]

Other books which are known to have been sold by many Colporteur firms were much like those in Streissler's list. Most were large, illustrated works of general-interest, non-fiction books—like Zimmermann's *Wunder der Urwelt* and other books published by Gustav Hempel, Herren and Ukert's *Staatengeschichte*, and the Schönlein Publishing Company's *Library of Entertainment and Knowledge (Bibliothek der Unterhaltung und des Wissens)*, a series of booklets costing 75 *Pfennig* apiece. Issued at the rate of 13 booklets per year from 1877, the *Bibliothek* included novels, essays, popularizations of science, and other things which were intended to appeal to the kind of people who loved the *Gartenlaube* magazine. Twenty-six Colporteur firms got 15,790 subscriptions for the *Bibliothek*. All of Germany's book stores together got less than 10.[80]

## The "Travelling Book Trade"

Even narrower than the selection of books offered by the Colporteur Book Trade was that offered by the fourth branch of the Itinerant Book Trade. This was known as the "Travelling Book Trade" *(Reisebuchhandel)*. It was often confused with the Colporteur Book Trade, since it too used salesmen equipped with sample copies of books as its major sales' weapon. But it differed from the Colporteur Trade in some respects. It sold complete books rather than books in sections. Moreover, the firms of which it was comprised were all large, heavily capitalized operations.[81]

They had to be big and well-financed operations in order to stock the expensive books which they sold—large encyclopedias, multi-volume world histories, and the like—and in order to offer their customers credit. Credit had to be given because the books which were sold by the Travelling Trade were too costly for most Germans to pay for all at once. A bound set of Meyers *Konversationslexikon* sold for 160 Marks in the mid-1880s, for example. The purchaser made a cash down payment of 53 Marks and paid the rest in monthly installments. The usual monthly payment for works sold by the Travelling Trade was five Marks. The salesmen who sold *Meyers Konversationslexikon* were under contract to the Bibliographisches Institut to approve credit only for people who looked like they could keep up the monthly payments.[82]

If tightly run to minimize the incidence of dead-beat customers and of salesmen who absconded with books or money, a Travelling Trade operation could be very profitable, and most were. Fewer than 100 titles were handled by this trade, the mainstays being the perpetually beloved large encyclopedias published by Brockhaus, Pierer, Herder, and the Bibliographisches Institut. Margins were high and no discounts were given to customers. A dealer had to pay only 96 Marks for the bound set of *Meyers Konversationslexikon* which he sold for 160 Marks.[83]

## Ire of conventional book shops

The growing importance of the Travelling and Colporteur Book Trades in the regular book market was wormwood to the operators of conventional book shops. To be sure, some of them joined rather than battled the trend by establishing their own Colporteur operations, but they did not like to see what the Itinerant Trade appeared to be doing to book shops. What made the traditional retailers most bitter was that the Itinerant Trade siphoned off sales of popular books, which could have provided a steady income to book-shops. Worse, the itinerant dealers were not the only ones who took the sale of popular books away frombook stores: there were also religious and cultural organizations, teachers' groups, government agencies, publishers who dealt directly with the public, and ruthless, price-cutting, big city dealers.

Of the religious and cultural groups, the most active in the regular market were the Catholic Borromäus Society, the Protestant Gustavus Adolphus Society, and the Society for Mass Education. The Borromäus Society had been a subject of complaint by conventional retailers for decades. Of the teachers groups, the Pestalozzi Society plagued book shop owners the most; of the government agencies, the postal service was said to do the most harm. Rarely did any of these organizations sell books to non-members or non-employees, but since each of them had so many employees or members of their own, and since they sold books at considerable discounts, the number of books which they sold was large. They were able to sell books cheaply because they bought them from publishers in large lots at wholesale prices. In 1873, for example, employees of the post office were offered a large "work of general interest"[84] for 28 Thaler; the regular selling price of the work was 40 Thaler. Credit was available for postal employees who did not want to pay for the book all at once. It should be noted that not all publishers would sell to the post office or other organizations unaffiliated with the book trade. The Bibliographisches Institut stopped selling to the post office in 1873. Similarly, not all publishers would sell books directly to individuals not connected with the trade. But enough publishers would sell books to non-members of the trade to create a real threat to conventional book stores.[85]

## "Discount Mongers"/"Cash Booksellers"

Another threat came from the discount booksellers who centered in a few large cities and sold books all over Germany by mail. Usually called "Discount-Mongers" *(Schleuderer)* by the traditionalist elements in the trade, these retailers preferred themselves to be known as "Cash Booksellers". Some of them owned large book shops, others were book wholesalers, and still others were Modern Antiquarian dealers. Among the best known of them were the Leipzig firms of R. Streller, P. Ehrlich, G. Boehm, and J. Drescher, all of which were founded in the mid-1870s. Many of them located in Leipzig to avoid paying shipping costs on books which they received from publishers; it was an old trade custom that publishers either kept stocks in Leipzig or would send them there at their own expense. Most of the Cash Booksellers who were not in Leipzig were to be found in Berlin, which was becoming Germany's greatest publishing center (Leipzig's ascendancy was in distribution, not in publishing). In Berlin, they would not have to pay any shipping costs on the books published in the city.[86]

Had the Cash Booksellers sold books only in Berlin and Leipzig, much less would have been heard about them. As it was, however, they took all Germany for their market, using the new national postal system to send out "reams of offers every day … to professors, students, teachers,"[87] binders, librarians, and other potential book buyers. Their customers in turn ordered books by mail and received them quickly by means of the new parcel post service which the Imperial Post had established. Sending books via parcel post was cheap.[88]

The Cash Booksellers were an outgrowth of the Modern Second-Hand Trade, which had been flourishing for several decades before the unification of Germany. Some even called themselves "Modern Antiquarians." The principal difference between the two was that the Cash Booksellers dealt almost exclusively in brand-new books, while the Modern Antiquarians worked with books which had been in print for some time but not sold. Most of the business methods of the Cash Booksellers were inspired by, and patterned after, those of Modern Antiquarian masters like Gsellius: they bought up huge lots of broad-appeal books at wholesale prices from publishers, then sold them for about 25 percent less than the publishers' retail selling price—a fact which they trumpeted to the world in their heavy advertising. The Cash Booksellers operated in open violation of the hallowed book trade principle that the publisher and only the publisher could determine the retail-selling price of a book, and that the book had to be sold at this price everywhere in Germany. When the Leipzig Discount-Monger Streller was attacked in the *Börsenblatt* for his flagrant violation of the principle, he replied by sneering that it was hopelessly outmoded, that modern conditions demanded low prices and small margins, and that since most publishers would not set retail prices at an intelligently low level, the job had to be done by enterprising retailers like himself. "Low prices are an irresistible inducement to purchase," maintained Streller; "[they] get [people] used to buying more frequently; they are always welcome to book-buyers, whose moderate means impel them to always consider how much things cost. This is the unconditional truth."[89]

Although publishers must have winced at such arrogance, and smarted at the loss of their traditional role in pricing books, the big orders placed by Streller and his colleagues must have sweetened the air, and made remonstrance seem like mere self-destructive pomposity. Publishers continued to accept orders from the Discount-Mongers. The orders grew larger and more frequent every year.[90]

With their aggressive methods, and their scorn for many of the traditional conventions of the book trade, the Cash Booksellers were the culmination of all the aggressive innovation, all the disdain for genteel but inefficient practices, which had been growing up in the trade throughout the nineteenth century. The Cash Booksellers were on the side of "progress [and] ... modern merchandising principles,"[91] observed a university librarian who studied the trade in the early 1880s, while conventional book shops were on the side of tradition and older merchandising principles.

In the 1880s as in the 1820s, the practices of Germany's conventional book stores were based upon the approval system, which was unique to Germany.[92] This system allowed retailers to order books from publishers on approval; the retailers in turn allowed prospective customers to examine the books on approval. The only major change in the system from earlier in the century was that by the 1867–1888 period, most book shops would take on approval only those books which they themselves had requested from publishers. The old practice whereby publishers sent out books scattershot to any and all book stores, whether the stores had asked for them or not, was dying out.[93]

The reason why fewer and fewer retailers accepted unrequested books was that as both the number of publishers and of books published increased, retailers feared that they would be overwhelmed with books, too many of them unsaleable, unless they took only those which they themselves had ordered.[94]

The approval system allowed any bookseller, no matter how small or how remote his shop, to deal in practically any book published in Germany. By allowing retailers to order books on approval—and therefore on credit—rather than having to pay for them, it made it possible to set up a book shop for far less capital than would otherwise have been the case. The approval system was a major reason why Germany had many book shops in small provincial towns and cities as well as in metropolises.[95]

This approval system, however, had one big drawback—it was clumsy and expensive. To "progressive" souls in the book trade, its costliness and inefficiency made it outmoded, a burden upon the trade, a hindrance to growth. It was costly to send a book from the publisher to Leipzig, have it forwarded from Leipzig to a book store somewhere, and then give it to a prospective buyer to examine in his leisure. There was no guarantee that the customer would even buy the book; no one felt compelled to actually purchase books which he had requested on approval, and many books sent out on approval had to be sent back to Leipzig. The approval system entailed high costs for transportation and paperwork. To cover these costs, the prices of books had to be set higher than they would otherwise have been.

The apostles of Modern Merchandising Principles believed that high prices deterred sales. Furthermore, they argued, the approval system required too much use of credit, with book stores obtaining books on credit from publishers and in turn letting their customers have books on credit. Since Germans were notoriously slow to pay for books, book stores suffered from a

shortage of ready cash; their inability to pay publishers on time deprived pub
lishers of needed capital.

To the "progressive," the whole conventional system of book retailing
appeared to reward the timid, protect the incompetent, and enchain the able.
The "progressives" believed that unrestrained competition was the key to
economic growth and progress. They were particularly galled by the custom
that only the publisher could set the price of a book, and that this price
should allow a 33.3 percent margin for the retailer; (the margin was needed
to cover the costs of the approval system). If the book trade were to achieve
its true potential, said the "progressive," the publisher-established price would
have to be abandoned, as would the clumsy approval system and the heritage
of genteel bookselling that went with it. If abandoning these practices
doomed the provincial book store and turned the metropolitan store into a
cold, cash-oriented, purely functional place, that was the price of progress.[96]

In the two decades after 1867, it was more and more evident that progress
was exacting just that price. Itinerant booksellers, who were anything but
genteel, and Cash Booksellers, who set their own prices, grabbed an ever-
larger share of the market. Since the market grew fast there was still plenty of
business for the conventional booksellers, but their share of the total market
declined. The increase in the number of book shops during the decades
heightened the sense of competition and of pressure among both veteran and
new book shop owners. Disquiet at the activities of the itinerant booksellers
and Discount-Mongers grew into paranoid frenzy in many retailers when
they realized that there were so many new book shops also trying to cut in
on the market. Many of the new booksellers had come in from other, grosser
and less refined trades, and they lacked both the feeling of collegiality and the
gentlemanly restraint which had once been fairly common among book shop
operators. As an 1868 essay in the *Börsenblatt* characterized the newcomers to
the retail trade in Munich:

> They all want to shove forward, to make business boom, to see money
> cascade into their coffers, and thus to achieve these ends they shower the
> public with new books on approval, bringing them door to door, offer-
> ing them madly, forcing them upon people.[97]

Fearful of going under, enraged at their competition, many retail shop owners
took (in self-defense) to aggressive tactics, especially in the large cities. Curi-
ously, these tactics often seemed to be directed more at rival book shops than
at Cash Booksellers and Colporteurs. To wither the competition with daring
price cuts seemed to have become the aim of many. Established firms lowered
prices to undercut new firms, new firms lowered them to break into the
markets of the established shops. Book shops in the big cities turned to the
mail-order discount trade which the Cash Booksellers had pioneered.
Numerous booksellers who had no desire to do mail-order discounting
believed that they had to do it to remain solvent.[98]

So pervasive had price-cutting by book shops become, that the custom of the publisher setting the price of a book appeared to be headed for extinction. Emil Strauss, a "progressive" Bonn bookseller, saw the portent of this trend when he wrote in 1879:

> I see in the spread of price-cutting [by the retailers] the ruin of the book store in its present form ... nothing can make the traditional practices of the retail book store viable anymore ... the future belongs to the book store operated according to the principles of modern business practice.[99]

Such a book store would be a big city operation relying upon aggressive salesmanship and cash-only sales.

The small city and town book shop, on the other hand, would have no place in the future which Strauss envisioned.[100] It lacked the specialized markets upon which big city (and university and residence city) book shops could count; the specialized markets, e.g., for scholarly books, were never as torn with competition as was the market for general books. The provincial book shop lacked the capital which enabled shops in Berlin and in Leipzig to purchase huge stocks of books for cash at low prices. Its clientele expected to be given credit and it had to rely upon the traditional 33.3 percent margin to cover its costs. Increasingly, it saw its regular customers order popular works by mail from Berlin and Leipzig. Of course, its customers still ordered some works from it, books of local interest for example, but that was not enough. In the 1870s and 1880s, the *Börsenblatt* was filled with apocalyptic lamentations from provincial booksellers.[101]

Apocalyptic complaints were nothing new, as we have repeatedly seen in the course of this volume. Often they were just so much hot air, manifestations of indigestion, of crotchety old age, or the like. But these complaints of the 1870s and 1880s had real substance. Karl Dziatzko, the Chief Librarian at the University at Breslau, studied the book trade in the early 1880s and found the complaints by provincial retailers "so frequent and widespread ... that [their] validity ... and the existence of a genuine ... state of need cannot be doubted."[102] Within the book trade, publishers began to realize that the provincial shops were in great danger. Some were concerned, others not, but all were drawn up into a great debate and struggle: would the trade act to preserve its traditional retail structure or would it let this die in the interests of "progress."

The main thrust of the nineteenth-century development of the trade had been to undermine the traditional system. The ideal of economic freedom, unrestrained by either government or guild, the idea that unrestrained competition led to betterment of the trade—these concepts had gained more and more adherents in the trade as the century progressed.

## Rescue of conventional book shops: the "Kroner Reforms"

Nevertheless, the traditional retail organization of the trade was rescued. In 1880 many publishers followed the lead of B. G. Teubner and forbade retailers to publicize discounts on their books; they also forbade discounts of higher than 10 percent off the retail price set by the publisher. Within the Exchange Union of German Booksellers, the increasingly powerful national trade organization, the anti-discounting forces grew strong under the leadership of the Stuttgart publisher Adolf Kröner, a man whose forceful temperament and diplomatic skill won him the title, "the Bismarck of the German Book Trade."[103]

In September of 1887, at a famous meeting held in Frankfurt/Main (considered friendlier territory than Leipzig or Berlin by the anti-discounting forces), the Exchange Union threw the full weight of its sanction behind Kröner. It banned discounting. Effective from the Easter Book Fair of 1888, no member of the Union could sell a book at less than the publisher's retail price and publishers could not sell books more cheaply to large customers than to small. A book published anywhere in Germany was to be sold everywhere in Germany at the same retail price. To back up its rules, the Union forbade its members to have business transactions with those who violated them, whether they were Union members or not. Moreover, those who broke the rules were to be denied the use of such vital institutions as the Leipzig Order House, the central clearing house for most publisher–retailer transactions.[104]

There were exceptions made and soft spots left in the so-called "Kröner Reform." To secure the cooperation of the Berlin book dealers, Kröner, conceded to them the right to sell books at up to a 10 percent discount. However, the discount applied only within the Berlin city limits. Some Berlin book shops continued to sell at discounts to customers outside of Berlin anyway. In 1889 the Leipzig dealers unilaterally granted to themselves the same rights as their Berlin colleagues and the Exchange Union could do nothing about it. The 1887 rules permitted publishers to make special deals with government agencies, institutional buyers, and other large, organized groups. They allowed regional associations of book dealers to weaken the ban on discounting within the regions which they represented. Despite these exceptions and concessions, the Kröner, Reform was effective. In the two decades after 1887, the concessions and exceptions were eliminated. The Exchange Union proved so effective at enforcing its rules and thereby restraining competition that it was soon accused of being a cartel.[105] The Kröner Reform saved the provincial book store.

Since the prohibition of discounting seems to go counter to the whole trend of nineteenth-century development in the trade, the motivation behind it deserves careful explanation. The important thing to realize is that while some of the support for Kröner's proposals was purely sentimental conservatism—a feeling that good old German institutions like the small city book store should be kept robust because they were good old German institutions—most of Kröner's support was rooted in hard-headed calculation. Kröner, himself believed that if the book trade did not put itself in order by curtailing ruinous competition, the government would stomp in to do it. Many publishers came to the belief that to let the provincial book shop die was to destroy an important part of the market; most of the thousands of titles published in Germany every year were sold only through book stores and could only be sold through book stores, since Cash Booksellers, itinerant booksellers, and the like made it a principle to deal in only a small number of titles. Thus if only discounters and itinerant booksellers survived, many publishers would perforce be excluded from the market. This was especially true of publishers of serious and scholarly works. As one writer expressed it in 1887:

> Owing to the existence of the ... sale or return [system, i.e., approval system], the smallest bookseller is enabled to lay before his customers for inspection the latest books in their respective branches [fields]. This system of literary irrigation must be preserved in the interests of education and culture as well as in those of publishers and agents, *both of whom are dependent upon the retailer for their existence.*[106]

Dziatzko wrote of "the great exposure and myriad opportunities for sales given [a] publisher's books by the great network of book stores, a network which extends down to the smallest places."[107]

Numerous publishers felt that the sales methods of the conventional book shops, while rather passive, were more effective than "progressive" critics imagined. An 1882 article in the *Börsenblatt* told of a single retailer who sold 5,000 Marks worth of a single title by giving copies on approval to his customers.[108] Finally, it has to be realized that the ideal of unfettered competition held so fervently by German businessmen both within and without the book trade at mid-century was no longer embraced by so many in the late 1880s. The trend towards cartelization in the book trade represented by the Kröner Reform was part of a trend which swept over many German trades and businesses at that time.

## Notes

1  The Bundestag's action on the classics was part of a law giving copyright protection until 30 years after an author's death. The works of writers who had previously been granted copyright protection in the entire confederation, i.e., the most famous of the classic writers of the late eighteenth and early nineteenth centuries, were to be protected for 30 years from November 9, 1837, if the writers had died before that date. See "Die deutschen Classiker und der Buchhandel," *Börsenblatt* 1867, Nr. 221, pp. 2371–2372.

2  Ibid., p. 2371.

3  At first Cotta had set a price of two Reichsthaler for the 1867 Schiller edition. He was forced to lower it when a Leipzig publisher named A. H. Payne announced that he would soon be offering a set of Schiller's complete works for one Reichsthaler to those who subscribed to his popular periodical, *Das Familie Journal*. See: "Schillers saemmtliche Werke fur einen Thaler," *Börsenblatt* 1867, Nr. 239, p. 2583.

4  Quoted in Schulze, *Der deutsche Buchhandel*, pp. 210–211.

5  Ibid., p. 487.

6  The Menz figures are cited in E. Umlauff, *Beitrige zur Statistik des deutschen Buchhandels*, Leipzig 1934, p. 159.

7  "Zur Statistik," *Börsenblatt* 1869, Nr 208, p. 2870.

8  In 1869, for example, there were 12 German book stores in New York City and 10 each in London, Paris, and St. Petersberg. There were many in the Austro-Hungarian monarchy, too. See "Zur Statistik des Buchhandels," *Börsenblatt* 1869, Nr. 208, p. 2870.

9  "Dresdens Buchhandel," *Börsenblatt* 1884, Nr 176.

10  Figures for 1875 and 1882 from *Umlauff, Beitraege zur Statistik des deutschen Buchhandels*, p. 52. Figures for 1888 from "Buchhaendler Geographie," part VI of the Adressbuch des deutschen Buchhandels, Jg. 51 1889 pp. 401–466.

11  These restrictions had been ended by several of the German states earlier in the decade.

12  According to Goldfriedrich, *Geschichte*, p. 489, in 1867 about 30 of every 100,000 Germans were university students; in 1885, 57 were.

13  In 1870 about 36 percent of the German population was urban, in 1880 42 percent, and in 1890 47 percent. In 1870 every twentieth German lived in a large city; in 1900 every fifth did. See Goldfriedrich, *Geschichte*, pp. 488–489.

14  E. Johann, *Die deutsche Buchverlage des Naturalismus und der Neuromantik Weimar*, 1935, pp. 14–16.

15  Uhlig, *Geschichte des Buches und des Buchhandels*, pp. 64, 68.

16  See: d., "Statistisches zur Misere des deutschen Buchhandels," *Börsenblatt* 1872, Nr. 95, p. 1559.

17  The Bibliographisches Institute's series of classics was called the "Bibliothek der deutschen National-Literatur," Hempel's was called the "Bibliothek der Gesammtliteratur".

18  On Hempel and the *Nationalbibliothek* see: Muehlbrecht, "Der Feldzug der deutschen Verleger," *Börsenblatt* 1867, Nr. 59, p. 627. On Mueller-Grote see the article "Carl Mueller-Grote," *Adressbuch des deutschen Buchhandels*, 1913.

19  Jaeger and Langewiesche, *Geschichte des Deutschen Buchhandels im 19. Und 20. Jahrhundert*, 2001, p. 21.

20  Meiner, *Reclam*, pp. 16–19, 27–29.

21  A. Last, "Der Einfluss der Leihbibliotheken auf den Roman-Absatz," *Börsenblatt* 1884, Nr. 162, pp. 3247–3248.

22  Ibid., p. 3248.

23  Ruprecht, *Vaeter und Soehne*, pp. 214–215.

24  "Carl Mueller-Grote," pp. v–i.

25  *Börsenblatt* 1878, Nr. 67, p. 1134.

26  A. Spemann, *Wilhelm Spemann, Ein Baumeister unter der Verlegern*, Stuttgart 1943, pp. 142–154.

27  Both series were printed by the same printer, which is one reason for the similarity of type.

28  Lohrer, *Cotta*, p. 136.

29  X., "Weihnachtskatalog," *Börsenblatt* 1888, Nr. 221, p. 4646.

30  *Börsenblatt* 1877, Nr. 257, p. 4291, Nr. 286, p. 4919.

31  Seemann, "Noch etwas Ueber den Illustrierten Weihnachtskatalog," *Börsenblatt* 1872, Nr. 47, p. 722.

32 It covered books published during the current year up until September (when the catalog went into print).

33 The publisher Gustav Langenscheidt sent 1,912 review copies to 415 newspapers between 1869 and 1878. Of the 1,912 copies: 590 were reviewed, 60 were not reviewed but returned to Langenscheidt. 1,262 were neither reviewed nor returned; Langenscheidt assumed that these books were either enriching the newspaper editors' home libraries or were sold to Modern Antiquarian book dealers. See G. Langenscheidt, "Zum Capital der Recensionsexemplare," *Börsenblatt* 1879, Nr. 53, pp. 898–899.

34 "Grober Unfug," *Börsenblatt* 1886, Nr. 60, p. 1355.

35 *Börsenblatt* 1872, Nr. 13, p. 195.

36 Quoted in Spemann, *Wilhelm Spemann*, pp. 102–103.

37 Quoted in ibid., p. 103.

38 Meiner, *Reclam*, p. 50. Reclam experimented with the dye on his cheap Shakespeare edition of 1865–1867.

39 C. Mueller-Grote, *Adressbuch des deutschen Buchhandels*, 1913, p. vii.

40 G. Schmitz, *Funfundsiebzig Jahre George Westermann, Braunschweig*, Brunswick 1913, pp. 63, 86.

41 *Börsenblatt* 1884, Nr. 138, pp. 2776–2777.

42 Krieg, *Materialien zu einer Entwicklungsgeschichte der Buecher-Preise*, p. 32.

43 In 1869 the *Börsenblatt* (Nr. 230, p. 3195) reported that Gustav Freytag and his publisher, the Weidmann Publishing Company, had borrowed ideas from England to sell his novels in large editions at low prices.

44 F. Vincentz, "Die Entwicklung der deutschen Buecherpreise," *Börsenblatt* (Frankfurt edition) Nr. 18, March 1958), p. 265.

45 Data from ibid., p. 265. The mean selling price of all German books considered together remained almost constant from 1860 until the mid-1880's: Since, however, real incomes rose during these years, it grew progressively easier for people to afford books.

46 *Börsenblatt* 1876, Nr. 38, p. 583.

47 Last, "Der Einfluss der Leihbibliotheken," *Börsenblatt* 1884, Nr. 162, p. 3248.

48 R., "Hohe Buecherpreise," *Börsenblatt* 1874, Nr. 131, pp. 2109–2110; J. Petzholdt, "Was macht in Deutschland die Buecher theuer?," *Börsenblatt* 1882, Nr. 224, pp. 4117–4118. However, M-r, "Hohe Buecher-preise," *Börsenblatt* 1874, pp. 2079–2080, argues that inflation had made books cheaper by lowering their real prices.

49 T. Petermann, "Der deutsche Buchhandel und seine Abnehmer," *Jahrbuch der Gehe-Stiftung zu Dresden*, vol. XII Dresden 1906, pp. 19–20.

50 Moritz Brand, "Unsere Volksliteratur," *Deutsche Buchhandler-Akademie*, V, 1888, pp. 224–229.

51 Franzos, "Autorrecht und Leihbibliothek," *Börsenblatt* 1884, Nr. 11, p. 179. During the 1880s, authors began agitating to make lending libraries either pay more for books than private individuals—with the extra charge going to authors—or pay royalties to a book's author each time it was lent out. But the agitation came to nothing.

52 *Börsenblatt* 1884, Nr. 206, p. 4000. It should be noted that mass-circulation magazines like the *Gartenlaube* (1879 circulation 375,000 copies per issue) printed a great deal of fiction; they were the cheapest source of run-of-the-mill fiction, and their popularity gives credence to the argument that publishers could have sold much more fiction had they priced it more cheaply.

53 "Fuer und wider die Leihbibliotheken in frueheren Tagen," *Börsenblatt* (Frankfurt edition) 1957, Nr. 38, pp. 582–583.

54 Seemann, *Fingerzeige zur Abschaetzung von Sortiments – (Antiquariats) und Verlagsgeschiften*, pp. 24–26.

55  K. Heinrici, "Die Verhaeltnisse im deutschen Colportagebuchhandel," *Schriften des Vereins fuer Sozialpolitik*, LXXIX; *Untersuchungen ueber die Lage des Hausiergewerbes in Deutschland*, vol. III Leipzig 1899, p. 193. These are very conservative figures, based on the annual trade *Adressbuecher*, which did not include all the firms which were actually engaging in the trade.

56  The best sources on the branches of the Itinerant Book Trade are: Heinrici, "Die Verhaeltnisse im deutschen Colportagebuchhandel," pp. 184–188; and A. Vogel, *Die Beschraenkungen des Wanderbuchhandels in Deutschland. Historisch-kritische Darstellung* (Dissertation for Tuebingen University, published Kirchhain, 1906), pp. 1–14.

57  R. Ackerrmann, *Ueber den deutschen Colportage-Buchhandel*, 1876, pp. 3–4.

58  Ibid., pp. 3–4.

59  Berger, "Der Buchhandel in der Lausitz," *Börsenblatt* 1876, Nr. 216, p. 3320.

60  Drahn, *Geschichte des deutschen Buch-und Zeitschriften-handels*, pp. 56–57, estimates that there were 3,000 firms employing a total of 6,000 salesmen in the Colporteur Book Trade in the mid-1880s. The General Union of Colporteur Book Dealers in the German Empire, in an 1886 pamphlet, maintained that there were 8,000 firms and 35,000 salesmen, a figure which probably includes all branches of the Itinerant Trade.

61  Elsner, *Beitrige und Dokumente zur Geschichte des werbenden Buch-und Zeitschriftenhandels*, vol. I, pp. 37–38.

62  As a rule, Colporteur firms bought from wholesalers rather than directly from publishers. The wholesalers grew powerful and arrogant as time went on, selling on whatever terms they chose and foreclosing mercilessly on their debtors. See Elsner, *Beitrage zur Geschichte des werbenden Buch-und Zeitschriftenhandels*, vol. I, pp. 50–51.

63  Elsner, *Beitrage zur Geschichte des werbenden Buch-und Zeitschriftenhandels*, vol. I, p. 38.

64  Eisner, *Beitraege*, pp. 42, 121–122.

65  Streissler, *Der Kolportagehandel*, pp. 8–11.

66  Vogel, *Die Beschrankungen des Wanderbuchhandels*, p. 3.

67  Streissler, *Der Kolportagehandel*, pp. 8–11.

68  Vogel, *Die Beschrankungen des Wanderbuchhandels*, p. 7.

69  Ibid., p. 3.

70  "Zum Colportagewesen," *Börsenblatt* 1876, Nr. 83, p. 1295.

71  The deposit could be money, a watch, a ring, or something similar.

72  All itinerant book salesmen were covered under Sections 42, 44, and 55 of the Gewerbeordnung of June 21, 1869. A revision of this law in 1883 tightened the requirements and conditions for traditional book peddlers who carried books on their backs but did not apply to salesmen who sold subscriptions.

73  Another factor which tarnished its image was the Colporteur Trade's reputation for selling obscene and socially corrosive literature to the masses.

74  "Zum Capitel der Colportage," *Börsenblatt* 1880, Nr. 226, p. 4852.

75  Drahn, *Geschichte des deutschen Buch-und Zeitschriftenhandels*, p. 56.

76  *1863–1963. Hundert Jahre Loewes Verlag Ferdinand Carl Stuttgart*, Stuttgart 1963, pp. 21–22.

77  Elsner, *Beitrige zur Geschichte des werbenden Buch-und Zeitschriftenhandels*, p. 65.

78  Streissler, *Der Kolportagehandel*, pp. 2–3.

79  Ibid., pp. 46–69.

80  R. Trenkel, "Zur Abwehr," *Börsenblatt* 1873, Nr. 53, p. 849.

81  "Ein neuer Modus, Geschaefte zu machen," *Börsenblatt* 1883, Nr. 152, p. 2892.

82  Streissler, *Der Kolportagehandel*, pp. 22–23.

83  Vogel, *Die Beschraenkungen des Wanderbuchhandels*, pp. 8–10.

84  B., "Gegen ungehoerige Beeintraeichtigung des Sortimenters," *Börsenblatt* 1873, Nr. 172, p. 2724.

85 *Börsenblatt* 1873, Nr. 192, p. 3018.
86 Doctor Adalbert Brauer helped me track down information on the Discount-Mongers (Schleuderer). There is actually very little specific information on the Schleuderer considering all that was written against them. They were usually referred to as a monolithic block—"the Discount-Mongers" or "them". See: A. Klasing, "Die Sortimentgrossisten in Leipzig," *Börsenblatt* 1878, Nr. 98, pp. 1682–1684, for the best contemporary account of "them."
87 So said the Bonn publisher Emil Strauss in 1879; quoted in Goldfriedrich, *Geschichte*, p. 499.
88 Ibid., pp. 485, 498.
89 R. Streller, "Entgegnung," *Börsenblatt* 1878, Nr. 134, pp. 2278–2279.
90 Dziatzko, "Zur gegenwaertige Lage," p. 522.
91 Ibid., p. 532.
92 Ibid., p. 516, says that the institutions of the book trade may have been similar in Denmark.
93 Goldfriedrich, *Geschichte*, p. 496.
94 H. Blumenthal, *Die wichtigsten Arbeiten des Sortimenters* Iglau, Vienna, Leipzig, 1887, p. 8.
95 There is a good description on pp. 516–517 of Dziatzko, "Zur gegenwaertige Lage."
96 Blumenthal, *Die wichtigsten Arbeiten des Sortimenters*, pp. 115–116.
97 Junius, "Der Muenchener Sortimentsbuchhandel von heute," *Börsenblatt* 1868, Nr. 21, pp. 238–239.
98 Ibid., pp. 238–239. See also "Ein neuer Beitrag zur Schleuderer-Statistik," *Börsenblatt* 1879, Nr. 76, p. 1297.
99 Quoted in Goldfriedrich, *Geschichte*, p. 499.
100 A good contemporary discussion of price-cutting presenting various viewpoints is "Die 'Schleuderer,' das 'solide Sortiment' und die Literatur," *Börsenblatt* 1886, Nr. 60, p. 1355, Nr. 66, p. 1499.
101 For some examples see: "Fort mit dem Kundenrabatt! Epistel eines saechsischen Provinzial-Sortimenters an seine Leipziger Collegen," *Börsenblatt* 1873, Nr. 219, pp. 3463–3464.
102 Dziatzko, "Zur gegenwaertige Lage," p. 519.
103 Lohrer, *Cotta*, p. 144. Kroener is supposed to have convinced Bismarck to write his memoirs, which Kroener published; it seems unlikely, however, that Bismarck needed much convincing.
104 The most complete accounts of the Kroener Reform and the events leading up to it are Goldfriedrich, *Geschichte*, pp. 497–573 and G. Jaeger, D. Langewiesche, and W. Siemann, eds., *Geschichte des deutschen Buchhandels im 19. Und 20. Jahrhundert*, Frankfurt/Main 2001.
105 Most notably by a Leipzig professor named Karl Buecher in his *Der deutsche Buchhandel und die Wissenschaft* (3rd edition, Leipzig, 1904). Buecher's book unleashed a furious controversy, which produced reams of pamphlet literature.
106 Hase, *Development of the Book Industries of Leipzig*, p. 54. Emphasis mine; I have changed a few words to make Hase's clumsy English more lucid.
107 Dziatzko, "Zur gegenwaertige Lage", p. 518.
108 "Der Kampf ums Dasein," *Börsenblatt* 1882, Nr. 187, p. 3395.

# 8  The mass book market explodes, 1870–1890

The early 1870s are the great divide in the history of the mass book market, setting it apart from the earlier market. Before 1870 or 1871 the market's growth had been steady; after, it was explosive—the boom of the regular trade was paralleled by that of the mass trade. Before the early 1870s, the reading tastes of the masses had been conservative, confined to things which had been popular for decades or even centuries; after, they broadened to take in new kinds of books and new forms of reading matter. Again, before about 1870 only a minority of lower-class Germans had been involved in the market; after 1870, a majority were.

Yet while both the growth of, and the changes in, the mass book market after 1870 set it apart from the mass market existing before the time of German unification, these were not sudden, revolutionary phenomena. They were the fruition of long-underway developments in press technology, demography, economics, education, and in the mass book trade itself. The potential that was presented by these developments was realized by innovative and aggressive marketing.

By 1870 printing technology had advanced to the point where it was both fast and cheap to turn out huge editions of books. High-speed, steam-driven presses, refinements of König's designs, were in use all over Germany. Into these presses could be fed inexpensive and plentiful wood pulp paper; it didn't matter that this paper looked cheap and disintegrated in a few decades, because the mass book trade did not produce for eternity. Illustrations could be done on the high- speed lithographic presses invented by the Frenchman Henri Voirin in 1860, where previously they could only by produced on slow hand presses. In the 20 years after 1870, moreover, important new inventions made it still cheaper to print material for the mass market. In 1873 Germany's first rotary press was constructed, and others quickly followed. Rotary presses were ideal for fast runs of newspapers and periodicals. Shortly after 1873, ways were devised to make lithographic plates of zinc rather than of stone; the zinc plates could be used in rotary presses. Finally, type-casting machines were put into operation in the early 1880s making it possible to eliminate the slower and less reliable hand labor.[1]

The possibilities given the mass trade by the new printing technology were enlarged by the demographic and economic changes of the era. Germany urbanized rapidly, workers' incomes rose, and the working week (for urban workers) was shortened.[2] Although modest, the rise in incomes and the reduction of working hours gave workers more disposable income and more leisure time. And since these workers were in urban environments, it was more likely that some of the money and some of the time would be spent on reading matter. As had long been true, people read more in urban settings. A writer's description of Leipzig in the 1890s applies as well to any large German city in the 1870s and 1880s: "There is a constantly growing population, its desire to read either fully awakened or brought to the point where it is easily awakened, by the many stimuli which the big city offers."[3] The social reformer Otto v. Leixner wrote in 1891 that: "In small towns and in rural areas the urge to read has not grown so much [among the masses], but in the big cities it has assumed almost fearful dimensions."[4]

It was the big cities, cities whose population exceeded 100,000, that were the fastest growing urban areas in Germany, and urban Germany was growing much faster than rural Germany. In 1871, 36 percent of the country's population was urban, in 1880, 42 percent, and in 1890, 47 percent.[5]

With more time to read, more money to spend on reading matter, and very often more desire to read, the German masses were also more capable of reading than they had been earlier. Literacy was more prevalent. Rudolf Schenda, the leading German scholar of the mass book trade, estimates that as of 1870, about 75 percent of the Central European populace was made up of actual or potential book readers.[6] For Germany alone the figure would be higher. The Prussian census of 1871 revealed that roughly 90 percent of all male citizens over nine years of age was "literate." Had it not been for the large, ill-educated Polish population in the Kingdom's eastern reaches, the figure would have been higher. Areas of Prussia, with few Poles, had higher incidences of literacy than the Kingdom as a whole and were most representative of the rest of Germany.[7] Only 2.05 percent of Berlin's population was illiterate according to the 1871 census, while the figures for the provinces of Saxony and Brandenburg were, respectively, 3.63 percent and 7.02 percent. Of course these numbers refer only to males. The 1871 census indicated that there were over twice as many illiterate females as males, most of them doubtless older women who had grown up before girls were expected to attend elementary school.[8]

Already high in 1871, the rate of literacy increased after that. Statistics on recruits into the Imperial Army show that in 1875, 2.5 percent were illiterate, in 1880, 1.6 percent, in 1889–1890, 1.3 percent, and in 1889–1890 0.51 percent. Only Sweden and Denmark had lower incidences of illiteracy than Germany in the 1880s.[9]

It does have to be kept in mind, however, that none of these statistics reveal anything about semi-literacy; many of the people whom the statistics cheerfully classified as "literate" were actually semi-literate. Professor Theodore

Hamerow has estimated that one in 20 male Germans was semi-literate at the time of national unification.[10] Yet even if 20 percent of the males—and 30 to 40 percent of the females—were semi-literate, it remains that two-thirds to three-quarters of the population were neither illiterate nor semi-literate. A substantial majority were genuinely literate, genuinely capable of reading at least simple material.

Most of these people had attained literacy in the state elementary schools, the only schools which nine-tenths of all Germans ever attended. Earlier in the century many children had not attended school at all, but by 1870 almost all did. Earlier in the century many more boys than girls had gone to school, but with the passage of time the gap between the number of boys and the number of girls attending school had continually shrunk. In the 1870s and 1880s it shrank further. Thirty thousand more boys than girls were enrolled in Prussia's elementary schools in 1864; 22 years later, when the total enrollment in the Kingdom's elementary schools had increased by over 2,000,000, there were only 6,000 more boys than girls attending. Since lower-class females, like their sisters in the middle and upper classes, tended to read more than males, the great increase in the number of girls going to school was fortunate for the mass book trade.[11]

In the 1870s Prussia remedied some of its earlier financial neglect of the elementary schools. In 1871 the kingdom spent almost as much on its seven universities with their 7,000 pupils as upon its 25,000 elementary schools with their nearly 4,000,000 pupils. Six years later, however, the funding for elementary schools was almost three times as large as that for the universities.[12] The pupil–teacher ratio declined for the first time in the century.[13] In addition, from 1871 to 1878, the salaries of elementary school teachers increased significantly. The man responsible for all these reforms was the scourge of the Papists, Adalbert Falk, who was Minister of Public Worship from 1872 to 1879.[14]

Despite Falk's efforts, however, Prussia continued to have a shortage of teachers and classrooms—a shortage of 11,015 teachers and 9,825 classrooms as late as 1891. The teachers' salaries which Falk raised were lowered within a few years of his leaving office. These facts are indications that Prussia, like the other states in the Empire, would go just so far in supporting elementary schools. It never had been the function of mass education to break down class barriers; it did not become so after 1870. The elementary school in the 1870s and 1880s had the same function as had the elementary school of the 1790s or 1820s—to give lower-class Germans sufficient skill in reading and calculation to do their jobs efficiently and to instill in them piety and patriotism. When curriculum changes were made, as for example in the Decree of October 15, 1872, their intent was to make the children better able to work with the new technologies sweeping trade, agriculture, and industry, and better able to resist the blandishments of Socialist agitators, not to enrich them with humanistic culture.[15]

Thus the graduate of a German elementary school in 1875 or 1885 was no more *gebildet*, no more cultivated in the humanistic tradition, than elementary school graduates had ever been. He (or she) lacked that conviction of the value of reading, that obsession to read (or seem to read) as much as possible, which characterized the middle-class German. He would find it difficult to comprehend why anyone would want to read Goethe or Schiller; she would feel the same about von Scheffel.

The lower-class German was not antipathetic towards reading—he simply did not consider it as important as did middle- and upper-class Germans. But he would read some. Peasants and artisans had long read to obtain useful information, delving into occupational handbooks, medical and dream books, lottery guides, and the like. They had long read for spiritual edification and consolation. Reading merely for entertainment, on the other hand, had never been much practiced by lower-class Germans. Yet the popularity of folk stories and Knight/Bandit/Ghost tales among them earlier in the century indicated that they might read more for diversion if material suitable to their tastes and means were made available. Moreover, by the 1870s the custom of extensive reading—the reading of many books once rather than a few over and over again—had become well entrenched among the German masses, just as it had among the middle and upper levels of society during the late eighteenth and early nineteenth centuries.[16]

It is obvious that the German masses constituted a book market of enormous potential in the early 1870s. While their per capita outlays for reading matter could not approach that of their betters, there were many more of them. But it should also be obvious that this market would not grow of itself, untended and uncultivated: reading was not that important to the masses and no lower-class German would voluntarily walk into a book store. The social taboo which kept lower-class people out of book stores meant that the trade had to go directly to them, usually in the form of an itinerant book-seller. Of the branches of the Itinerant Trade, the Colporteur Book Trade proved best suited to reaching the mass public, especially that in urban areas.

Even the glibbest Colporteur salesman, however, could not long succeed unless he had appealing reading material. This material had to be generated by publishers, who were keystones to the mass trade as they were to the regular trade. The mass trade required publishers who could comprehend and cater to lower-class tastes, which were very different from middle- and upper-class tastes. In 1870 there were a number of publishing houses which had been successfully catering to the masses for a long time. They included: B. G. Teubner in Leipzig, Winter in Frankfurt/Main, Beck in Nordhausen, G. J. Manz and Friedrich Pustet in Regensburg, Wolff and Rieger in Augsburg, and Ensslin and Laiblin and Fleischhauer and Spohn in Reutlingen. Well entrenched, long since having achieved the needed understanding of the mass mind, these firms continued active after 1870.[17]

But the field was not left to them alone. They were joined by a great influx of speculative publishers, men of varied and sundry pasts, from crimi-nals and men of sleazy cunning, to sincere little businessmen, to men of piety. Many of these people could not have entered the publishing trade before the advent of industrial freedom ended the old entry requirements. They gave to the mass book trade a powerful jolt of energy and new ideas like those received by the regular trade in the 1820s and 1830s.[18] Because they belonged to the mass trade, however, they have been deemed worthy of study neither by contemporaries nor by later scholars. They included: Werner Grosse of Berlin, Hermann Oeser of Neusalza, A. Weichert of Berlin, Hermann Dietrich of Dresden, and H. G. Münchmeyer of Dresden. Münchmeyer is probably the best known of them, but more for trying to browbeat the famous writer Karl May into marrying his sister than for his work as a publisher.[19]

For all the dearth of biographical information on mass trade publishers, there is no doubt that they were the central figures of the trade.[20] Rarely did they wait for manuscripts to be offered to them. Instead, they initiated plans for books, sometimes going so far as to draw up detailed outlines which they commissioned hacks to execute. Karl May, for example, was hired by Münchmeyer to write a total of six novels.[21]

Once a publisher had decided to have a book done, he expected copy to be turned out at a fast clip by his writers. And some of the writers working the mass trade obliged with astonishingly prolific production, almost as if they were mass-producing reading matter. One Franz Pistorius turned out nearly 2,000 (printed) pages between 1885 and 1888. W. Frey, who wrote for the same publisher, produced 194 stories between 1875 and 1888, each from 60 to 65 printed pages in length. Frey's total output for those 13 years was therefore about 12,000 pages; that they were small 12 mo pages detracts little from his sheer physical achievement. A writer named Fritz Möhrlin turned out six chatty agricultural manuals for a Stuttgart publisher between 1876 and 1878. Karl May's total output was immense. It is likely that books turned out so fast differed little from one another, but that mattered little to mass trade publishers—if the same basic story could be sold 20, or 40, or more times, masquerading as that many different stories, it was all money in the bank.[22]

The mass trade allowed authors no time to agonize over the "right word" or profound symbolism, no time to rummage deeply in source materials. Mass trade publishers kept a close reign upon their writers, treating them like wage laborers. Even a stellar performer like Karl May saw his manuscripts altered in a cavalier manner by a publisher. The procrastination and independence that publishers of scholarly and reference works for the middle- and upper-class market often had to endure from their authors, the self-indulgences and eccentricities that publishers of "serious" literature sometimes suffered from the writers whom they published—such things were not tolerated in the mass book trade. A letter from a publisher of crime thrillers to a writer he had under contract read:

> We're now up to your fourth instalment … and it's still too insipid, it doesn't grip and terrify [the reader]. How much longer can this go on? When at last is there going to be a murder or some spicy scene to make the story exciting? We're almost to the point where we regret having

placed our trust in you. Your broad, cozy description of family life doesn't appeal to the tastes of our readers at all.... The end of the seventh installment must have a detailed, exact description of a murder or other gruesome act, which will be further developed in the eighth installment and concluded in the ninth.[23]

It is unfortunate that the identity of the publisher who wrote this letter is not known, for he demonstrates a superb understanding of what the German masses liked and did not like in their fiction. He, and some other mass trade publishers, had a feel for their market which rivalled that of Friedrich Arnold Brockhaus or Joseph Meyer for the middle-class market; and they too were imitated by the unoriginal majority of their publisher-peers.

The smartest of the mass trade publishers sensed that the lower classes, particularly those in cities, were ready for new reading matter. They were ready for reading matter which was new in two respects: (1) dealing with topics hitherto not seen in books for the mass market, or dealing with traditional topics in untraditional ways, and (2) packaged in new ways, for example as illustrated magazines and newspapers. To realize the masses' readiness to absorb new reading matter would require new marketing techniques. In the early 1870s the ablest of the mass trade's publishers did a great deal of pondering and experimenting with new books and new marketing devices.

The first wave of experimentation came with the so-called "Colporteur novel." "Colporteur novels" were novels which were issued in numerous installments at regular intervals. Each installment was from eight to 12 pages long. Normally there were from 50 to 150 installments, but some novels stretched to 200 or even 250. An installment retailed for 10 Pfennig.[24]

"Colporteur novels" had actually appeared first in the mid-1860s, but became much more common after 1870. They were sold mainly by the salesmen of the Colporteur Book Trade, hence their name. Rarely were they sold by the old-style "Colporteurs" (i.e., peddlers) who carried their wares upon their backs and who circulated in rural areas. This point was not that clear to middle-class contemporaries. In respectable and cultivated circles it was common to refer to "Colporteur novels" as "trashy literature" and as "back stairs novels," the latter name derived from the widely accepted supposition that the books were sold furtively to servants on the back stairs by sinister characters. As a writer for the *Gartenlaube* expressed it, "A large part of the [middle and upper class] German public can associate the words 'Colporteur' and 'the Colporteur Trade' only with shadowy figures who slither up and down the back stairs."[25] "Colporteur novels" were also known by the neutral term "10-Pfennig novels."

These novels were directed, observed a contributor to the *Börsenblatt*, "at a public which has hitherto not even existed for the book trade, [that is,] the broad masses, the lower orders of the populace, who previously hardly even knew what the word 'book' meant, let alone purchased books."[26] Somewhat overstated, the point was nonetheless well taken. The publishers of "Colporteur novels" did cater to the broad masses. Aware that the masses were intimidated by books, especially big and elegant-looking books, they had their novels deliberately printed in a crude style reminiscent of old-fashioned devotional works and schoolbooks—physically reminiscent, in other words, of books to which the lower classes had long been exposed.[27]

Moreover, the "Colporteur novel" came to the lower-class German in small segments that were suggestive of the pamphlets that had long circulated among the masses. Even the poor reader turned out by the state elementary schools could expect to have mastered one installment by the time the next one was delivered to his house. Had the publisher issued the novel as a single volume, or even as two or three volumes as was common in the regular trade, its size would have scared off many potential customers.[28]

Similarly, had publishers demanded that the total price of a "Colporteur novel"—frequently 10 to 15 Marks—be paid at once, no one could or would have paid it. But the worker or artisan would have 10 Pfennig in his pocket to pay for each chapter as it came. Publishers calculated that he would be too simple to figure out the total cost of the novel. In a better world, the worker or artisan would have quickly seen through the publisher's sham and freed himself from such exploitation; but in the real world of the 1870s and 1880s nothing of the kind happened, and the lower-class German sometimes ended up spending more for reading matter than many middle- or upper-class people. A maid in the employ of the social reformer Heinrich Fränkel in the 1880s for example, spent over 5 Marks in a single three month period on "Colporteur novels."[29]

As to the content of the "Colporteur novels," publishers strove for a product which was simple in its diction, blunt in its narrative, concrete in its images, and exciting in its effect. Otto Glagau, in a fascinating essay published in the *Börsenblatt* in 1870, asserted that:

> No story [in a "Colporteur novel"] can be without ghosts and magic, murder and manslaughter, for the masses have a burning craving for simple facts, [for] compact and unadorned incident, for an uninterrupted and relentless pace, for a riot of ever-new twists and turns of plot, the wilder and more improbable the better. They don't want to be given the opportunity to linger and to reflect, but rather want to be perpetually surprised and dazzled, to be dragged through a labyrinth of incident, and to be shocked and stunned by ceaseless, explosive, and unexpected swerves in the plot.[30]

A Colporteur Trade handbook cautioned against letting any event in a novel run on too long, lest reader ire erupt; the readers of "Colporteur novels" followed the plots intently, and if "in the 60th installment the sweet, innocent Wanda is still languishing in the dungeon of the repulsive, lecherous Count Kuno von Rechenfels,"[31] there would be vociferous complaints and threats of cancelled subscriptions made to the salesman and delivery boys.

The people whom publishers contracted to write "Colporteur novels" were, according to Glagau, well suited to turning out exciting copy. Many had only to draw upon their own tumultuous lives for ideas and inspiration:

> As a rule all of them ... have one thing in common, a thing which while not absolutely necessary for the work which they do, is nonetheless desirable and advantageous: almost all of them have a more or less eventful life behind them, a life which has tossed them about a good deal and has thus enabled them to accumulate a rich treasury of experience. Among them are for example many ex-soldiers and former Foreign Legionaries,... former merchants and seamen, [former] actors and artists, waiters and artisans, retired bureaucrats and bureaucrats fired from their posts, decadent students and scholars, and in general many ruined people from all levels of society.[32]

Others had lived less turbulent external lives, but could draw upon inner creative reserves and the like:

> Among the Colporteur writers there are also utterly solid, even stuffy (*stockspießbürgerlich*) people who've never drunk anything but ... beer their entire lives..., men who do their jobs ... all day long and only pick up the pen during their leisure hours motivated to do so perhaps by some inner compulsion, perhaps [merely by the desire] to earn some money. The most popular Colporteur author in Berlin ... a man whose publisher cherishes him as he does his own wife and daughter, is presently a clerk who spends his days working behind the counter and writes his novels only in the still of the night.[33]

For all this great reservoir of creative talent, most of the early "Colporteur novels" were little more than old tales recast in endless installments–old Knight/ Bandit stories, old ghost stories, old mushy love stories, and trashy old French novels. New editions, of *Rinaldo Rinaldini* and new biographies of Schinderhannes entertained the masses as earlier ones had. One publisher's *Schinderhannes—the Greatest Robber Captain of the 19th Century (Schinderhannes, der größte Räuberhauptmann des 19. Jahrhunderts)* brought him a profit of two million Marks.[34]

The persistence of traditional stories was probably more the result of deliberate calculation by the publishers than of their (and their authors') inability to think up new ones, however. Reasoning that the masses would want the familiar at first, they chose familiar stories and decked them out with the familiar old-fashioned double titles:

- *Redhanded Hugo, or the Dancing Corpses on the Rabenstein (Der rothhandige Hugo, oder die tanzenden Leichen auf dem Rabenstein).*
- *The Beautiful Girl from Samos, or Nights of Horror in the Prisons of the Seven Towers of Constantinople (Das schöne Mädchen von Samos, oder die Schreckensnächte in den Gefängnissen der sieben Thürme zu Konstantinopel).*

- *America's Children of Hell and the Dark Ghosts of Europe, or the Battle for Human Rights (Amerikas Kinder der Hölle und finstern Geister Europas, oder der Kampf um Menschenrechte).*
- *White Slaves, or a Victim of the Church (Weisse Sklaven, oder ein Opfer der Kirche).*
- *The Count of Steinfels, or Murderer of Women (Der Graf von Steinfels oder Frauenmörder).*[35]

Yet despite the familiar elements, there were differences which set the "Colporteur novels" apart from earlier mass fiction. For one thing, they were more bloodthirsty, as publishers after 1870 noted that the masses liked ever-stronger doses of gore. Moreover, by the mid-1870s publishers, experimenting with lures, had come up with new themes and topics to supplement the old ones. The most-used of the new concepts were: (1) the novelization of spectacular contemporary events and (2) novels about crime and/or scandal with contemporary settings.[36] Works based upon these concepts were among the most successful "Colporteur novels" ever published.

The contemporary events which were most often novelized were those involving the mysteries and misfortunes of royalty. Whether coincidentally or not it is difficult to say, but Europe's crowned heads did provide an unusual number of thrills for novelists to work upon during that era—when else had there been such juicy scandals, such touching suicides? The tragi-comic career of Louis Napoleon inspired things like *The Ill-fated Bride, or Secrets of Emperor Napoleon III (Die Schicksalsbraut, oder die Geheimnisse des Kaisers Napoleon's III)*, a novel which also dwelt at length upon the fates of Maximilian of Mexico and his wife Carlotta. Maximilian was a popular topic in his own right, too. The 1868 Spanish Revolution, made spicy by the revelation of scandals concerning the deposed Queen Isabella, gave the German masses *Isabella, Spain's Deposed Queen or Secrets of the Court of Madrid (Isabella, Spaniensverjägte Königin, oder die Geheimnisse des Hofes yon Madrid).*[37]

Closer to home, the big topics were the suicide of the Austrian Archduke Rudolf at Mayerling in 1889 and the escapades of mad King Ludwig II of Bavaria, who killed himself in 1886. In Berlin alone 50,000 copies of *Secrets of the Royal Palace or Revelations about the Life and Death of Ludwig (Die Geheimnisse des Königschlosses oder Enthüllungen über Leben und Tod Ludwigs)* were sold, and it was only one of 13 "Colporteur novels" about the insane Bavarian king. Twenty-two novels about the Mayerling tragedy were published, the most popular of them being bought by 80,000 Germans.[38]

Even commoners could hope to be novelized—if they were involved in gruesome murders and crimes. "Dozens" of novels were inspired by the evidences of unspeakable horrors discovered at a cloister in Cracau in the 1860s, according to Glagau.[39] The exploits of a murderer named Schentz were recounted in several novels; Schentz always murdered women. Then there were the "Colporteur novels," which were based upon composites of many murders and murderers than upon specific cases. An example of such a book was the immensely popular (140,000 copies sold) *The Murderer of Women and his Victims (Der Frauenmörder und seine Opfer).*[40]

A veritable *Grand Guignol* of horrors made Victor von Falk's *The Executioner of Berlin (Der Scharfrichter von Berlin)* the most beloved of all "Colporteur novels." At least 260,000 copies were sold during its first year of publication, and estimates of its total sales run to over one million copies. It may have been the biggest-selling novel of the nineteenth century in Germany. Three thousand pages long, supposedly based in part upon the true life of a Berlin hangman named Krauts, its plot unfolded in such settings as: disreputable taverns, the dwelling of a madam, the home of the executioner, a usurer's house, a counterfeiter's workshop, an insane asylum, and the palaces of nobles. Its first 240 pages flung readers through: an orgy in a bandit hideout, a patricide, the hanging of an innocent maiden, an attempted poisoning, a revolt, and a grave robbery; while subsequent pages kept excitement high with: espionage, the hypnotism of a maiden, the kidnapping of a child and preparations for its murder, a train crash, divorce, a trapeze artist's fall, vows of vengeance, the burial of a living person, a duel, and more. The dialogue matched the events in its vigor. "Get dressed or I'll beat you bloody, you treacherous whore!" was the way one character expressed himself.[41]

The publisher of *Der Scharfrichter von Berlin* made a profit of three million Marks from the book.[42] Few publishers were near that fortunate, of course. Countless "Colporteur novels" flopped in the marketplace. Many were abandoned by their publishers after 50 or 80 of a projected 100 or 150 installments. A careful study done early in the twentieth century showed that of approximately 636 "Colporteur novels" published between 1860 and 1903, only 85—15 percent in other words—had had sales of more than 10,000 copies. The sales of many were under the 5,000 copies necessary to cover costs.[43]

To publish a "Colporteur novel" was a gamble. It was a bigger gamble than any other kind of book because the size of these novels and the way in which they were sold required large capital outlays before any sales had materialized. Contemporary trade literature indicates that it cost about 25,000 Marks to produce and market a "Colporteur novel" on a national scale in the 1870s. By the end of the decade of the 1880s, that sum would only yield a small novel to be marketed on a small geographic scale, for example only in Lusatia. The publisher who wanted to market all over Germany had to lay out as much as 150,000 Marks.[44]

The reason for these large investments was not author royalties. It was printing costs. Tremendous numbers of the initial five to seven installments of a "Colporteur novel" had to be printed so that Colporteur salesmen could distribute them gratis to as many people as possible. These free copies were supposed to hook people into subscribing to and paying for all the subsequent installments. The first installment was a prospectus giving a glowing overview of what was to come, while the next few were supposed to heat up the plot to a fever of irresistible intensity.

As it was considered the most crucial element in the marketing campaign, the first installment was drafted with care and cynical cunning. Just as the American pornography publishers of a few decades ago covered their book jackets with set phrases certain to arouse potential buyers, phrases like "lust slave" or "orgy girl," so the German publishers of "Colporteur novels" filled their first installments with vivid stereotyped words and phrases, pyrotechnical verbiage like: "cup of poison, deadly sins, sacrilege, . . . night of madness, gruesome grave, bloody ghost, frightful skeleton, devil in human form, [and] bandits' grotto."[45] Then, there were sweet idyllic set phrases used to describe the romances which were to come in later installments: "forest stillness, tumultuous ocean, fragrant glades of lemon trees. . . angel of peace, triumph of love, voluptuous beauty, enchanting charm, and boiling blood."[46]

Believed to be imbued with the power to loosen lower-class purse strings, these phrases were always used; at times they were strung together to form some of the most mindless prose ever printed. A first installment issued about 1870 crooned:

> Come out of the sweet stillness of the forest's solitude, dear reader *(Leserin)*, come to the shore of the tumultuous ocean, open your ears to the powerful roar of the storm-driven wild waves, and it will seem to you, even if you are from a small village as if you are making your first entry into the noisy, bustling, lively streets of a great city. Come now, take my hand, be guided by my experienced and sure hand into these streets by opening the pages of the first installment of a surging work, a work awaited with great expectation in all the lands where the German tongue resounds—*The Secrets of a Great City, or Sinners and Penitents*. It will reveal to you everything which your curiosity and your desires make you want to know: The Seven Deadly Sins of Devils in Human Form; The Hero; the Passions and Miseries in the Cottages of the Poor, in the Bandits' Grotto, in the Palaces of the Mighty. Yes, here will be unveiled before you all the Secrets Of This Earth in all their marvelous riches; here in a single work, *The Secrets of a Great City, or Sinners and Pentinants* you will be initiated into the knowledge of all these mysteries.[47]

Had the German language ever been debased into sentences so ridiculous? This passage, however, was representative of the prose used to sell "Colporteur novels." "One prospectus i.e., first installment was more fraudulent than another," admitted an apologist for the mass trade later.[48]

From 100,000 to 1,500,000 copies of each, such prospectuses were printed up for distribution by Colporteur Trade salesmen. The number printed decreased with each succeeding installment, a process which continued even after people had signed up for the novel—few subscribers saw these books through to the end. Below are some figures on a "Colporteur novel" unleased by a large Berlin publishing house.

*Table 8.1* Printing "Colporteur novels"[49]

| Number(s) | Installment | |
|---|---|---|
| | Quantity printed | |
| (Numbers 1–5 were distributed gratis) | 1 | 1,500,000 |
| | 2 | 215,000 |
| | 3 | 190,000 |
| | 4 | 180,000 |
| | 5 | 175,000 |
| Total for 1–5 | | 2,260,000 |
| | 6–8 | 70,000–75,000 |
| | 9–15 | 60,000–70,000 |
| | 16–28 | 50,000–60,000 |
| | 29–45 | 40,000–50,000 |
| | 46–70 | 30,000–40,000 |
| | 71–110 | 20,000–30,000 |
| | 111–120 | 18,000–20,000 |
| | 121–130 | 16,000–18,000 |
| | 131–136 | 15,000–16,000 |
| | 137–146 | 14,000–15,000 |
| | 147–150 | 13,000 |
| Total for 6–150 | | 4,600,000–5,000,000 |

Note
Figures from "Von der Kolportage," *Börsenblatt* 1892, Nr. 123, p. 3226.

Despite the large numbers of installments which had to be printed and distributed to generate the relatively few enduring sales, this novel produced for its publisher a profit of at least 80,000 Marks.[49]

What publisher would not be willing to gamble for a chance at profits like that? In the 1870s, when the "Colporteur novels" were the hottest item on the mass market, as many as 200 publishers tried their hand at them. Most produced novels which were turgid, dreary, boring, and silly even by the unsophisticated standards of the German masses. The usual practice was to attempt to veil these failings with misleading and exciting titles and with extravagant and often deceitful offers of premiums to subscribers.[50]

## Using premiums to sell books

Dangling premiums before people to induce them to order books was nothing new, nor were frauds involving the promised gifts. But these practices, infrequent before the era of German unification, suddenly became common during it as a result of the ambition of the publishers of "Colporteur novels" (premiums do not appear to have been offered on a large scale for any other type of book during the 1870s). Pictures were the most commonly offered premiums; subscribers were assured that the value of the pictures exceeded the entire selling price of the novel. In some cases the pictures were "free" for subscribers, in others they could be had for a tiny fraction of the "true" value. The masses had been buying pictures since the Middle Ages, so there was a real demand for them.[51] Most of the pictures they were offered as premiums were cheap lithographs, but they were not told that. Instead, they were told, to cite one example, things like:

> In addition to this gripping novel the distinguished subscriber will receive two masterfully executed masterpieces which will give ineffable beauty to any room: 'Galileo Explaining the Revolution of the Earth' with the tenth installment, and 'Columbus Refuses to be Unchained' with the final installment. Each of these [pictures] may be had [by subscribers] for ... only 7½ Silver Groschen.[52]

The second most frequent premium involved special benefits in lotteries; the masses were addicted to lotteries. Sometimes publishers instituted their own lotteries and allowed only subscribers to enter them, at other times they gave subscribers tickets to state lotteries; in either case the subscriber's chances of striking it rich were said to be excellent.[53]

Not to be outdone, some publishers promised more tangible premiums: Swiss watches, silver and gold utensils, new clothing, and teams and carriages. One promised a country house on the Rhine. Few such premiums ever materialized. If they did, the subscriber was sure to have paid more than they were worth. Yet the publishers responsible for such things could rarely be prosecuted for misrepresentation because they worded their promises in ways that made legal redress impossible. Fine-print disclaimers absolved them from backing up any verbal promises made by the salesmen who sold the novels door to door.[54]

It was too much: the publishers of the "Colporteur novels" had gone far too far to suit those respectable elements that concerned themselves with the welfare of the lower orders. Outrage at the "Colporteur novel" phenomenon welled up throughout the 1870s, strongest among Catholic leaders but also gripping the Lutheran clergy, government officials, social reformers, and cultural figures. As early as 1873 the Secretary of the "German Society Against the De-Christianization and Moral Corruption of our People" petitioned the Prussian Landtag to cut off the flow of this moral poison.[55]

The prevalence of fraud and chicanery involving premiums gave the opponents of the "Colporteur novel" an excellent reason to demand restraints on those who published and manufactured the books. Their real interest, however, was less in cleaning up premium frauds than in cleaning up the content of the novels.[56] Many believed that "Colporteur novels" glorified and therefore incited criminal behavior:

> The "Colporteur novel" arouses sympathy and admiration for criminals and thus becomes a school for criminality. And, thanks to the enterprising activity of the Colporteur [Book Trade], the spread of this poison has

assumed huge, daily more huge, proportions. In the cottages of the poor, in the dwellings of the worker, among the families of petty artisans— everywhere we find the colored installments, their outward appearances as repulsive to cultivated taste as their contents.[57]

This argument was strengthened by well-publicized cases in which criminals confessed that reading "Colporteur novels" had first led them astray.[58]

Criminality was not the only evil attributed to "Colporteur novels." A religious leader declared that "because of it socialism attains grosser and more dangerous dimensions; the shocking rise in the suicide rate is to a large extent a fruit of these, 'thriller Colporteur novels'."[59] Retail book shop owners asserted that they were facing ruin because people bought "Colporteur novels" from itinerant booksellers and refused to buy anything else.[60]

The chorus of outrage grew louder each year. By the late 1870s it could generate more than angry words. In 1879 the Saxon government began denying peddlers' licenses to subscription collectors. In the Imperial Reichstag, the lead against the "Colporteur novel" was taken by the Catholic Center Party, with the blessing of the Right and of the government. The Center's proposals were embodied in an Amendment to the Industrial Laws, which was put before the Reichstag in April 1882 for debate and discussion. The Amendment would have permitted itinerant salesmen to sell only: Bibles, religious and patriotic works, schoolbooks, maps, and calendars. It would have made obtaining peddler's licenses much more difficult, banned the use of premiums, and required the publishers of installment works to print the total price of the works on each installment.[61]

The proposal was strongly opposed by the National Liberals, who found it atavistic, a return to the bad old days of heavy censorship, and by the Itinerant Book Trade, which found it a threat to its existence.[62]

The Amendment, which finally passed the Reichstag in 1883, was more a victory for the National Liberals and the Itinerant Trade than for the Center, though it really satisfied nobody. It banned premiums, required that a book's total price be printed on every installment, and forbade the sale of printed matter and pictures which were offensive to morality and religion. Old-style book peddlers had to submit lists of the books they intended to sell to government authorities for approval. The subscription collectors and salesmen of the Colporteur Book Trade, however, were exempted from this requirement, even though: (1) they were much more numerous than the old-fashioned peddlers, whose numbers were actually declining, and (2) they sold most of the "Colporteur novels"—peddlers seldom carried them.[63]

Much of the Amendment was too nebulously worded to be effective.[64] It did not say exactly what made books offensive to morality and religion. Confusion as to whom it pertained and as to what it actually meant, made manifest by a welter of conflicting court decisions, led to enforcement problems as prosecuting authorities became hesitant to invoke any but its most lucid, clear-cut parts. It neither slowed the production of "Colporteur novels" nor induced publishers to tone them down in any way, and hence did not satisfy opponents of these books.[65] A blow to the already-declining, old-style book peddlers, the Amendment did not hurt the more modern and vigorous Colporteur Book Trade at all. Colporteur Trade salesmen quickly found ways to circumvent the ban on premiums.

On the other hand, these circumventions removed much of the gross fraud from the premium offers. The 1883 law, combined with an internal clean-up movement already underway in the Colporteur Trade, did eliminate the worst excesses in the merchandising of "Colporteur novels," and helped stave off stronger repressive legislation for slightly over a decade.[66]

By 1883 the heyday of the "Colporteur novel" was past anyway. No longer so easily gulled, the masses were no longer as likely to sign up for these books. Genuinely exciting and/or intensely topical ones could still attract hordes of subscribers, but the more usual offerings found fewer customers every year. By 1890 only about 15 heavily capitalized publishers did "Colporteur novels" with any regularity. From comprising as much as 90 percent of the total sales of the Colporteur Book Trade in the decade of the 1870s, they declined to 10–20 per-cent by the decade of the 1890s.[67]

## Periodicals gain market share

The paramount position in the mass book market was taken by newspapers and magazines during the course of the 1880s. Few publishers were upset by the change, for they found in newspapers and magazines inexhaustible lodes of profit. What kind of newspapers and magazines? They were simple and illustrated, pitched to the same simple level as the "Colporteur novels." Newspapers might be simple local sheets or simple partisan papers put out by or for such special interest groups as the SPD (Social Democratic Party) or the Catholic Church. The most popular newspapers, however, were the new mass-circulation illustrated yellow journals. They were more an expression of Anglo-American commercial genius than of something uniquely German, but the love of blood and scandal which gave them their (still-enduring) popularity knows no national borders. In Germany they made the fortunes of publishers like August Scherl and Hermann Ullstein, just as they did of Alfred Harmsworth in England and William Randolph Hearst in the United States.[68]

Even rural Germany, which had been largely untouched by the "Colporteur novel," succumbed to the newspaper. A Thuringian pastor wrote sadly in the early 1890s:

> Previously the newspaper had less influence (than the Bible and song-books) over the religious and moral attitudes of our peasantry.... Yet even then the pernicious effects of the anti-Christian press could be perceived often enough..., and this has increased with the yearly spread of newspaper reading among all circles of rural folk.[69]

The popular newspaper and the illustrated magazine were the all-conquering literary innovations of the nineteenth century, as the novel had been of the eighteenth.[70]

But if the newspaper and magazine came to overshadow the older forms of reading matter, they by no means eradicated them: it would be more accurate to say that they supplemented them. The masses of this era read all sorts of things, some old and some new. Books, pamphlets, and other forms of reading matter which had traditionally figured large in the mass trade still did, turned out now by steam-driven presses on wood pulp paper rather than by hand presses on rag paper—but still turned out and still purchased by rural Germans, who were more insulated from modern "literary" trends and from secularism than their urban brethren. Between 1868 and 1888 five publishers produced editions of the old folk story of the Palatine Countess Genovesa, three publishers brought out the story of the *Four Heymonskinder*, and two the story of Til Eulenspiegel.[71]

## Religious books

After two and a half centuries of pre-eminence in the market for Lutheran devotional works, Johann Arnd's *True Christianity (Wahres Christentum)* and *The Garden of Paradise (Paradiesgärtlein)* were still being reprinted, though not as frequently as in the earlier decades of the nineteenth century. The devotional works of Johann Friedrich Starck, on the other hand, retained the full measure of their earlier popularity. Over 20 editions of Starck's *Daily Handbook (Tägliches Handbuch)* were published between 1868 and 1888, a few of them by religious institutions which did not have to worry about profits but most by commercial publishers. The publishing house of A. Gotthold in Kaiserslautern produced two editions, with a total of 40,000 copies between 1884 and 1888. Another devotional classic, Karl Heinrich v. Bogatsky's *Golden Treasure Chest of God's Children (Güldenes Schatz-Kästlein der Kinder Gottes)*, remained on the book market in a variety of editions done by two publishing houses, Bertelsmann in Gütersloh and the Orphanage in Halle, while J. F. Steinkopf of Stuttgart published an edition of Bogatsky's hymns.[72]

The most frequently printed book of all was the Bible, just as it had been since the invention of printing in the fifteenth century. The Prussian Bible Society, one of several non-profit institutions which printed and sold Bibles, distributed 80,694 Bibles and 16,706 New Testaments during the single calendar year 1885; it distributed nearly 750,000 Bibles between 1885 and 1894. Germany probably absorbed over 500,000 Bibles each year during the 1880s. It should be noted, however, that Bibles were frequently sold for less than cost by religious societies just to get people to take them. By the 1870s and 1880s, religious societies produced the bulk of the Bibles sold in Germany; commercial publishers produced only a small part.[73]

## Other popular mass-market items

In addition to devotional works and Bibles, such traditional mass-market items as vocational manuals, calendars, picture sheets *(Bilderbogen)*, and pamphlets *(Heftchen)* continued to play important roles in the mass book trade. If anything, these types of reading matter were produced in larger numbers after 1870 than before.[74]

In the late 1880s, for example, the bookman Gustav Uhl estimated that 18,000,000 calendars were sold in Germany annually.[75] The content of these calendars was the hallowed blend of fiction, advice, and chronological data. A few had yearly sales approaching 500,000 copies, though most had to be content with sales of from 30,000 to 100,000 copies, and some never caught on with the public at all.[76]

Always competitive, the calendar market became more so in the 1870s, when Prussia lifted her requirement that calendars carry government stamps. Literally hundreds of publishers tussled with one another in this market. Few of them had anything original to offer the public, so they copied, imitated, and repeated one another. Between 1875 and 1879, 42 "People's Calendars" *(Volkskalender)* were tossed onto the market; between 1885 and 1888, 44 of them. They included "People's Calendars" with "Christian," "German," "humorous," and other slants as well as illustrated "People's Calendars" for every major geographic/political region of the Empire.[77]

Sometimes calendars were alike in more than title: late in the 1870s, two Berliners were discovered to be publishing the same calendar under two different titles: (1) the *Deutscher Kalender* (100,000 copies) and (2) the *Berliner hinkende Bote* (80,000 copies). These two titles would appeal to different tastes, hence total sales would be higher—an ingenious segmentation of a market.[78]

Whatever their titles, calendars were purchased by more Germans than any other type of reading matter. Vocational manuals, on the other hand, were bought by a more limited clientele. They were of little use and hence rarely purchased by those with the lowliest jobs—common laborers, factory drones, and many farm workers. But they were useful to and therefore purchased by independent farmers, artisans, and skilled workers.[79] The rapid pace of technological advance which characterized the late-nineteenth century made up-to-date manuals increasingly important to such people, and the market for them grew accordingly. Several publishers brought new series' of agricultural handbooks onto the market, for example. In the mid-1870s Schotte and Voigt of Berlin issued a 54-volume series called the *Agricultural Library (Landwirthschaftliche Bibliothek)*, while Ulmer of Stuttgart put out a *Library of Agricultural Manuals (Bibliothek landwirthschaftliche Lehrbücher)*. Both series were composed of straightforward manuals covering all aspects of farming, from bookkeeping to the uses of dung.[80]

Ulmer also published a unique and highly popular series for farmers and their families to read on those long winter nights. Aptly titled *Des Landmannes*

*Winterabende*, it was aimed at the still-numerous class of small farmers. It contained books on raising crops and livestock, but also homely didactic fiction like Fritz Möhrlin's *Peter Schmid the Progressive Farmer* (*Peter Schmid, der Fortschrittsbauer* 164 pages, 9 woodcuts). For the farmer's wife there was Susanna Müller's *The Housewife on the Land* (*Die Hausfrau auf dem Lande* 176 pages). The volumes of the series averaged about 180 pages in length and sold for one Mark to 1.20 Marks. Forty-one volumes were published between 1876 and 1889.[81]

## Pamphlet fiction

Publishing creativity like that which underlay *Des Landmannes Winterabende* was evident also in some of the pamphlet series' of fiction done by a variety of publishers after 1870. As a physical form, the pamphlet or booklet between 30 and 80 pages had long been a staple of the mass book trade; according to Rudolf Schenda it was "probably the most popular printed matter of the 18th and 19th Centuries."[82] Fiction pamphlets continue to play a big role in German publishing to this day, when they are most often found at railroad station book and periodical shops. The pamphlet format was not restricted to fiction—many vocational manuals, health guides, dream books, and the like were, physically speaking, pamphlets rather than books. The most interesting developments in the pamphlet format after 1870, however, came in the realm of fiction. Unfortunately, this fiction received little attention from educated contemporaries and less from later scholars. It is ironic that "Colporteur novels," which were often little more than pamphlets strung together on a thin and absurd thread of plot, set off a huge furor, while pamphlet fiction on identical themes handled in the same elemental manner was ignored.

Ignored—but not by the masses. They loved the little story booklets. Their patronage made several series of these pamphlets among the most widely circulated publishing ventures of the century. The dimensions attained by several of the series are astounding.[83]

In addition to these big series, there were several smaller ones. Examples include: the *Christliche Volksbibliothek* published by the Society for Christian Devotional Writings, the *Duetsche Volksbücher* (18 volumes, 1877) published by Zwitzler of Wolfenbüttel, and the venerable *Die deutschen Volksbücher* published by Winter of Frankfurt/Main. Composed mainly of traditional folk stories like "Tristan and Isolde" and "King Appolonius," Winter's series had been popular for decades before it expired at around 1880.[84]

With the exception of the *Christliche Vo1ksbibliothek*, all of the successful pamphlet fiction series were commercial and secular undertakings. The *Volksbibliothek des Lahren hinkenden Bote* was directed at the upper educational levels of the masses and also at the middle class; it included works by Schiller, Hauff, Uhland, Kleist, E. T. A. Hoffmann, Körner, Shakespeare, Kotzebue, and retellings of Greek myths alongside of works by authors like Karl May and Christoph v. Schmid. The other big pamphlet series were pitched towards a lower level of cultural refinement, offering rich quantities of such conventional mass fiction as pirate stories, stories about gypsies, stories about foundlings, Knight/Bandit stories, ghost yarns, and stories in which chaste heroines endured incredible peril before being rewarded with mushy love.

These series also offered their readers newer themes and thrills in abundance, as publishers experimented widely. There were stories set in the Argentine Pampas, in Africa, in China, in jungles; there were stories about Moors, Lapps, gorillas, Incas, slaves, African chiefs, South Sea islanders, sultans, Australian aborigines, eskimos, and General Gordon, to cite a handful.[85]

## The "Wild West" conquers the German masses

But the most numerous of all were the stories about the American "Wild West," especially its Indians. Here are a few representative titles from Spaarmann's *New Peoples' Library (Neue Volksbibliothek)* and *Library of Interesting Stories (Bibliothek interessanter Erzählungen)*, and the *Little People's Stories (Kleine Volkserzählungen)* of the Bagel Publishing Company:

* *The Magic Bird or the White Girl of the Monitaris Indians. Episodes from a Summer Stay among Indians of the Rocky Mountain Territory (Zaubervogel oder des weiße Mädchen der Mönnitarrisindianer. Episoden aus einer Sommeraufenthalt unter Indianern des Rocky Mountain Territoriums).*
* *In the Canyons of the Colorado. Story (Im Felsenthale des Colorado. Erzählung).*
* *Prairie Justice. The Gold Mine on the Colorado. Two Stories from the Texan Wilderness (Prairie-Justiz. Die Goldmine am Colorado. Zwei Erzählungen aus der texanischen Wildnis).*
* *Hawkeye the White Chief, or the Marvelous Rescue of Mary and Ellen. An Indian Story (Falkenauge, der weiße Häuptling, oder Mary's und Ellen's wunderbare Rettung. Eine Indianererzahlung).*
* *The Snowy Grave in the Sierras or Starving in the Silver Mine, A Story from America (Das Schneegrab in der Sierra oder verhungert in der Silbermine. Eine Erzählung aus Amerika).*
* *Sitting Bull the Indian General. A Story from the Indian War in the Year 1876 (Sitting Bull, der Indianer-General. Eine Erzählung aus dem Indianer Krieg in Jahre 1876).*
* *Pocahontas the Indian Princess. A Historical Story from the Earliest Years of Settlement in America (Pokahontas, der Indianer-Prinzessin. Eine geschichtliche Erzählung aus den ersten Zeiten der Ansiedlung in Amerika).*
* *Death in the Wildernes. An Historical Story of Indian Life (Der Tod in der Wüste. Eine geschtliche Erzählung aus dem Indianerleben).*[86]

## Crime stories

Second to "Wild West" and Indian stories in popularity were crime stories set in gritty, un-glamorized contemporary settings. Characteristic titles from Bagel and Spaarmann were:

*   *The Executioner's Son (Der Sohn des Scharfrichters).*
*   *The Dead Hand. A Crime Story (Die Todtenhand. Eine Criminalgeschichte).*
*   *The Robbery Murder or the Discovered Testament (Der Raubmörder oder das gefundene Testament).*
*   *The Factory Owner and His Doppelganger. A Crime Story (Der Fabrikant und sein Doppelgänger. Eine Criminal-Erzählung).*
*   *A Dark Secret. A Crime Story (Ein dunkles Geheimnis. Eine Criminalgeschichte).*[87]

Neither contemporary crime nor the American West had been common topics in mass fiction before 1870. It was the many stories published after the unification of Germany that laid the foundations for that obsession with cowboys and criminals which persists strongly to this day in Germany. Few things that have ever appeared in print have filled the minds of so many people for so long.

## Notes

1   K. Faulmann, *Illustrierte Geschichte des Buchdruckerkunst*, Vienna, Pest, Leipzig 1882, pp. 539–550.
2   Hiller, *Zur Sozialgeschichte von Buch und Buchandel*, p. 102.
3   Heinrici, "Die Verhaeltnisse im deutschen Colportagebuchandel," p. 202.
4   O. Leixner, *Zur Reform unserer Volksliteratur*, Berlin 1891, p. 14.
5   Hamerow, *The Social Foundations of German Unification*, vol. I, p. 55.
6   Schenda, *Volk ohne Buch*, pp. 444–445.
7   Hamerow, *The Social Foundations of German Unification*, vol. I, p. 281; A. Jacobi, "Zur Analphabeten-Statistik," *Neue Zeit*, 13 Jg., 1894–1895, I, p. 656.
8   Jacobi, "Zur Analphabeten-Statistik," p. 656.
9   Ibid., pp. 657–658.
10  Hamerow, *The Social Foundations of German Unification*, vol. I, pp. 282–283.
11  P. Lundgren, *Educational Expansion and Economic Growth in 19th century Germany*, Princeton 1973, Table 2.
12  Tews, *Ein Jahrhundert preussischer Schulgeschichte*, p. 177.
13  Ibid., p. 257.
14  Ibid., p. 177.
15  Ibid., pp. 177, 196–197, 204.
16  Engelsing, "Die Perioden der Lesergeschichte in der Neuzeit," pp. 964–973.
17  These publishers are listed in the book trade *Adressbuch* for 1899, Part VI, pp. 403, 407, 456, 464.
18  The connection between industrial freedom and the new happenings in the mass book trade was perceived by a number of people, among them middle-class bookmen whose outlook was distorted by class bias, e.g., *Börsenblatt*, 1870, Nr. 44, p. 602. The least class bias is found in H. Blumenthal, *Der Colportagebuchandel und das buchhaendlerische Reisegeschaeft*, Iglau, Vienna, Leipzig n.d., but *c.*1897, pp. 18–19, 185.

19 Streissler, *Der Kolportagehandel*, p. 7.
20 Examining titles in *Heinsius Buecherlexicon* is a good way to see what tastes were being appealed to by mass-market publishers. Titles often had little relation to actual contents but do show to which tastes the publishers were trying to appeal.
21 See K. May, *Ich. Aus Karl Mays Nachlass*, pp. 459–467.
22 According to Uhl, "Vom Kolportage-Buchandel," *Deutsche Buchaendler-Akademie* V, p. 431, writers were expected to produce the equivalent of eight octavo-sized pages.
23 Quoted in Kellen, "Der Massenvertrieb der Volksliteratur," p. 86.
24 Each installment was composed of the equivalent of eight to 12 pages.
25 See Kellen, "Der Massenvertrieb der Volksliteratur," p. 87; R. Fullerton, "Creating a Mass Book Market in Germany," *Journal of Social History*, 1977, 10(3): 265–283.
26 Glagau, "Der Colportage-Roman," *Börsenblatt* 1870, Nr. 217, 2974.
27 Streissler, *Der Kolportagehandel*, p. 18.
28 Ibid., p. 18.
29 Fraenkel, *Ein neuer Weg*, p. 13.
30 Glagau, "Der Colportage-Roman," *Börsenblatt* 1870, Nr. 217, p. 2974.
31 Streissler, *Der Kolportagehandel*, p. 18.
32 Glagau, "Der Colportage-Roman," *Börsenblatt* 1870, p. 2023.
33 Ibid., p. 3023. Since he gives no sources it is difficult to know how far to believe Glagau. But in light of Schenda's description of popular mass-market writers (*Volk ohne Buch*, pp. 143–173), Glagau appears quite plausible.
34 Kellen and Maier, "Die Zahl der Kolportage-Romane," *Börsenblatt* 1903, Nr. 138, p. 4837.
35 Titles from: Glagau "Der Colporatge-Roman," *Börsenblatt* 1870, Nr. 217, p. 294, Nr. 221, p. 231; Baumbach, "Der Colportagebuchandel und die Gewerbenovelle," p. 12.
36 Schenda, *Volk ohne Buch*, p. 350.
37 Glagau, "Der Colportage-Roman," *Börsenblatt* 1870, Nr. 221, p. 3022.
38 Kellen and Maier, "Die Zahl der Kolporatge-Roman," *Börsenblatt* 1903, Nr. 138, p. 4837.
39 Glagau, "Der Colportage-Roman," *Börsenblatt* 1870, Nr. 221, p. 3022.
40 Ibid., p. 3022; Vogel, *Die Beschraenkungen des Wanderbuchandels*, p. 27.
41 Quoted in Schenda, *Volk ohne Buch*, p. 351. Only a few battered copies of this novel exist today.
42 Kellen, "Der Massenvertrieb der Volksliteratur," p. 90, says that the hangman actually contributed some sections of the manuscript—but received only 5,000 Marks.
43 Kellen and Maier, "Die Zahl der Kolportage-Romane," *Börsenblatt* 1903, Nr. 138, p. 4836.
44 Kellen, "Der Massenvertrieb der Volksliteratur," p. 87; "Von der Kolportage," *Börsenblatt* 1882, Nr. 128, p. 3226.
45 Glagau, "Der Colportage-Roman," *Börsenblatt* 1870, Nr. 217, p. 2974.
46 Ibid., p. 2974.
47 Quoted by Glagau, *Börsenblatt* 1870, Nr. 217, p. 2974.
48 Blumenthal, "Der Colportagebuchandel," p. 87.
49 Kellen, "Der Massenvertrieb der Volksliteratur," p. 87.
50 "Aus den Krise des Colpotagehandels," *Börsenblatt* 1873, Nr. 47, pp. 745–746.
51 Pictures had been sold by peddler-Colporteurs; buyers had used them to decorate the walls of their humble cottages for centuries. Other sellers included retail book shops and the newer branches of the Itinerant Book Trade. Subjects included: saints and other religious figures, royalty, famous statesmen, well-known battles, and landscapes.
52 Quoted from a publisher's prospectus by Glagau, "Der Colportage-Roman," *Börsenblatt* 1870, Nr. 217, p. 2975.
53 Elsner, *Beitrage und Dokumente*, p. 41; "Eine Notabene," *Börsenblatt* 1876, Nr. 230, p. 3566.

54 Vogel, *Die Beschraenkungen des Wanderbuchhandels*, p. p. 27.
55 "Aus den Kreise des Colportagehandels," *Börsenblatt* 1873, Nr. 47, pp, 745–746.
56 Vogel, *Die Beschraenkungen des Wanderbuchhandels*, p. 27.
57 Kellen, "Der Massenvertrieb der Volksliteratur," p. 83.
58 Vogel, *Die Beschraenkungen des Wanderbuchhandels*, p. 76, cites with skepticism a survey of 240 men who had entered Berlin prisons during one week; 36 of them said that they had first been led astray by Colporteur novels.
59 K. J. Mueller, *Die Kolportage christlicher Schriften*, Berlin 1890, pp. 3–6.
60 Typical of the outrage of retail shop owners was A. E., "Aus der Erfahrung. II. Colportage und Colporteure," *Börsenblatt* 1872, Nr. 85, pp. 922–923.
61 Heinrici, "Die Verhaeltnisse im deutschen Colportagebuchandel," pp. 193–197, 205.
62 Vogel, *Die Beschrankungren des Wanderbuchhandels*, pp. 29, 41–43.
63 The date of the amendment was July 1, 1883. See Vogel, *Die Beschrankungen des Wanderbuchhandels*, pp. 41–42.
64 It is likely that most of the Reichstag delegates had little if any awareness of the differences among the different branches of the Itinerant Trade, and thus in voting for close reins upon the book peddlers actually believed that they were putting close reins upon sellers of "Colporteur novels."
65 See the remarks by Franz v. Holtzendorff, a famous contemporary teacher of criminal law, as quoted by Schulze in his *Freie oeffentliche Bibliotheken*, p. 315.
66 Streissler, *Der Kolportagehandel*, p. 42.
67 The estimate that "Colporteur novels" made up 90 percent of the Colporteur Trade's sales in the 1870s is Vogel's, *Die Beschrankungren des Wanderbuchhandels*, p. 26. I think this estimate too high. On sales of "Colporteur novels" in the 1880s, see Heinrici, "Die Verhaeltnisse in deutschen Colportagehandel," p. 217.
68 Both Scherl and Ullstein added book publication to their operations after 1890; only Ullstein made money.
69 "Zur baeurlichen Glaubens-und Sittenlehre. Von einem thueringischen Landpfarrer," quoted in "Was liest der deutsche Bauer?," *Neue Zeit* Jg. 14 (1895–1896), I, pp. 213–214.
70 On the prevalence of newspaper reading among the masses see Rodenberg, *Die Druckkunst als Spiegel der Kultur*, p. 294.
71 *Heinsius*: XVI, vol. 2, pp. 684–685; XVII, vol. 2, p. 817; XVIII, vol. 2, pp. 781–785, 789.
72 *Heinsius*: XV, vol. 1, pp. 62–63; vol. 2, pp. 639–640; XVI, vol. 1, pp. 57, 179.
73 "Preussische Haupt-Bibelgesellschaft," *Börsenblatt* 1886, Nr. 247, p. 5907.
74 Schenda, *Volk ohne Buch*, pp. 272–276.
75 Uhl, "Vom Kolportage-Buchhandel," *Deutsche Buchaendler-Akademie* V, p. 382.
76 *Börsenblatt* 1886, Nr. 50, p. 1123.
77 *Heinsius*: XVI, vol. 2, pp. 687–689; vol. XVIII, vol. 2, pp. 786–788.
78 "Zur Kalendervertrieb," *Börsenblatt* 1882, Nr. 187, p. 3398.
79 "Die englische Presse ueber deutsche Literaturzustande," *Börsenblatt* 1876, p. 3250.
80 *Heinsius*: XV, vol. 1, p. 173; XVI, vol. 1, pp. 146–147.
81 *Heinsius*: XVI, vol. 2, p. 7; XVII, vol. 2, p. 10; XVIII, vol. 2, p. 9.
82 R. Fullerton, "Towards a Commercial Popular Culture in Germany," *Journal of Social History*, 1979, 12(4): 489–511.
83 *Heinsius*, XVI, vol. 2, pp. 143, 683.
84 *Heinsius*: XV, vol. 1, p. 169; XVI vol. 1, p. 143, vol. 2, pp. 683–687; XVII, vol. 1, p. 143.
85 *Heinsius* XVI, vol. 2, p. 685; XVII, vol. 2, p. 817.
86 Ibid., pp. 143, 683.
87 Ibid., pp. 143, 683; XVIII, vol. 2, pp. 784–785.

# Conclusion

We end the discussion just before the first courses analyzing marketing—usually called "commerce" at the time—were introduced in some German universities, followed a few years later by American courses taught by people who had studied in Germany.

These courses were heavily influenced by the German Historical School of Economics, which posited that by examining enough historical examples, one could derive economic laws. The school died out partly because Germany was defeated in the First World War and its thought came into discredit. But before it died out the last and greatest of the German historical economists—Joseph Schumpeter—went to the United States and became very famous there.

Whether or not one can derive universal rules from the evidence presented in this book, one can certainly argue that a great many of today's basic marketing concepts were illustrated by the German bookmen of the nineteenth century, especially publishers. A great deal of what is taught and practiced today was actively practiced by nineteenth-century German booksellers, especially publishers. Some examples are: public relations, cooperative advertising, direct selling, improved product appearance, display windows, and heavy advertising. Germany's bookmen knew a great deal about how to create and to market their products. The German publishers of the nineteenth century did an excellent job in responding to the needs and tastes of various publics. In some cases they sensed latent needs and responded to them. The German book markets grew enormously between 1815 and 1890; they grew faster than did the population, educational levels, and incomes. Where at the close of the Napoleonic Wars few Germans took part in the book markets, by 1890 most did. German home libraries in the 1880s were not large but they were common; in the 1820s they had been rare. Moreover, the home library of the 1880s was larger than that of the immediate post-Napoleonic years.

The key to the rapid growth of the German book markets is the spread of aggressive marketing, above all by publishers. The traditional passivity in which most German bookmen reposed early in the century was shucked off by more and more of them from the 1820s onward; the examples set by Friedrich Arnold Brockhaus, Josef Meyer, and others were followed by an increasing number of bookmen as the century progressed. Aggressive book-selling meant that bookmen not only responded to demands from their markets, they also stimulated them. Aggressive bookselling meant that they exploited the potentials presented by such phenomena as increased urbaniza-tion, decreased illiteracy, new occupations, and higher incomes. Publishers created new reading material such as trade manuals and new, enticing pack-ages for already-existing material; pocket books and cheap illustrated reading matter are examples. The traditional book store and Colporteur were supple-mented by newer places to retail books such as Discounters and Modern Antiquarian dealers.

Publishers played an increasingly dominant role in book marketing. Often coming up with ideas about what the public would like, they commissioned writers to produce books reflecting these ideas; there were a growing number of professional writers making their livings from what they wrote. Publishers were concerned with the quality of what they commissioned—but above all they were concerned with achieving financial success in the market. This development has been decried by many cultural purists—yet who can blame publishers for trying to make their businesses into going concerns. That books with low sales might be of the greatest cultural value is far too blanket a state-ment culturally, and an idiotic statement economically.

Was the growth of the book markets a positive development? I have assumed throughout that it was. While the motives of most nineteenth-century German bookmen were hardly as pure, i.e., non-commercial, as they sometimes pompously asserted, and while they in their cupidity did heave a good bit of ephemeral rubbish onto the book markets, they also made it easier for Germans to own worthwhile books. The greatest commercial successes in both the mass and the regular book market were not the colorful sensations of fiction, whether Sir Walther Scott's Waverly novels or knight and bandit sagas or Wild West tales, but rather were books which were considered to be practical and useful possessions, books which, as Johann Bergk so beautifully expressed it in 1825, "aid[ed] physical, cultural, and spiritual well-being." The bulwarks of the regular trade were such works as: encyclopedias, diction-aries, classics, cookbooks, health guides, textbooks for academic secondary schools and universities, and general works on topics like history, law, and natural science. Religious works were more important to the regular book market earlier in the century than later—falling from first to fifth place in the number of titles published from 1815 to 1879—but there was always a good market for editions of the Bible, the *Imitation of Christ* and the like. The bul-warks of the mass book trade were: devotional books, calendars, schoolbooks, manuals, handbooks, and news fliers (later newspapers); not until after 1870 did the sale of fiction amount to much.

Thus the home library of the characteristic nineteenth-century German, whatever his or her social class, was composed mainly of books which were believed to be of solid and enduring value. What little frivolity and fluff might be there was either borrowed from circulating libraries or had been given as gifts to amuse the women of the household. Compared to the home libraries in Britain, France, and the United States, the German ones were small; per capita ownership of books in Germany was never as great as in these three countries, even during the industrial boom after 1870. One reason was that most German books were more expensive, another was that Germans of the middle and upper classes, however wealthy, preferred to borrow most books from circulating libraries or to read them in reading societies rather than buy them.

Whether Germans read more or less than Englishmen, Frenchmen, or Americans cannot really be inferred from data on book purchases, for books can be purchased and never read, and read without having been purchased.

## Regular and mass book trades

The main market distinction, as we have repeatedly seen, was between the middle- and upper-class public served by the book store in its several forms, and the "mass" market composed of Germans who would never enter a book store, even a discount book store—workers, artisans, peasants, and their families. They purchased above all from itinerant booksellers; late in the century the railroad station bookstall supplemented itinerant sellers. Distinct from one another in tastes, the two markets reflected Germany's social divisions.

The reading tastes of both markets were fairly stable over the decades. This was especially true of the mass book market, which until after 1870 absorbed almost exclusively individual books and types of book which had been in circulation for centuries, for example devotional works, calendars, and dream interpreters. One big new type of book developed in the nineteenth century for the mass market was the self-help manual, which helped people to master old and new occupations. After 1870 the masses added illustrated newspapers and magazines, and fictional thrillers to their repertoire.

The middle and upper classes had begun to abandon such traditional reading matter as devotional works even before 1815 in favor of novels and encyclopedias. The ancient classics, however, retained the full measure of their old importance in the regular book market, aided of course by the fact that German academic education continued to be based largely upon them. Encyclopedias, cookbooks, novels, and the classics (modern as well as ancient) were the most representative middle- and upper-class reading matter throughout the century. The popularity of individual books naturally varied over time. Fiction was the most prone to increasingly rapid changes in fashion, the rage swerving from Knight/Bandit stories before 1830 to English and French novels in the 1830s and 1840s, to pseudo-Gothic verse epics in the 1850s—to cite some examples.

## Informal market research

I have not found any evidence of formal market research until late in the period, but there was considerable use of informal research based upon observation, intuition, and experimentation. How did Brockhaus know early in the period that he could make a success of an encyclopedia that had gone unsuccessfully through several publishers hands? His business experiences in England had convinced him that aggressiveness counted; his own observation told him that low prices could open people's wallets, so he priced low—and sales of his encyclopedia took off. How did the publishers of pamphlet fiction series late in the period know that America-based, Wild West stories would be more popular than stories set in Germany? They didn't in advance, but they experimented with several different types of story and found that the Wild West sold best. How did publishers after 1870 know that elaborately printed and illustrated "luxury" books would find a ready market? They didn't, but they sensed that such books might sell well amidst the expanding wealth and aggressively self-confident mood of the period, and they experimented. And so it went throughout the entire period: observation, intuition, and experimentation. For every success story there were also failure stories, of course—but that is true even today, despite incredible amounts of formal market research.

## Relation to larger economic developments

Historians from Werner Sombart onwards have characterized the nineteenth century as when High Capitalism had its advent. High Capitalism meant that aggressive and entrepreneurial attitudes towards business became widespread. We have seen this in the book trade, which was actually one of the first to show signs of it, in a process starting well before 1850.

## International influences

Germany's book trade did not exist in isolation. There were considerable influences across national borders. Some of the publishing innovations began in France, for example libraries of small-format books and gift books, and then spread to Germany. The pamphlet fiction so popular in the 1880s and beyond was inspired by British "penny dreadfuls," American dime novels, and the French *Bibliotheque Bleue*. The *Encyclopedia Americana* was an unauthorized translation of the German Brockhaus Encyclopedia *(Conversationslexikon)*. German publishers were active in the United States later in the nineteenth century. In 1869 there were 12 German book stores in New York City and 10 each in London, Paris, and St. Petersberg. There were many in the Austro-Hungarian monarchy as well.

## Jewish bookmen

More Jews began to emerge from isolation and ghettos in Germany. Many became largely secularized and began to enter various occupations. These included some of the most aggressive bookmen, especially the founders of "Modern Antiquarian" bookshops starting in the 1840s and those who sold books in their fast-growing department stores in the 1890s, which caused some anti-Jewish tirades—but others were less negative in their reactions. After all, the Jews were hardly alone in being aggressive businessmen. In the 1843 article "On Jewish Bookmen" *("Ueber die juedischen Buchhaendler,")*, it is emphasized that "Jewish book dealers do not want to know anything about Jews and Jewishness; they simply want to be German book dealers."[1] Historians generally accept that many nineteenth-century Jews went to great pains to act and think like true Germans. In the twentieth century, the association of Jewish merchants with aggressive practices that threatened small shop owners was one of the rallying cries of Nazi anti-Semitism, and the Nazis had a large following among small shop owners. But the Nazis came to power in a country that was very different than nineteenth-century Germany, a country which had to its surprise lost the First World War and then suffered from severe economic upsets in the years following, a country which had lost its monarch, a country which had seemingly lost its way.

## A final word

This has been a full, detailed, historical examination of the development of markets and marketing in one country. Similar studies could—and should—be produced of other industries in other countries. We should be highly skeptical of claims, whether by economists of different schools or by textbook writers, that sales just automatically grew in tandem with production until relatively recently. Historically, conscious and assertive Marketing has played a great role in increasing sales; it grew in tandem with increases in production.

## Note

1 Reprinted in the *Börsenblatt* 1845, Nr. 16, p. 183.

# Index

For Product Safety Concerns and Information please contact our EU
representative  GPSR@taylorandfrancis.com
Taylor & Francis Verlag GmbH, Kaufingerstraße 24, 80331 München, Germany

www.ingramcontent.com/pod-product-compliance
Ingram Content Group UK Ltd.
Pitfield, Milton Keynes, MK11 3LW, UK
UKHW020954180425
457613UK00019B/678